ROAD
ATLAS
OF THE
UNITED
KINGDOM

We are often asked by customers for a road atlas of Shell Service Stations in the U.K. well, here it is.

Shell is the U.K.'s largest and most widespread forecourt retailer with a network of some **2,500** Service Stations from the north of Scotland (and the Shetlands) to the tip of Cornwall, including Northern Ireland and the Channel Islands. Each offers Shell's quality fuels now recommended by more than **20** major car manufacturers.

A large number of Service Stations are open **24 hours** a day, and many have a **SELECT** shop offering a wide range of hot and cold foods, drinks, and everyday essentials. Customer toilets are checked hourly and staff at **SELECT** shops are specially trained to give you friendly and helpful service.
We at Shell give customer service the highest priority, so should you wish to talk to us, whether an enquiry, complaint or compliment, please ring us **FREE** at the Shell Customer Service Centre on **0800-010 100**.

Contents

This edition specially produced for Shell U.K. Ltd. by The Automobile Association.

© The Automobile Association 1993, © Shell U.K. Ltd. 1993, First edition © 1993.

Produced by the Publishing Division of The Automobile Association, for Shell U.K. Ltd., Shell Mex House, Strand, London WC2R 0DX.

Mapping produced by the Cartographic Department of The Automobile Association. This atlas has been compiled and produced from the Automaps database utilising electronic and computer technology.

Published by the Publishing Division of The Automobile Association, Fanum House, Basingstoke, Hampshire RG21 2EA.

Printed and bound by BPCC, Paulton Books Limited.

The contents of this atlas are believed correct at the time of printing, although the publishers cannot accept any responsibility for errors or omissions, or for changes in the details given.

How to use this Atlas

This atlas is divided into three principle sections:

1) 8 miles to 1 inch road maps of the U.K. and more detailed larger scale enlarged area maps, locating individual Shell Service Stations in major conurbations (page 4 - 69).

2) Index of place names (page 91 - 106).

3) Index of Shell Service Stations (page 107 - 142).

To help you find your way around the road maps we have individually coloured each **COUNTY.** Within each county we have individually numbered and located every **SHELL SERVICE STATION.** Cross reference this number with the **INDEX** of Shell Service Stations by looking up the county, which is in alphabetical order, and then the number of the location. Alongside this number you will find the name, address and telephone number for each Shell Service Station followed by a range of **INFORMATION** most frequently requested by customers. This includes;

- **Road Number,** where the Service Station is located on a major road
- **Telephone Number,** should you wish to contact the Service Station for more information
- **Fuels available;**　　　4 = 4 Star Leaded petrol
　　　　　　　　　　　　　U = Premium Unleaded petrol (min. 95 Octane)
　　　　　　　　　　　　　S = Super Unleaded petrol (min. 98 Octane)
　　　　　　　　　　　　　D = Diesel
- **Shell cards accepted;**　G = Shell Gold Card
　　　　　　　　　　　　　A = Shell Agency Card
　　　　　　　　　　　　　E = euroShell Card
- **24 Hour,** where the Service Station is open 24 hours a day for fuel (shop opening hours may vary)
- **H.G.V.,** where refuelling facilities are available for vehicles up to 38 tons
- **SELECT,** where there is a Select shop
- **Car Wash,** where there is a full roll-over car wash available

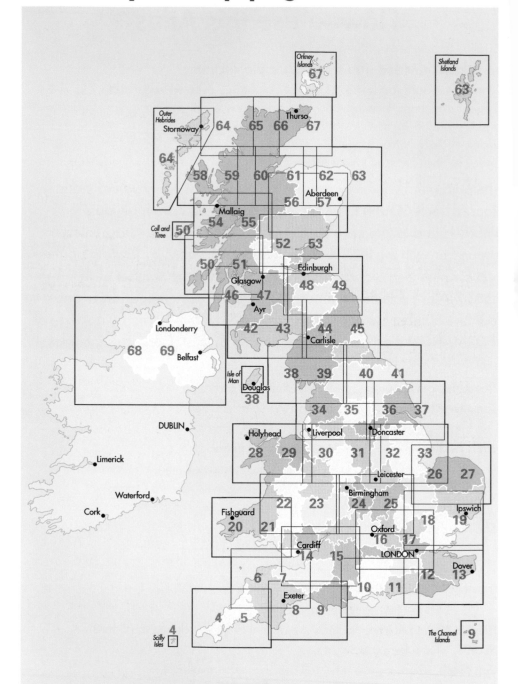

Key to map symbols

ROAD MAPS
Scale 1:500,000 approx 8 miles to 1 inch

| 0 | 5 | | 10 miles |
| 0 | 5 | 10 | 15 km |

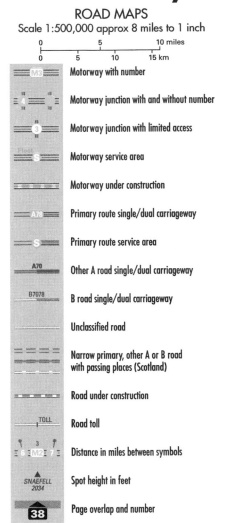

Motorway with number

Motorway junction with and without number

Motorway junction with limited access

Motorway service area

Motorway under construction

Primary route single/dual carriageway

Primary route service area

Other A road single/dual carriageway

B road single/dual carriageway

Unclassified road

Narrow primary, other A or B road with passing places (Scotland)

Road under construction

Road toll

Distance in miles between symbols

Spot height in feet

Page overlap and number

ENLARGED AREA MAPS
Scale 1:200,000 approx 3 miles to 1 inch

| 0 | 1 | 2 | 3 | 4 | 5 miles |
| 0 | 1 | 2 | 3 | 4 | 5 | 6 | 7 | 8 km |

Motorway with number

Motorway junction with and without number

Motorway junction with limited access

Motorway service area

Motorway and junction under construction

Primary route single/dual carriageway

Primary route service area

Other A road single/dual carriageway

B road single/dual carriageway

Unclassified road single/dual carriageway

Interchange/roundabout

Road under construction

Road tunnel

Steep gradient (arrows point downhill)

Road toll

Distance in miles between symbols

Railway line with station and level crossing

Tourist railway

Spot height in metres

SYMBOLS COMMON TO ALL MAPS

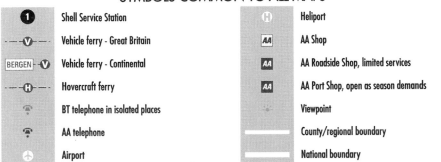

Shell Service Station

Vehicle ferry - Great Britain

Vehicle ferry - Continental

Hovercraft ferry

BT telephone in isolated places

AA telephone

Airport

Heliport

AA Shop

AA Roadside Shop, limited services

AA Port Shop, open as season demands

Viewpoint

County/regional boundary

National boundary

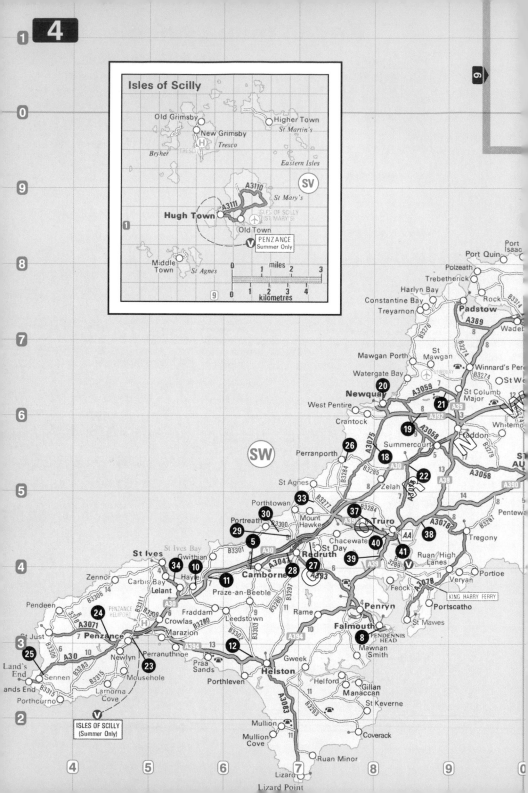

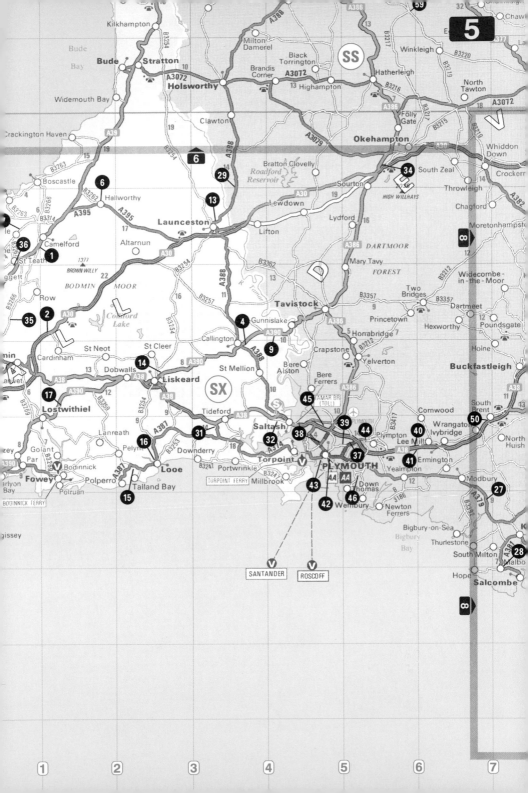

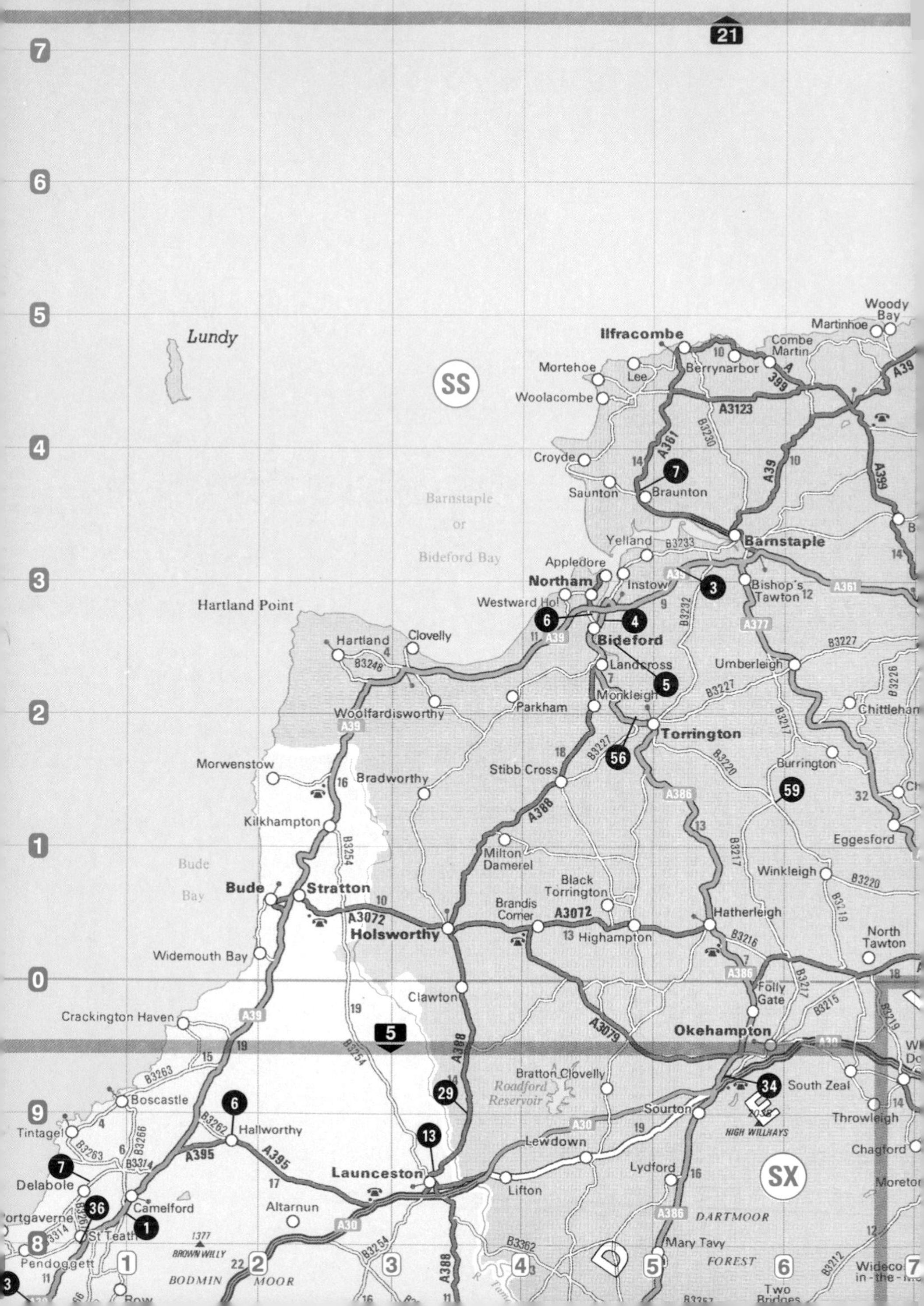

21

7

6

5

Lundy

SS

Woody Bay

Martinhoe

Ilfracombe

Combe Martin

Mortehoe

Lee

Berrynarbor

A

A3123

Woolacombe

B3230

4

Croyde

14

A361

7

10

A39

A39

A399

Saunton

Braunton

Barnstaple or Bideford Bay

Yelland

B3733

Barnstaple

14

3

Appledore

Instow

A39

3

Bishop's Tawton

12

A361

Hartland Point

Northam

Westward Ho!

9

B3232

A377

B3227

Hartland

4

Clovelly

11

A39

6

4

Bideford

Landcross

7

Umberleigh

B3227

B3226

Chittleham

B3248

Landcross

5

Woolfardisworthy

Parkham

Monkleigh

B3227

B3217

A30

2

A39

Stibb Cross

18

B3227

Torrington

B3220

Burrington

32

Ch

Morwenstow

16

56

Bradworthy

A386

13

59

Eggesford

Kilkhampton

B3254

Milton Damerel

A386

Winkleigh

B3220

1

Bude Bay

Black Torrington

B3217

North Tawton

Bude

Stratton

10

Brandis Corner

A3072

Hatherleigh

B3216

Folly Gate

Widemouth Bay

A3072

Holsworthy

13 Highampton

B3215

0

Crackington Haven

A39

Clawton

19

A388

A3079

Okehampton

A30

South Zeal

19

B3254

5

Bratton Clovelly

Roadford Reservoir

34

Throwleigh

14

Boscastle

B3263

6

Hallworthy

15

B3266

29

Sourton

HIGH WILLHAYS

Chagford

9

Tintagel

4

B3263

B3314

A395

A395

13

Launceston

Lewdown

A30

19

Lydford

16

SX

Moreto

7

Delabole

17

Altarnun

Lifton

A386

DARTMOOR

36

A388

B3362

Mary Tavy

FOREST

12

8

St Teath

1

Camelford

1377

BROWN WILLY

22

2

3

B3388

B3362

4

5

6

Wideco in-the-

ortgaverne

Pendoggett

11

1

BODMIN MOOR

Row

Two Bridges

B3357

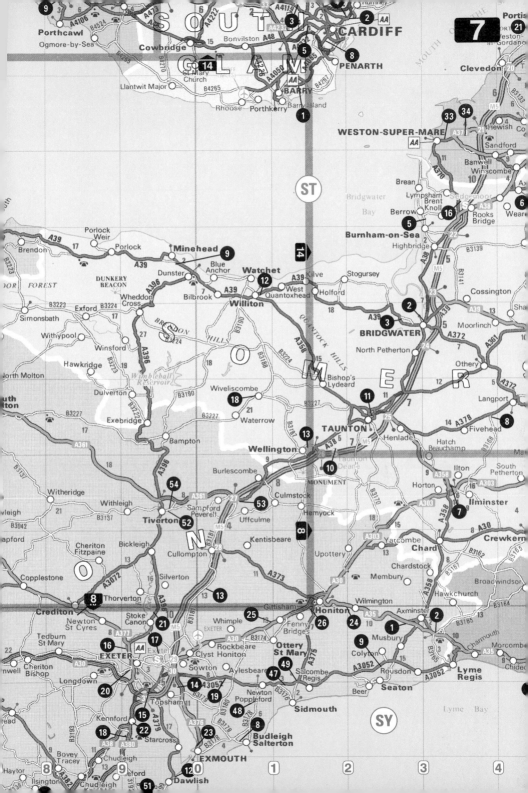

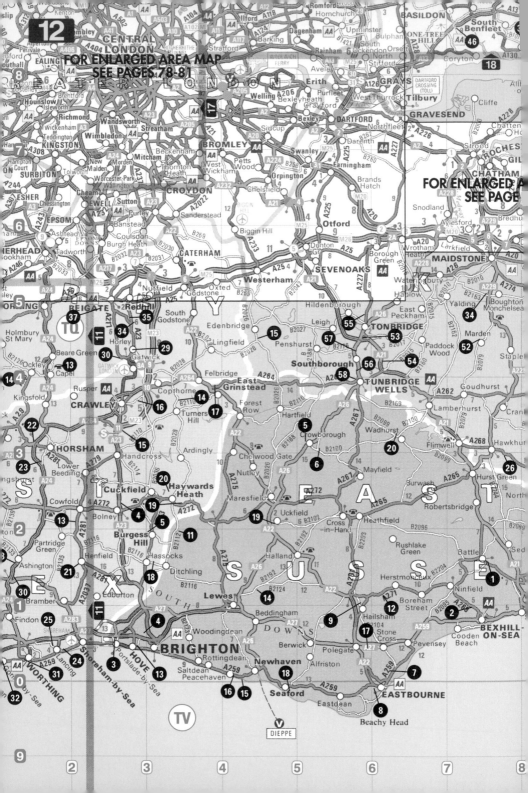

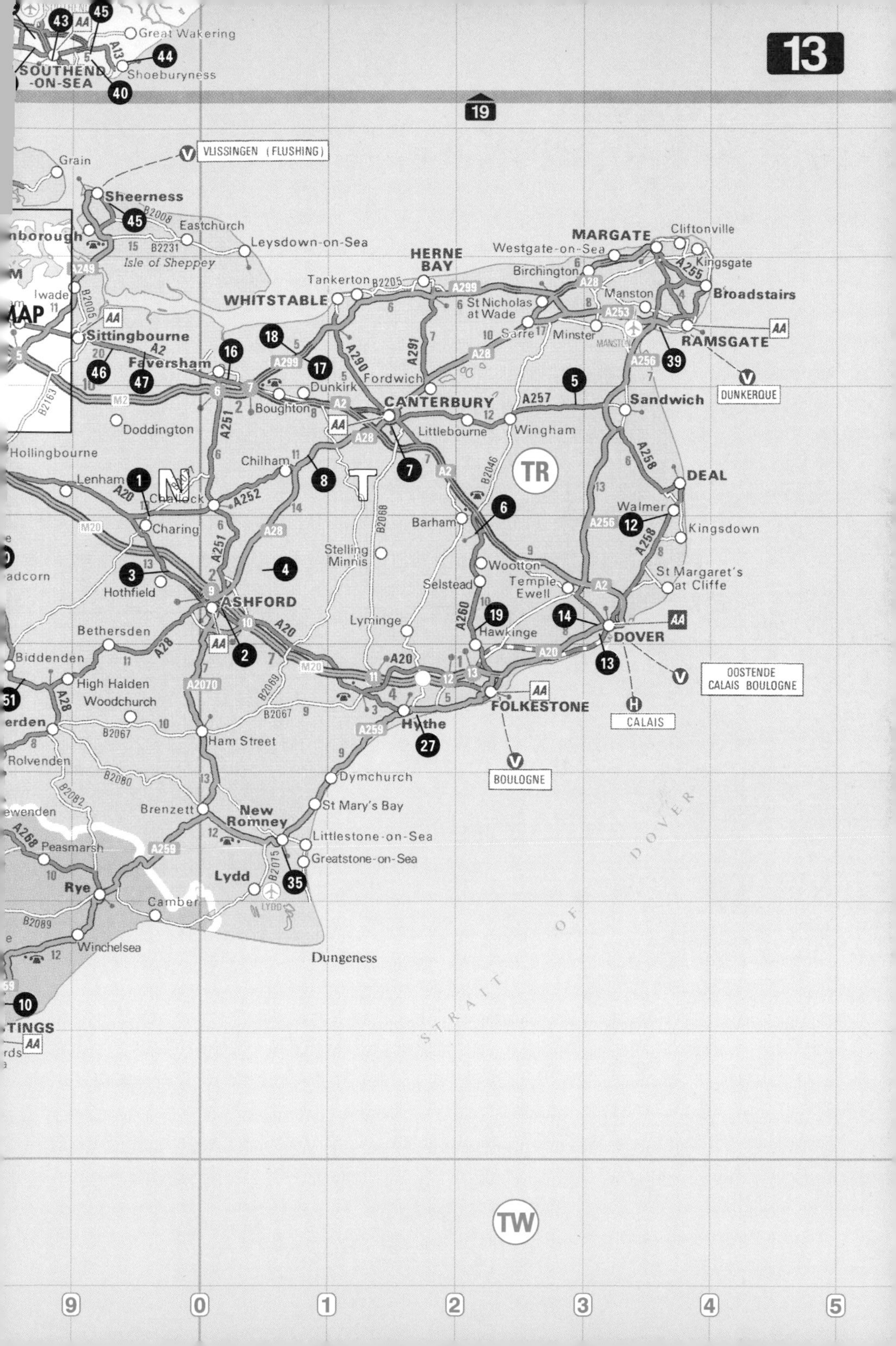

19

Grain

VLISSINGEN (FLUSHING)

Sheerness
45 B2008 Eastchurch
Leysdown-on-Sea
Isle of Sheppey
15 B2231

nborough
M
AP
249
Iwade
11
Sittingbourne A2
46 Faversham
47
B2163
M2 20
Doddington
Hollingborne
Lenham A20
N
Chellock
1
Charing
3 Hothfield
Bethersden
51 High Halden
Woodchurch
Biddenden
B2067
erden
Rolvenden
B2082
ewenden Peasmarsh
A268
Rye
B2089
Winchelsea
TINGS
AA
10

WHITSTABLE
16 18
A299
17 Dunkirk
Fordwich
Boughton
Chilham
A252
8
Stelling Minnis
ASHFORD
2
M20
B2080
Ham Street
13
Brenzett
New Romney
12
Lydd
Camber
Dungeness

HERNE BAY
Tankerton B2205
St Nicholas at Wade
Sarre
A28
Minster
CANTERBURY A257
Littlebourne Wingham
T
Barham
TR
6
Wootton
Temple Ewell
Selstead
Lyminge
A260
19 Hawkinge
14
A20
12
Hythe
27
Dymchurch
St Mary's Bay
Littlestone-on-Sea
Greatstone-on-Sea
35

MARGATE Cliftonville
Westgate-on-Sea Kingsgate
Birchington A255
A28 Manston
Broadstairs
Ramsgate AA
RAMSGATE
39
DUNKERQUE
5 Sandwich
DEAL
Walmer
12 Kingsdown
St Margaret's at Cliffe
A2
DOVER
13 V
OOSTENDE CALAIS BOULOGNE
AA
H CALAIS
V BOULOGNE
STRAIT OF DOVER

SOUTHEND-ON-SEA
43 AA 45
Great Wakering
44 Shoeburyness
40

TW

9 0 1 2 3 4 5

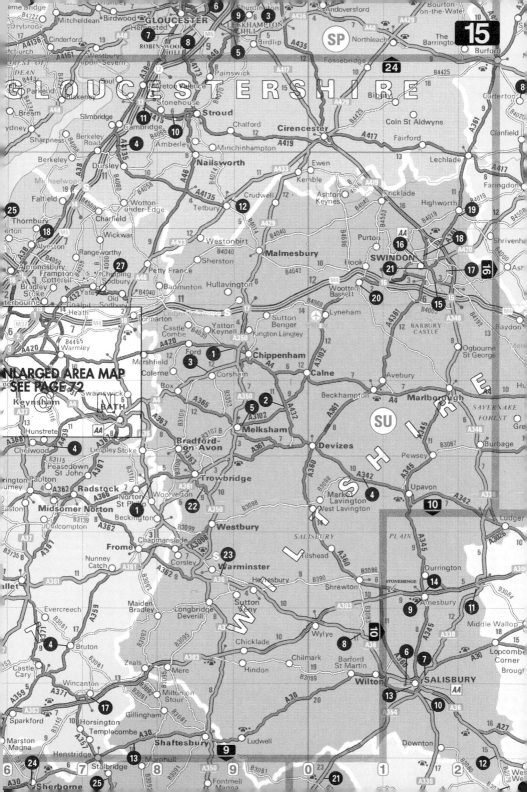

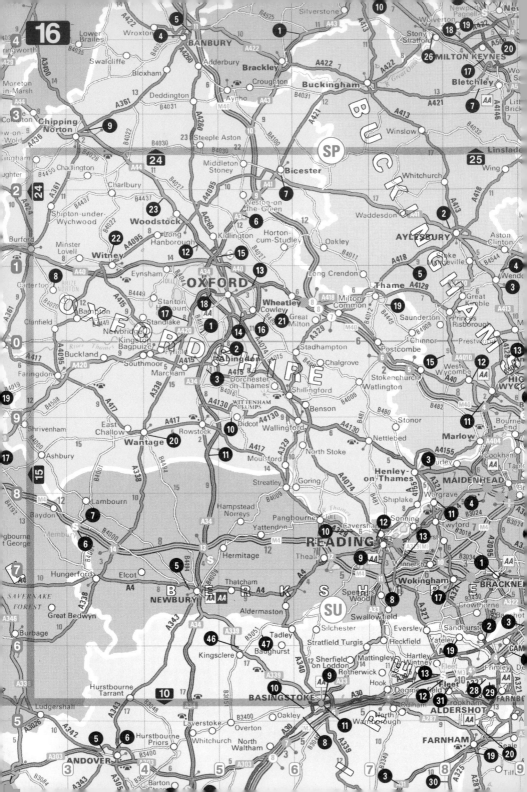

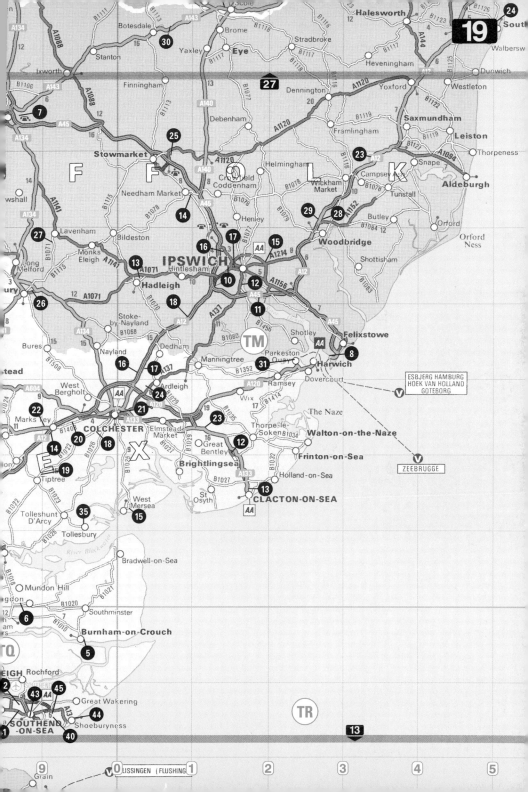

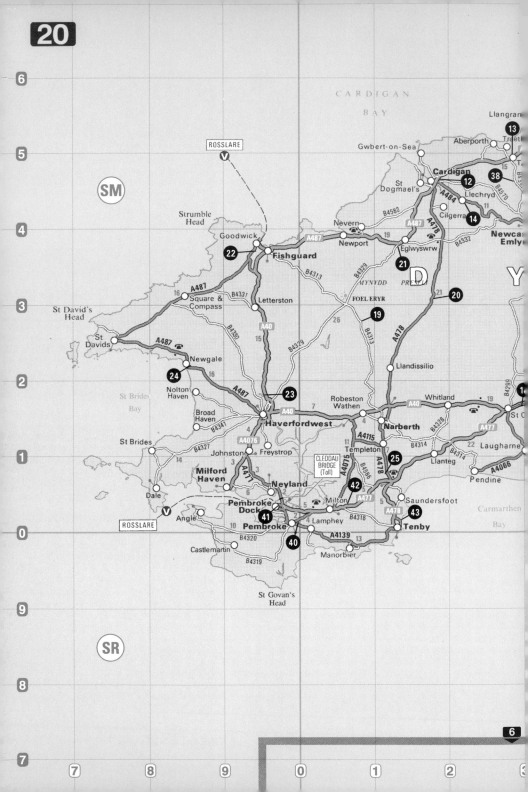

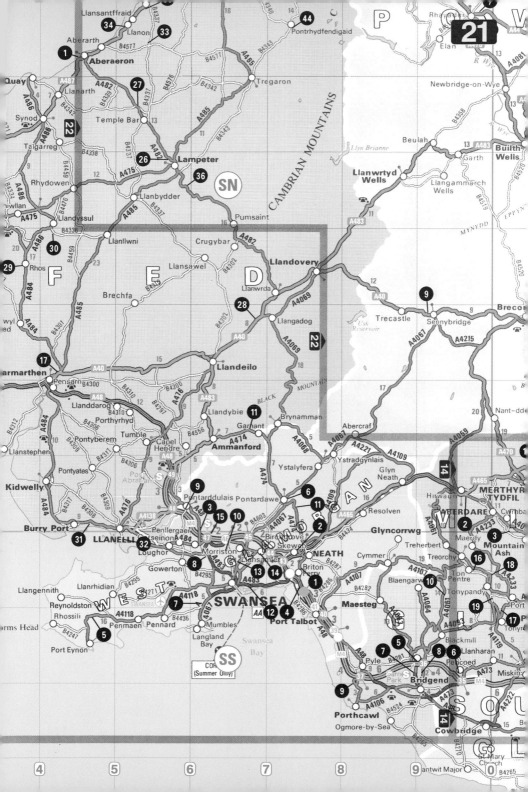

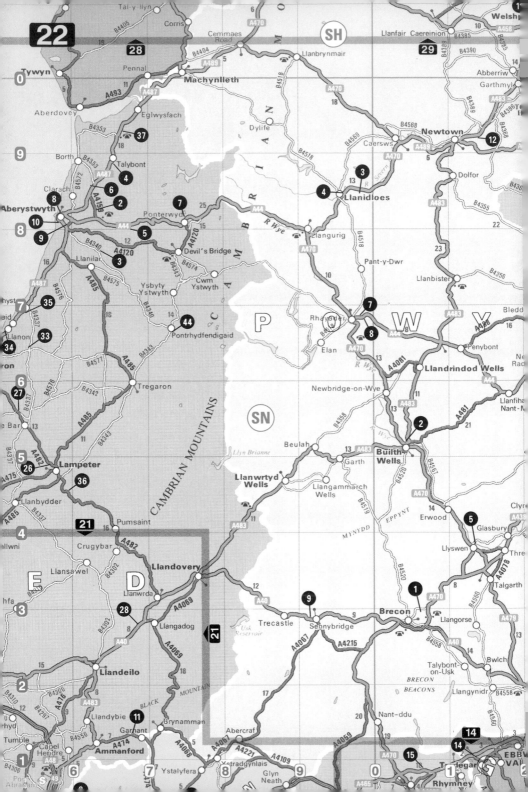

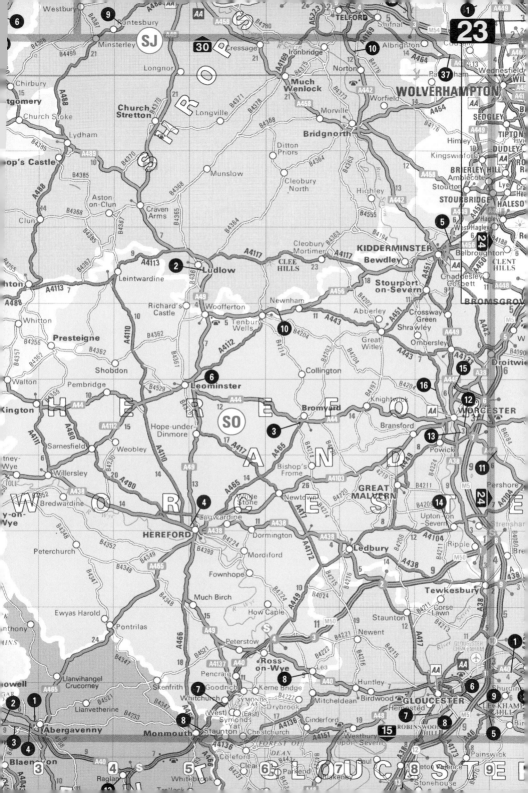

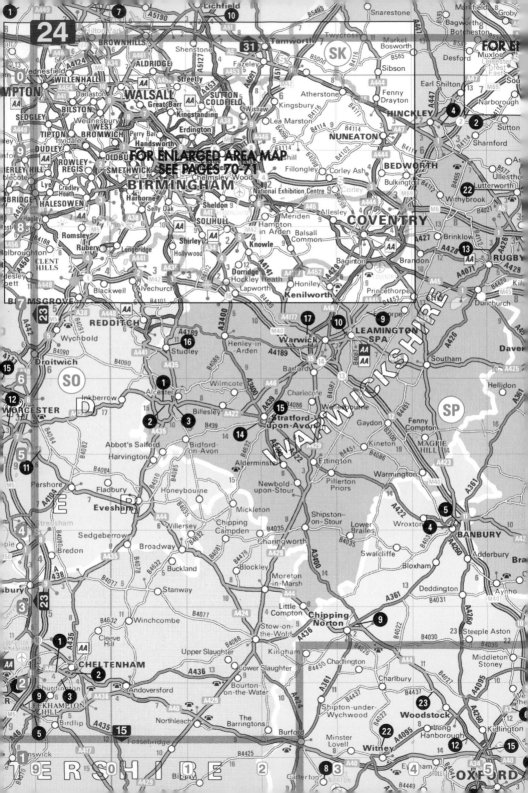

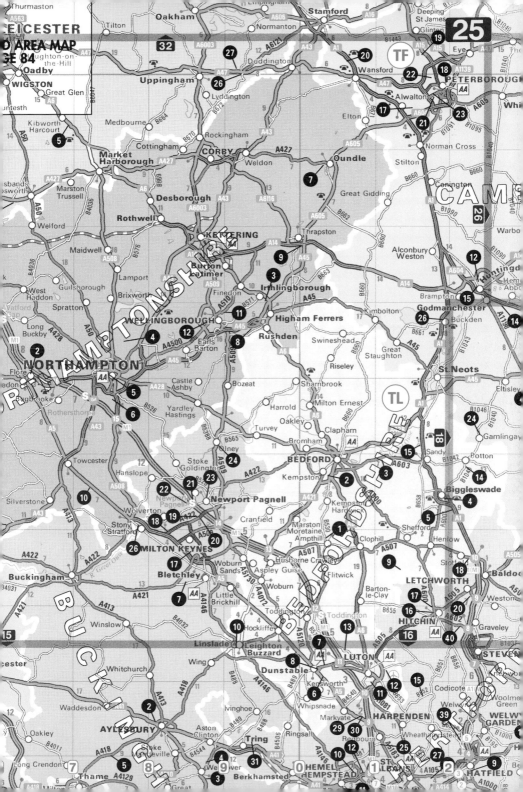

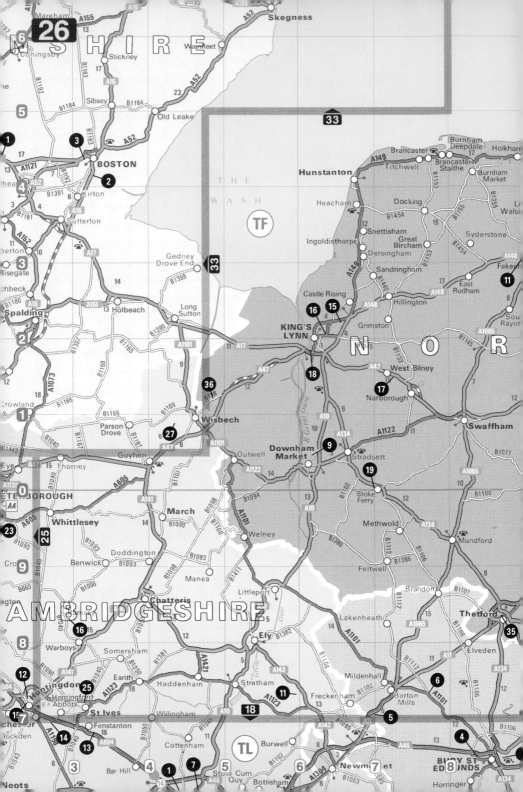

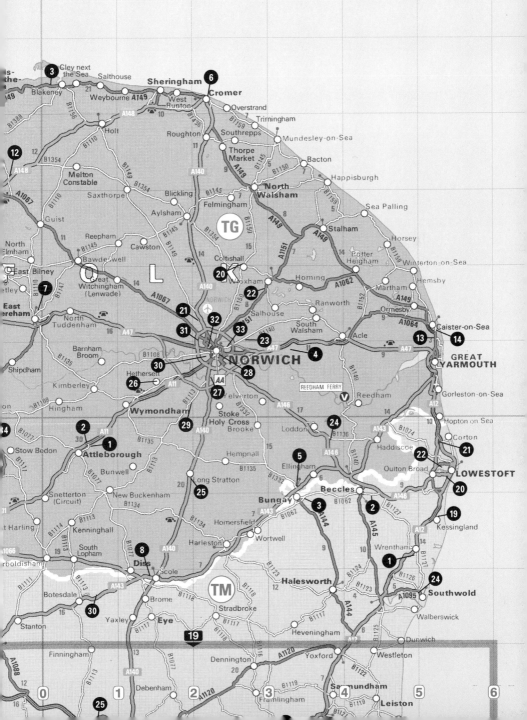

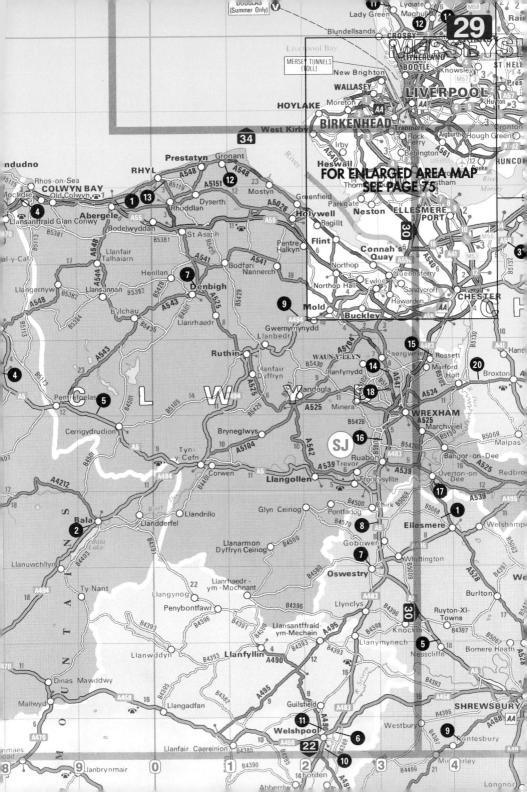

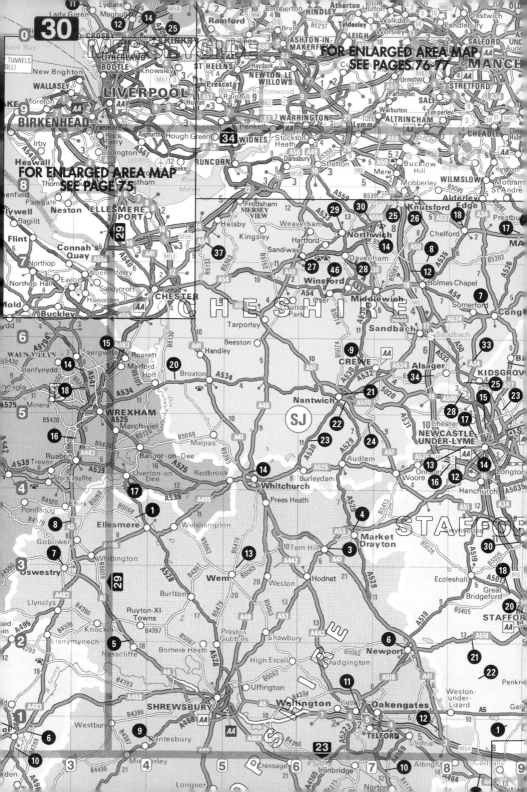

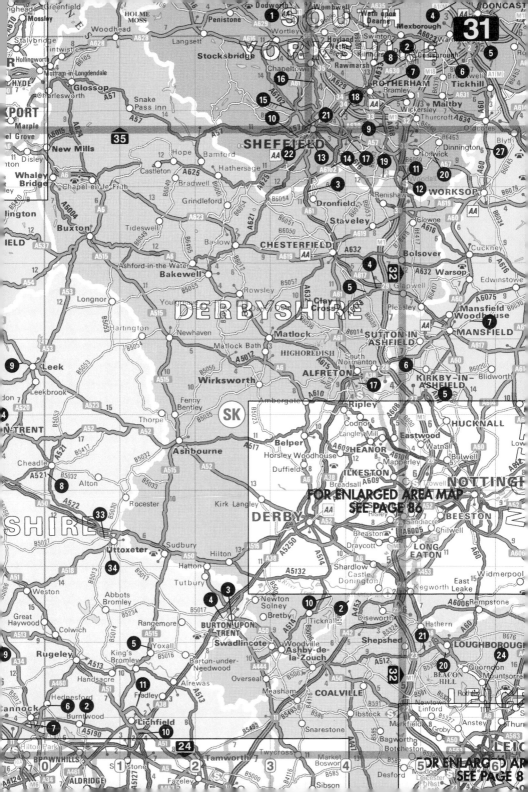

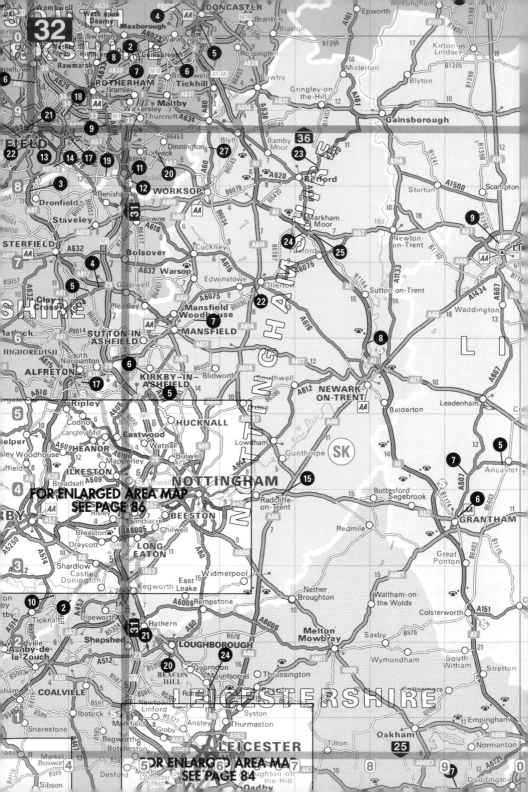

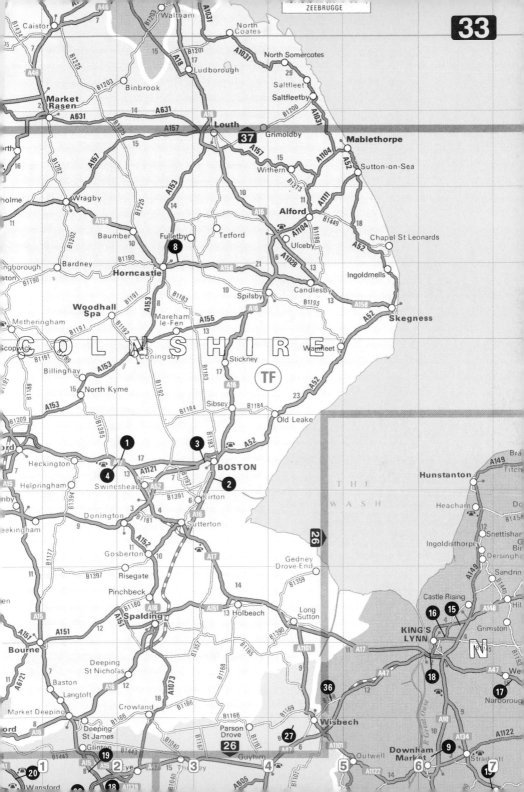

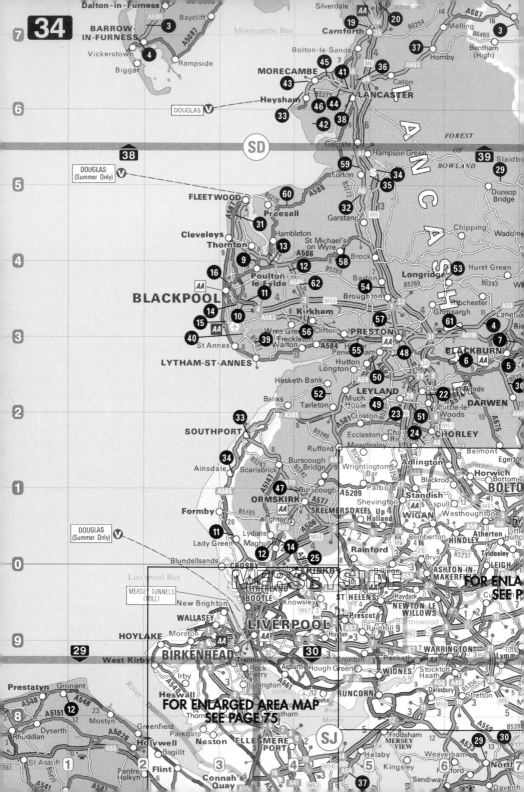

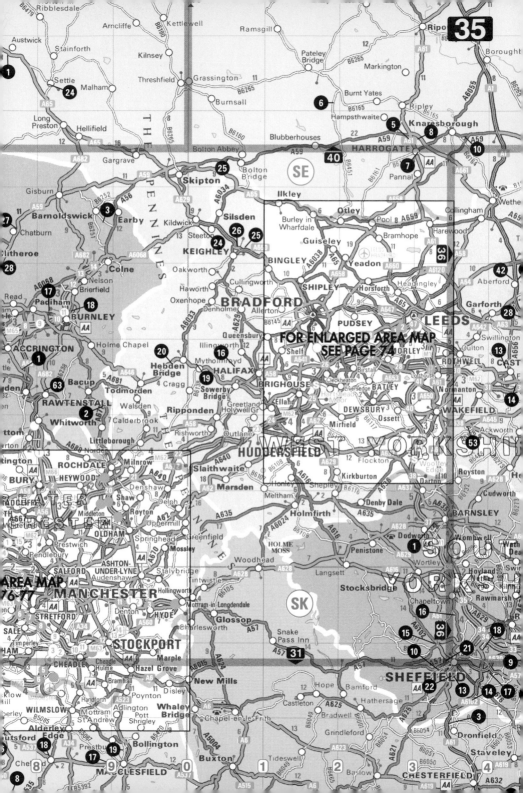

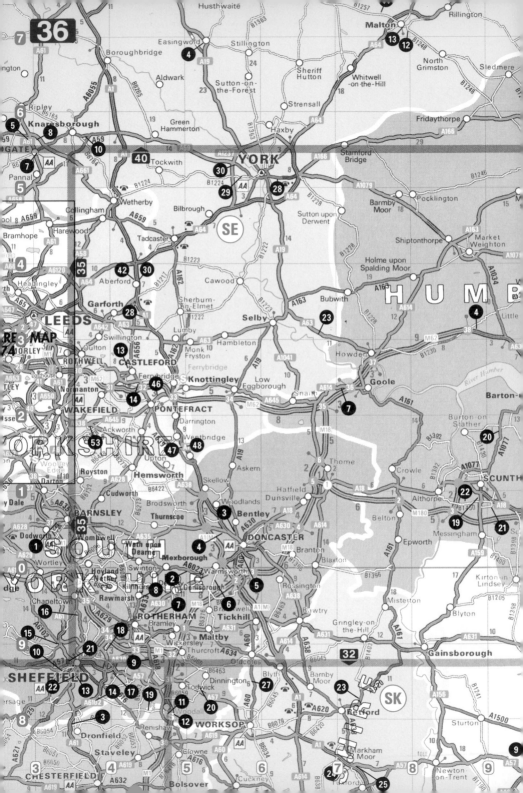

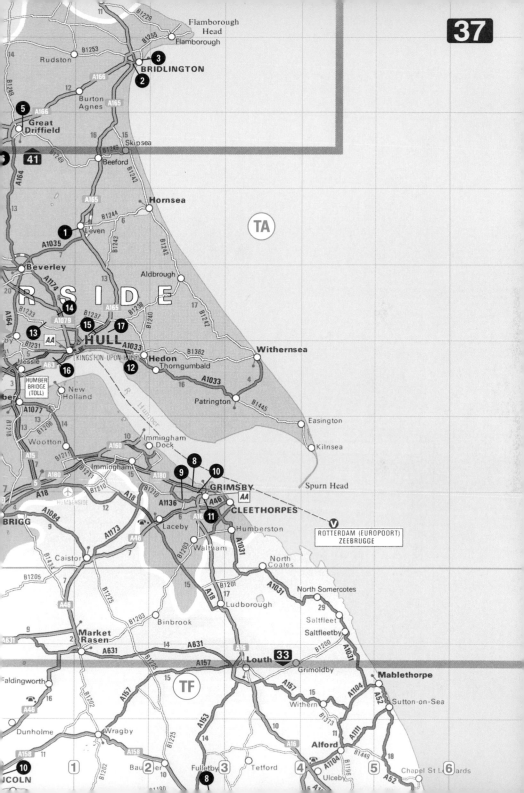

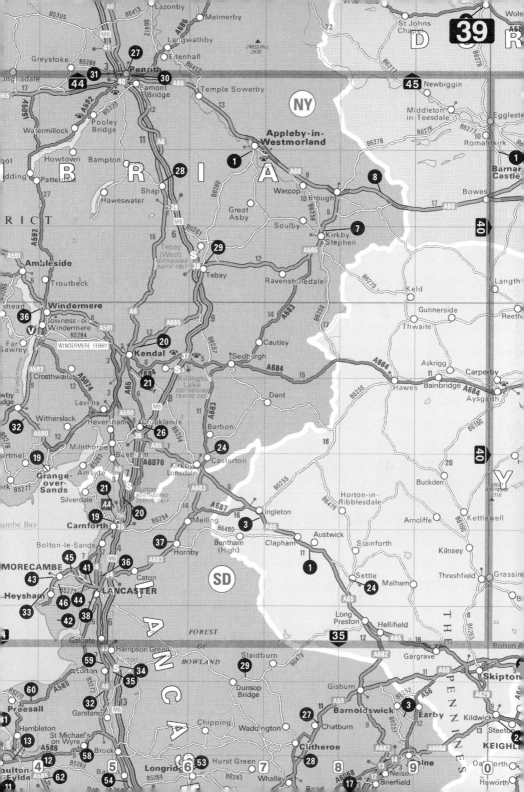

by the Sea

tton
Easingston Staithes
s
16
B1266 **A174** Sandsend
B1266
21 **A171** 27 Whitby
Ruswarp
Egton
Grosmont
Goathland
Robin Hood's Bay
Ravenscar
M O O R S
20
Rosedale Abbey
A169
20
Lastingham
Cloughton
Appleton-Le-Moors
Hackness
Wrelton
Scalby
20 SCARBOROUGH
3 **A170**
A170
Pickering
East Ayton
Wykeham 22
A169
Eastfield
Thornton Dale
Seamer
11
8
17
Snainton
B1261
Kirby
Misperton
Sherburn
A64
21
Filey
E
B1256
Staxton
A1039
7
B1257
14
Hunmanby
A165
Malton
Rillington
Reighton
13
B1248
12
A64
16
B1249
11
Flamborough Head
North Grimston
Sledmere
14
B1255
Flamborough
B1233
Rudston
B1253
3
Whitwell -on-the-Hill
B1248
B1753
Burton Agnes
Bridlington
2
TA
Fridaythorpe
A166
5
A166
Great Driffield
12
A166
Skipsea
37
Stamford Bridge
29
B1248
Bainton
6
A164
Beeford
A1079
Barmby Moor
Pocklington
18
Middleton on the Wolds
A165
Hornsea
15
B1248
13
B1244
A163
Shiptonthorpe
Market Weighton
1
Leven
6
A1035
B1243
B1242
Holme upon Spalding Moor
19
A1079
Beverley
Walkington
A1174
A1079
A164

H U M B E R S I D E

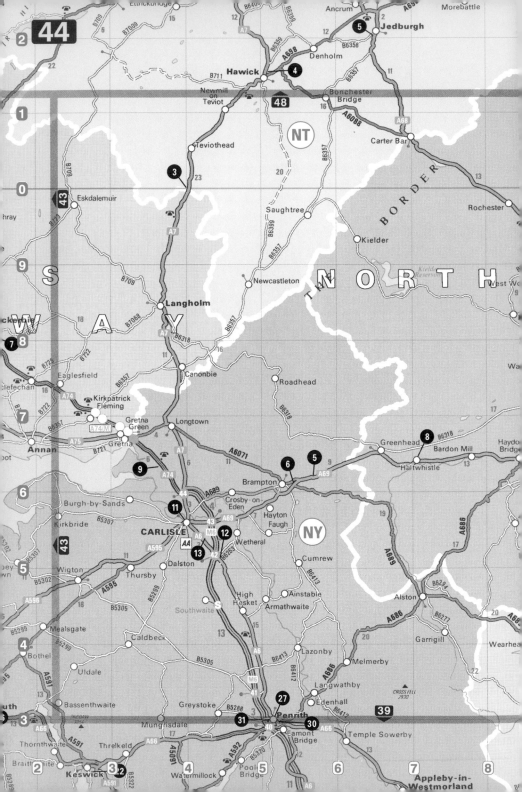

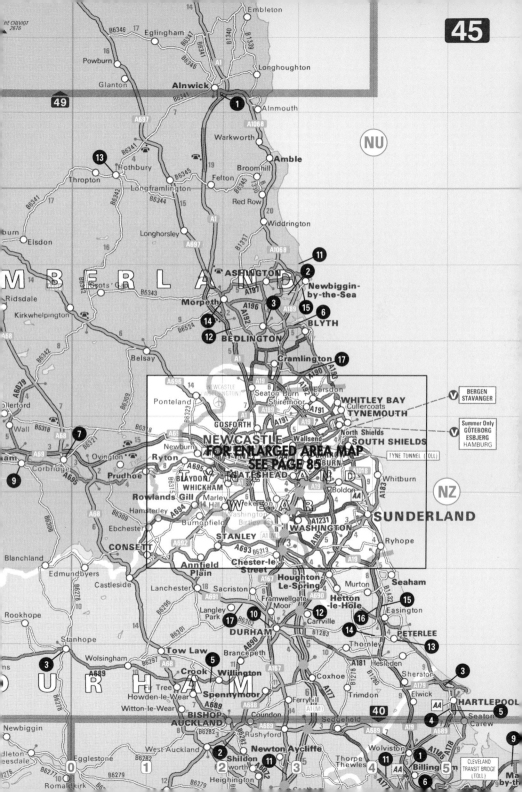

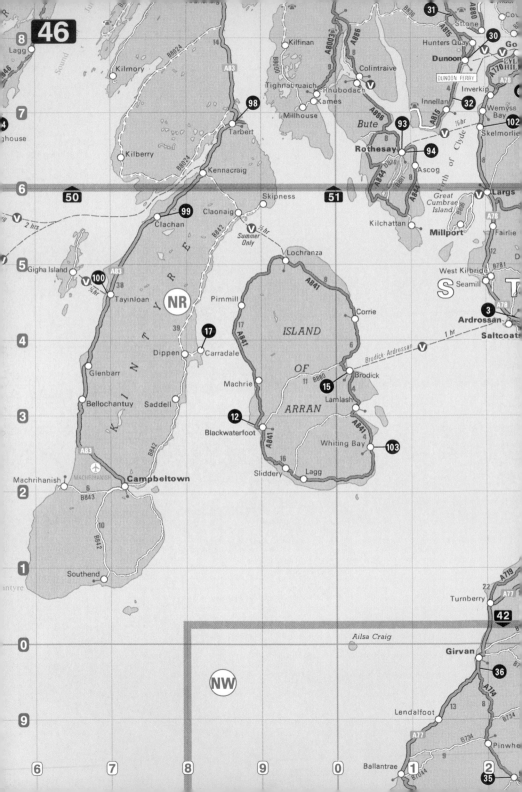

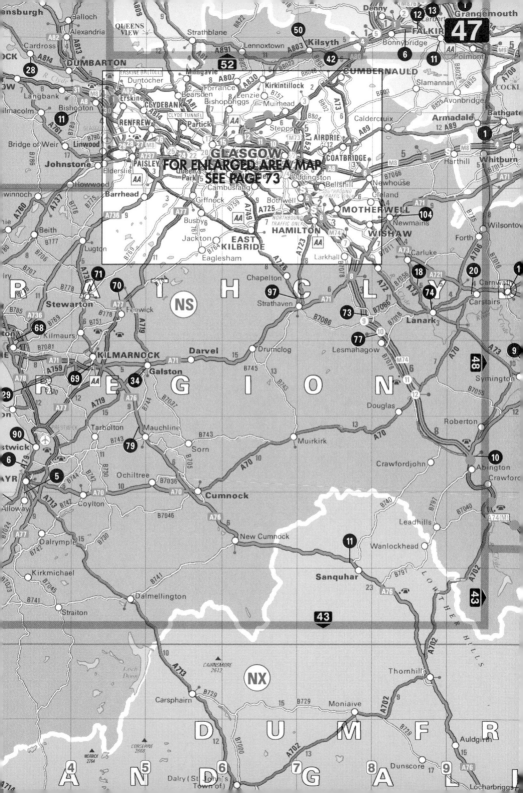

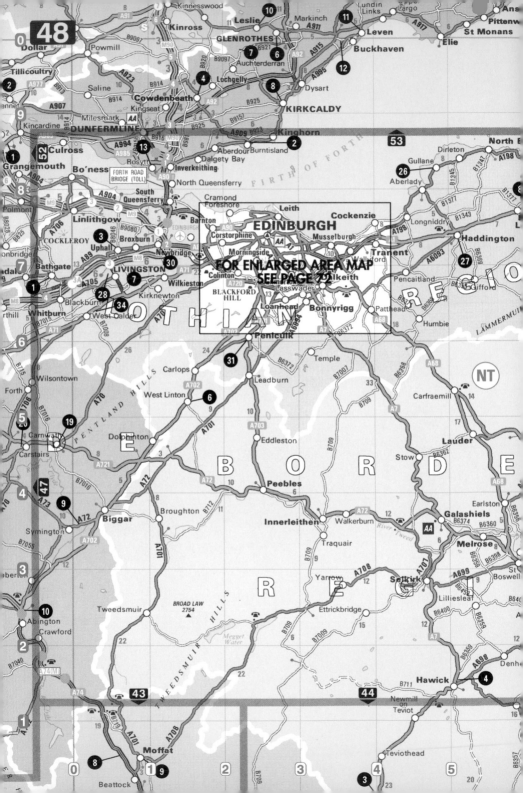

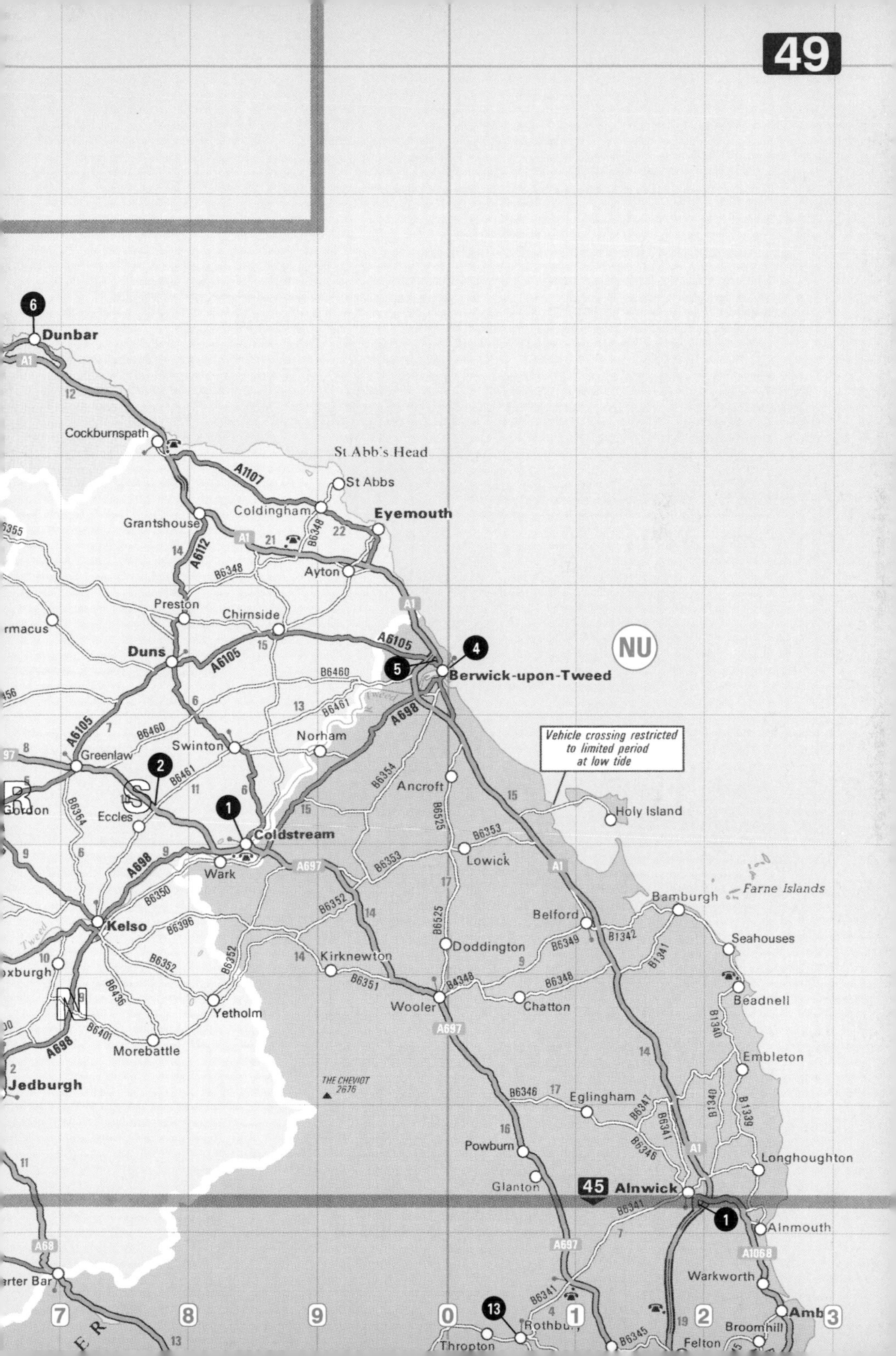

Dunbar

A1

12

Cockburnspath

St Abb's Head

A1107

St Abbs

Coldingham

Eyemouth

Grantshouse

A6112

14

A1 21

B6348

22

B6355

B6348

Ayton

Preston

Chirnside

A6105

Duns

A6105

15

B6460

A1

A6105

4

5

Berwick-upon-Tweed

A6105

7

B6460

13

B6461

A698

Greenlaw

A6105

8

2

B6461

11

6

Norham

Vehicle crossing restricted
to limited period
at low tide

NU

B6364

Gordon

Eccles

1

Coldstream

15

B6354

Ancroft

15

Holy Island

9

6

A698

B6350

9

Wark

A697

B6353

B6525

B6353

Lowick

A1

Farne Islands

Kelso

Tweed

B6396

B6352

B6352

17

B6525

Belford

Bamburgh

10

B6352

14

Kirknewton

B6349

B1342

Seahouses

xburgh

N

B6436

B6401

14

B6351

B6348

Doddington

9

B6348

Chatton

B1341

Beadnell

A698

Morebattle

Yetholm

Wooler

A697

B1340

Embleton

B1339

Jedburgh

THE CHEVIOT
2676

B6346

Eglingham

B6341

B6341

B6346

A1

Longhoughton

16

Powburn

B6346

11

Glanton

45 Alnwick

1

A697

7

Alnmouth

A68

B6341

A1068

rter Bar

Warkworth

13

Rothbury

Amb

7

8

9

0

13

1

B6345

2

Broomhill

3

Thropton

Felton

19

ER

13

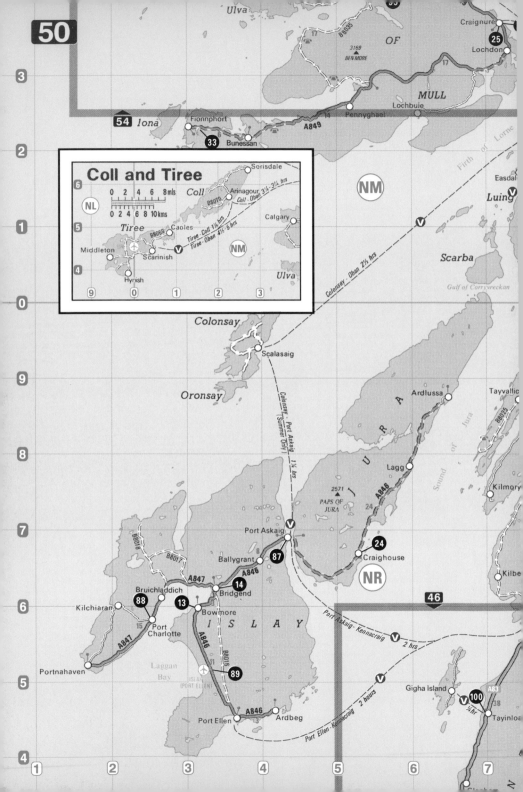

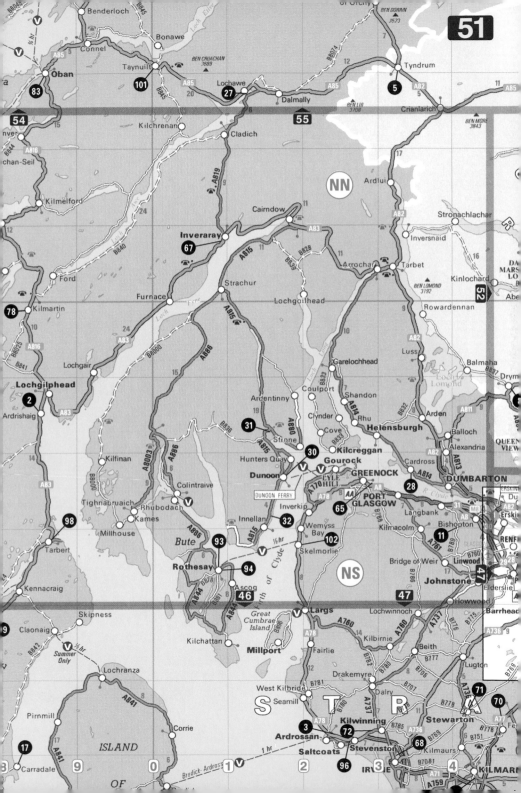

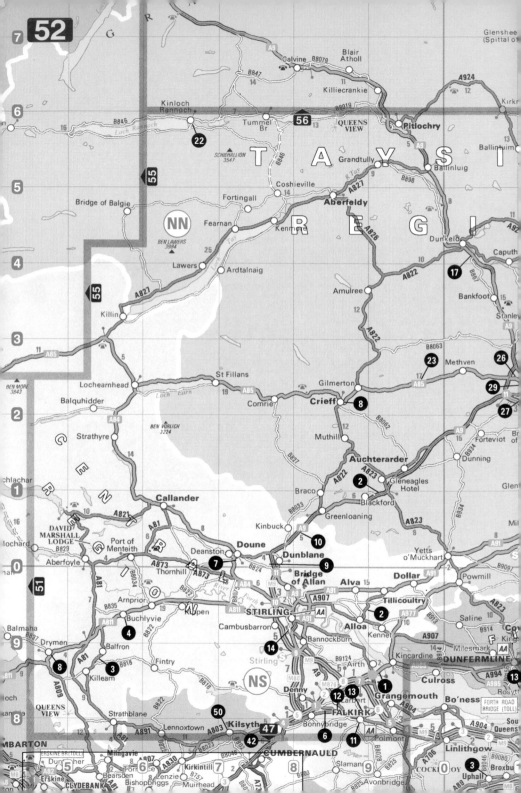

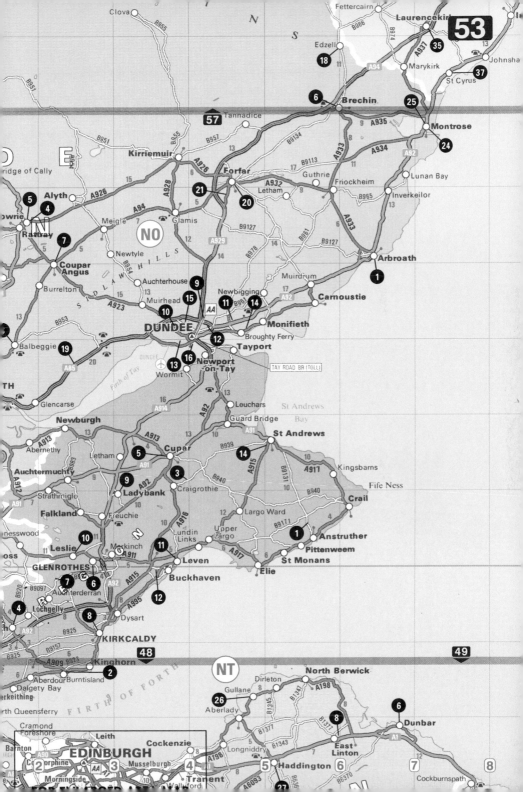

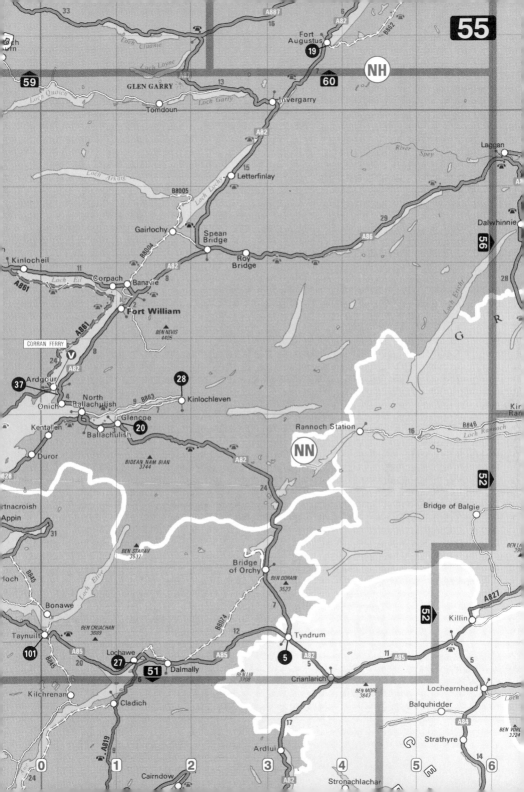

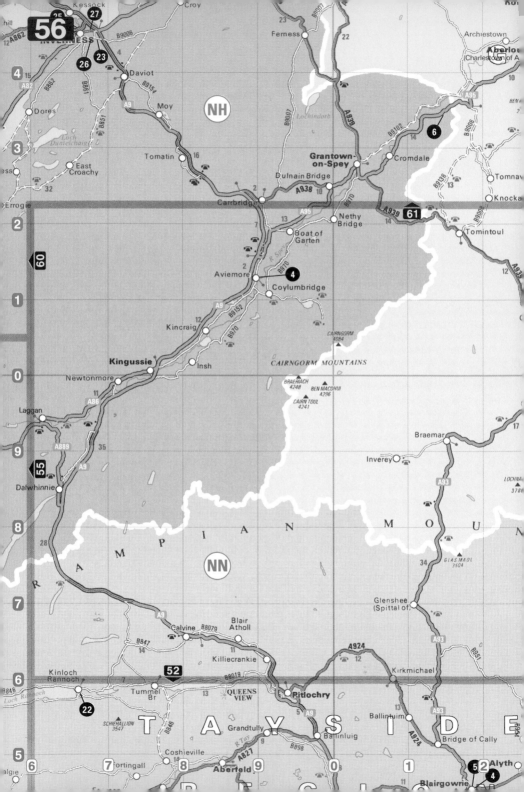

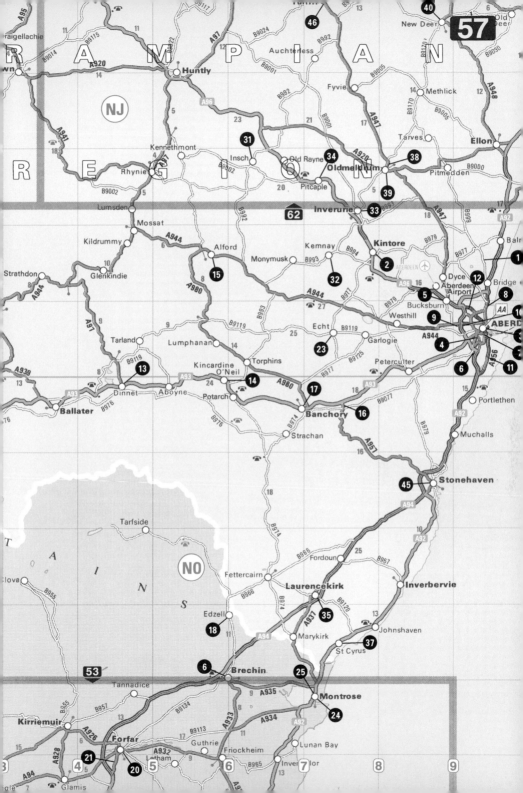

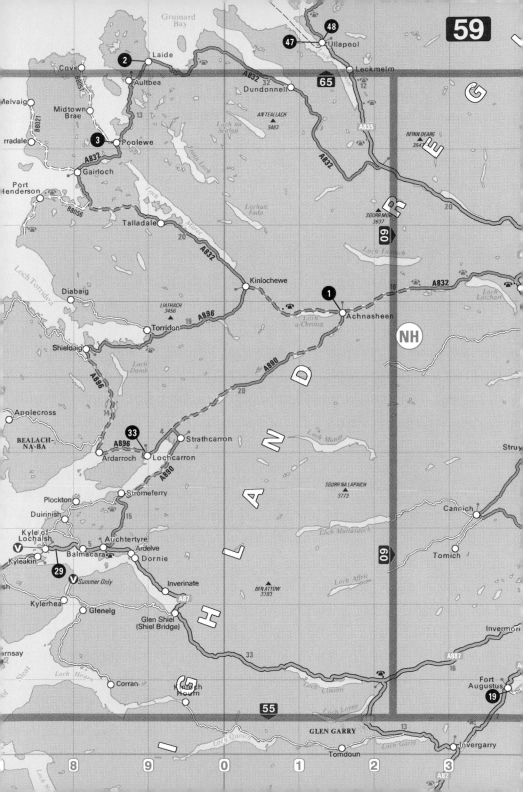

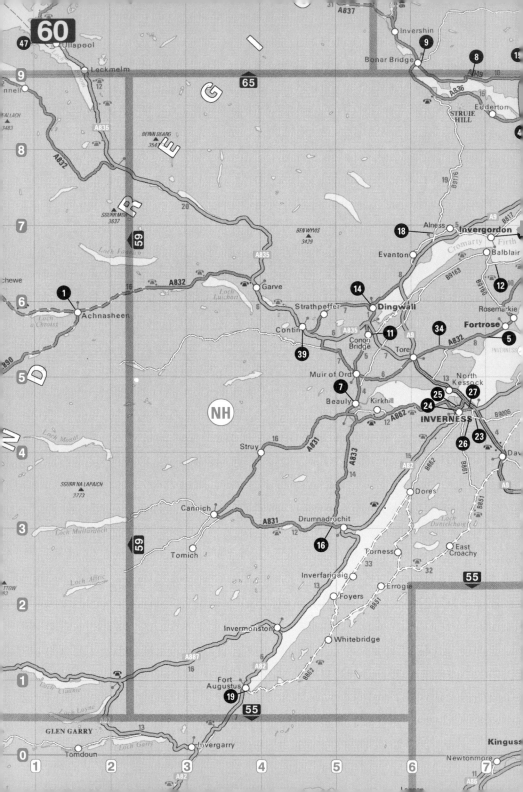

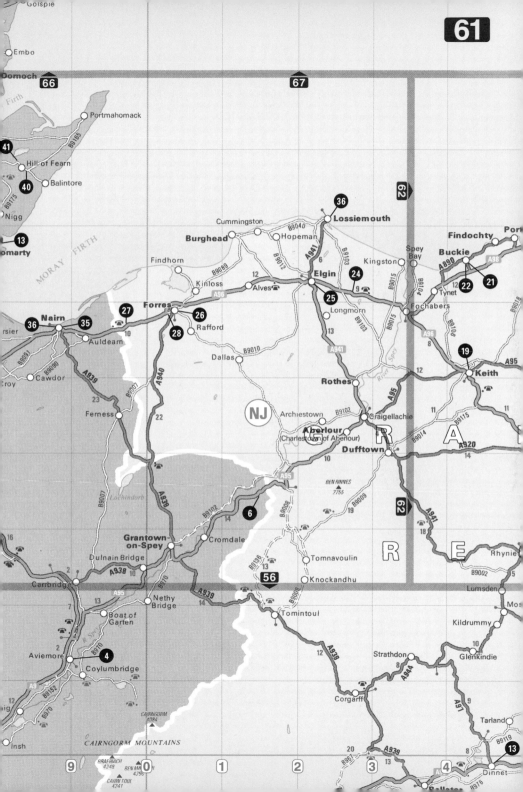

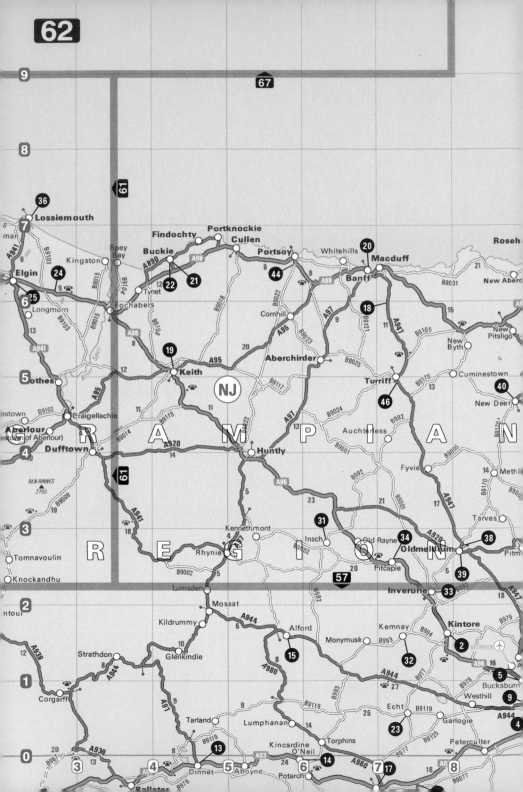

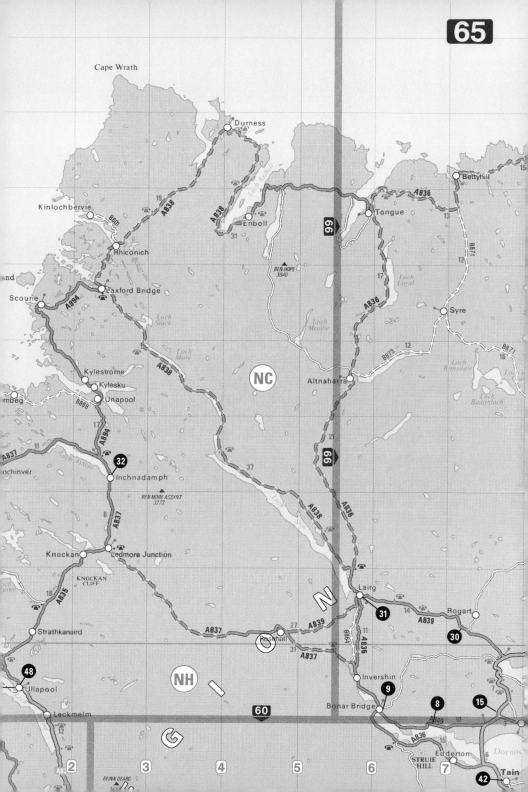

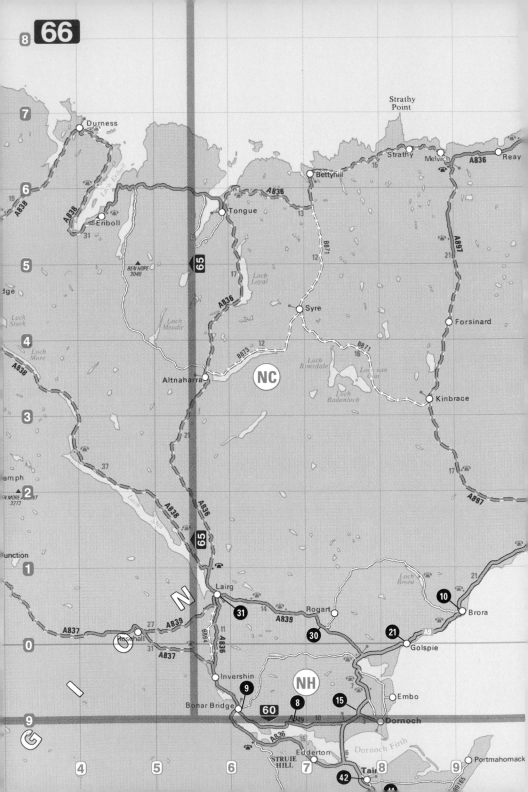

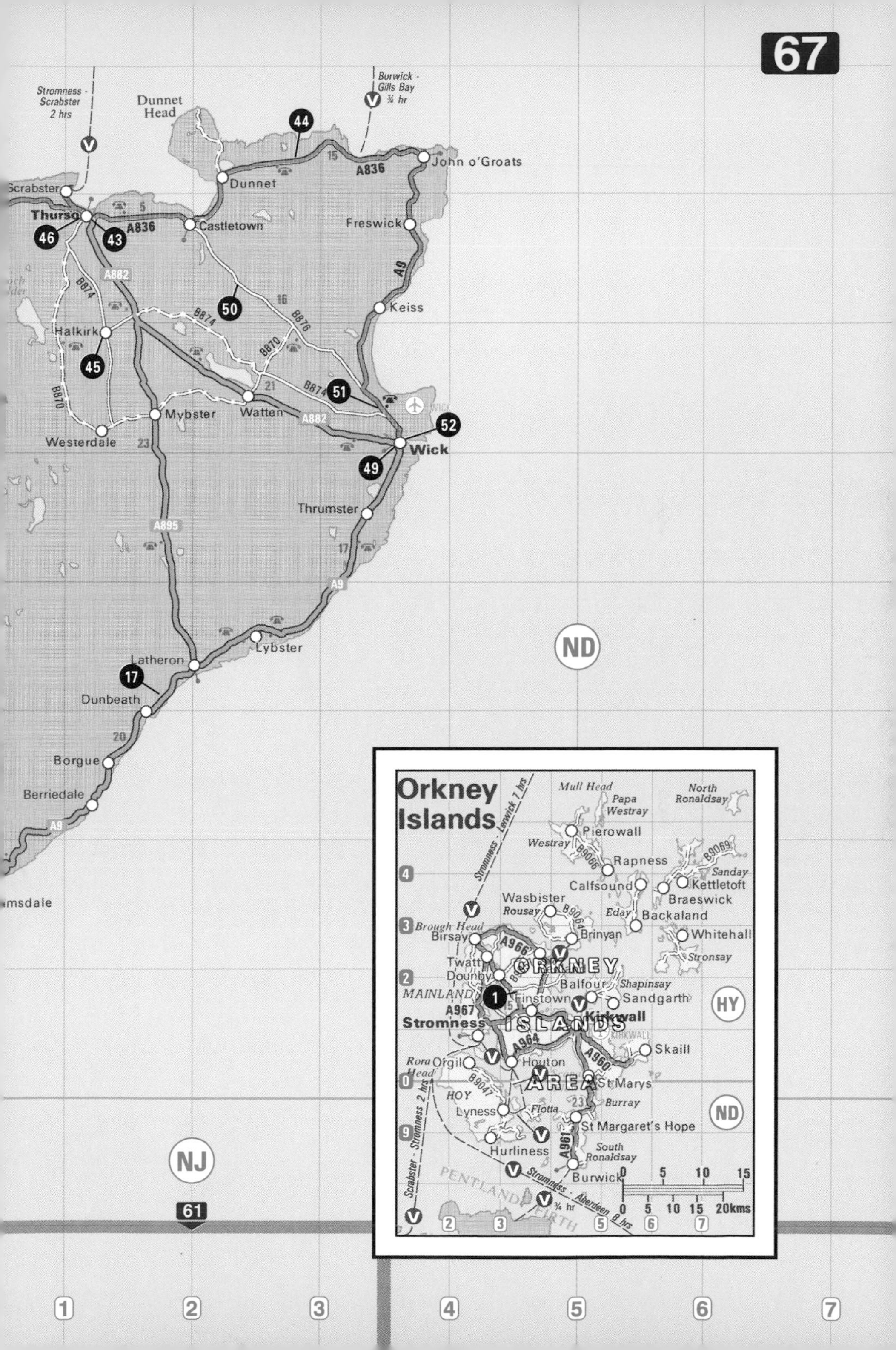

Stromness - Scrabster 2 hrs

Dunnet Head

Burwick - Gills Bay ¾ hr

44

15 **A836**

John o'Groats

Dunnet

Freswick

Thurso

46 **43** **A836**

Castletown

A9

A882

B874

50

Keiss

16 B876

Halkirk

B874

B870

45

51

B870

B874

A882

52

Mybster Watten

Westerdale 23

Wick

21

49

A895

Thrumster

17

A9

Lybster

Latheron

17

Dunbeath

20

Borgue

Berriedale

A9

msdale

ND

NJ

61

Orkney Islands

Stromness Lerwick 7 hrs

Mull Head

Papa Westray

North Ronaldsay

Pierowall

B9069

Westray

Rapness

Sanday

Calfsound

Kettletoft

4

Brough Head

Wasbister

Eday

Braeswick

3

Birsay

Rousay

B9061

Brinyan

Backaland

Whitehall

Twatt

A966

ORKNEY

Stronsay

2

Dounby

MAINLAND

Balfour

Finstown

Shapinsay

Sandgarth

1

ISLANDS

Kirkwall

HY

Stromness

A967

KIRKWALL

A964

Skaill

Rora Orgil

Head

Houton

A960

0

HOY

B9047

AREA

St Marys

ND

9

Lyness

Flotta

23

Burray

St Margaret's Hope

Hurliness

A961

South Ronaldsay

Scrabster - Stromness 2 hrs

Stromness ¾ hr

Burwick

Aberdeen 8 hrs

0   5   10   15

PENTLAND FIRTH

0   5   10   15   20kms

2   3   5   6   7

NJ

1   2   3   4   5   6   7

Scale 1:1,000,000 approx 16 miles to 1 inch

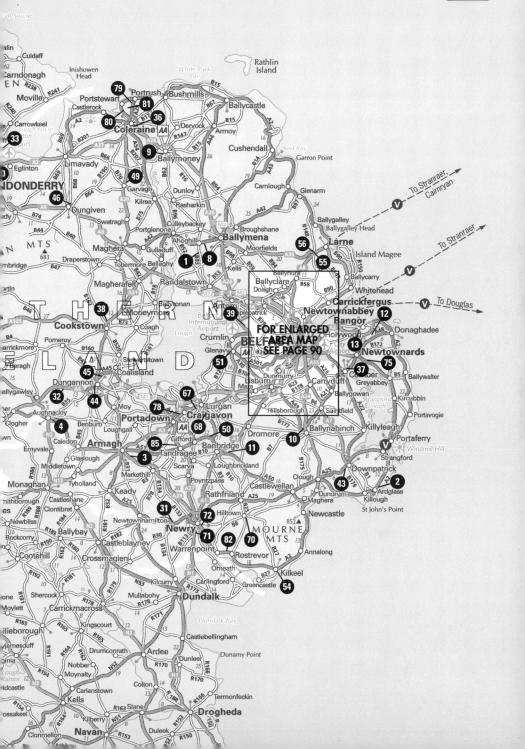

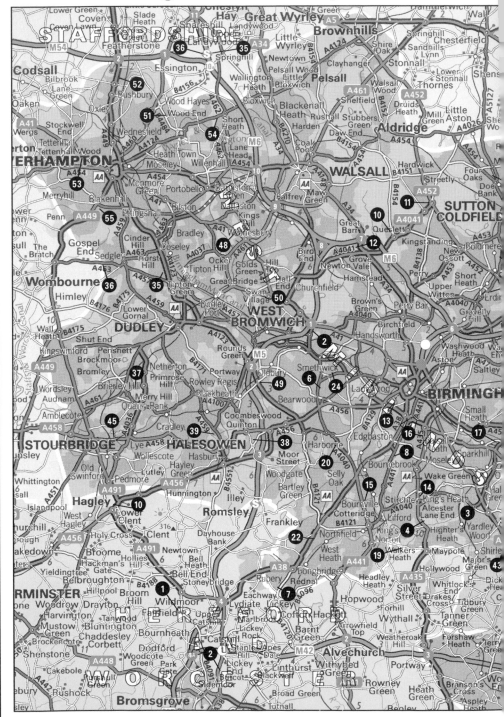

Wigginton
Seckington
Barton the Bear
A51
A513
B5493
Shuttington
Twycross
Shackerstone
Little Twycross
Congerstone
Veeford
Hopwas
Coton
Amington
Alvecote
M42
Warton
Twycross
Bilstone
Ca
Hints
Mile Oak
TAMWORTH
Bonehill
Glascote
Polesworth
Orton-on-the-Hill
Sheepy Magna
Sheepy Parva
Wellsborough
Market Boswort
Fazeley
Kettlebrook
Polesworth
Two Gates
Wilnecote
Hockley
Dordon
Bradley Green
B5000
Sibson
Ratcliffe Culey
Shenton
Drayton Bassett
Dosthill
A5
Grendon
Whittington
Atherstone
Higham on the Hi
A453
Whateley
Baddesley Ensor
Atherstone
Witherley
Atterton
Stoke Golding
Hine
Middleton
Cliff
Wood End
Baxterley
Fenny Drayton
A5
Stoke End
Hunts Green
Hurley Common
Mancetter
A446
Wishaw
Bodymoor Heath
Kingsbury
Hurley
Bentley
Ridge Lane
Oldbury
Hartshill
A444
Over Green
A38
Lea Marston
Marston
Nether Whitacre
Birchley Heath
Church End
Chapel End
Weddington
A47
Curdworth
Whitacre Heath
Botts Green
B4114
Anstey
Galley Common
Stockingford
NUNEATON
Water Orton
Hogrill's End
Whitacre Fields
Furnace End
Ballards Green
Arley
B4112
B4102
Attleborough
Blythe End
Gilson
Church End
Over Whitacre
Devitts Green
Gun Hill
Astley
Griff
Bram
Cole End
Shustoke
Astley
Marston Jabbet
B4112
Castle Bromwich
M42
Coleshill
Fillongley
Wood End
Bedworth Woodlands
Weston in Arden
Bulkin
Bedworth
B4029
Shard End
Maxstoke
Green End
Corley Ash
Goodyers End
Blackbank
Little Bayton
Barnacle
Kitt's Green
Bacon's End
M6
Corley
Ash Green
Exhall
Chelmsley Wood
A446
Little Packington
Chapel Green
Corley Moor
Keresley Green
Neal's Gn
Longford
Hawkesbury
Marston Green
Outwoods
Eaves Green
Hawkes End
Rowley Gn
Little
Aldermans Green
Sowe
Common
Sheldon
Elmdon
Bickenhill
Stonebridge
Meriden
Pinkett's Booth
Pickford
Keresley
Heath
Coleshill Potters Green
Walsgr on Sow
Elmdon Heath
Hampton in Arden
Four Oaks
Flint's Green
Pickford Green
Allesley
Stoke Green Heath Wyken
A46
Catherine-de-Barnes
B4102
Berkswell
Eastern Green
A45
A4114
COVENTRY
A428
LIHULL
Eastcote
A452
Reeves Green
Tile Hill
Canley
Earlsdon
Pinley
Binley
Brando
Copt Heath
Barston
Balsall Common
B4101
Westwood Heath
Kirby Corner
Stivichall
Willenhall
Ryton-on-Dunsmore
Knowle
Balsall Street
Carol Green
Catchem's Corner
King's Hill
Tollbar End
Temple Balsall
Balsall
Burton Green
Baginton
Brand
Dorridge
Darley Green
Fen End
Stoneleigh
A445
Four Ashes
Chessetts Wood
Chadwick End
Meer End
A452
The Spring
Crackley
A46
Stareton
Bubbenhall
Hockley Heath
Honiley
Baginton
A423
Lapworth
Haseley Knob
Kingswood
Wroxall
Kenilworth
Beausale
Windy Arbour
Weston under
Princethorpe
Kingswood Brook
Baddesley Clinton
Fiveways
Ashow

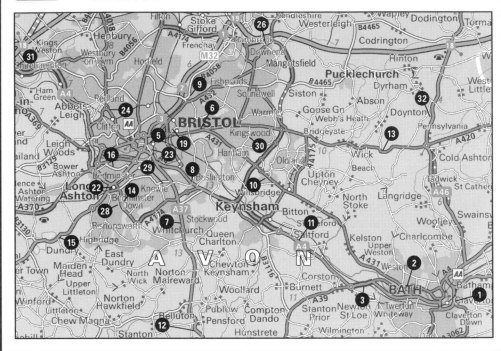

Edinburgh

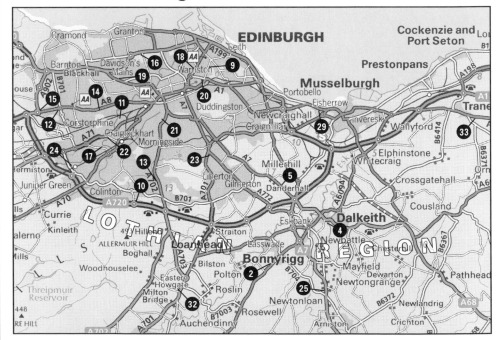

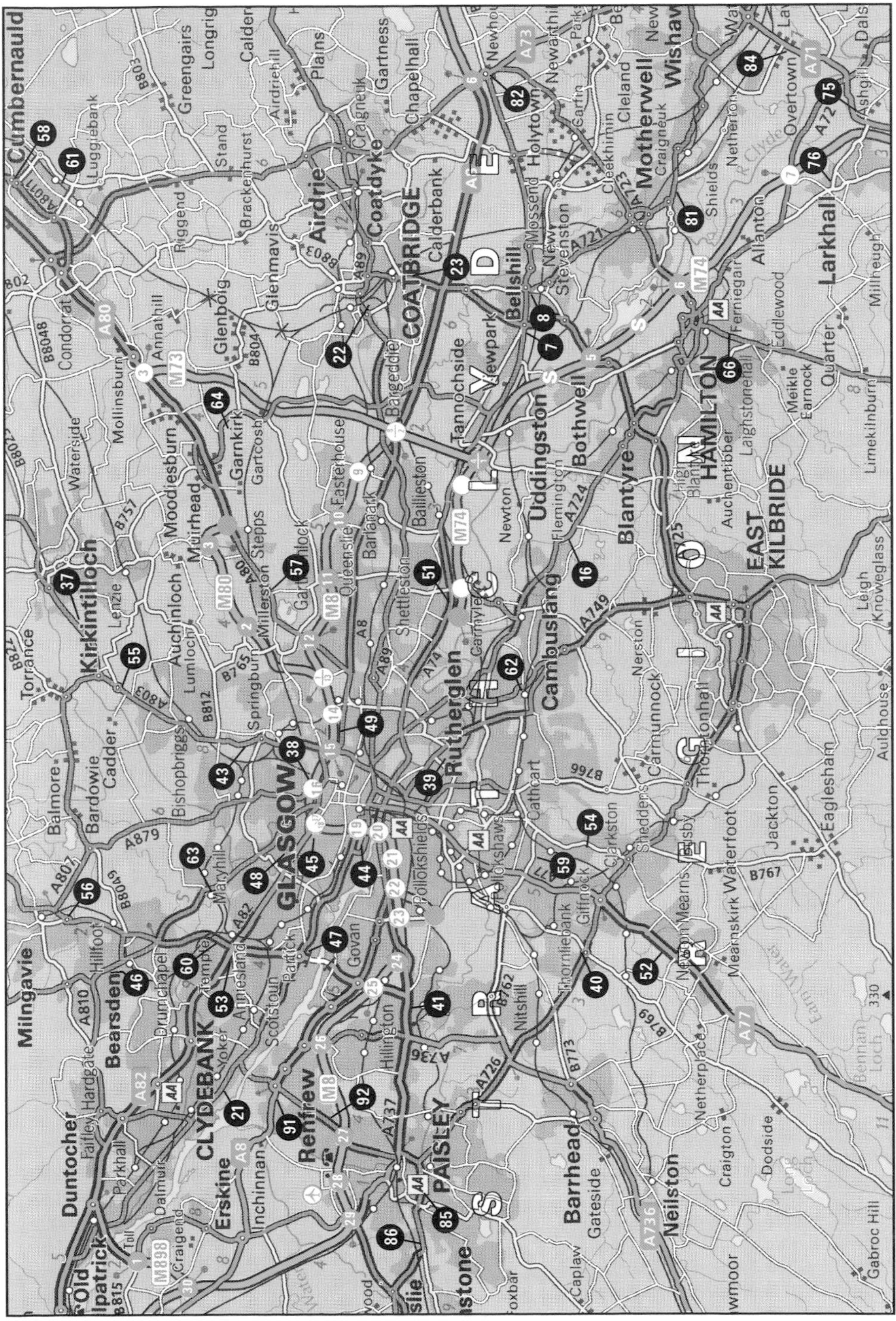

Cumbernauld
Luggiebank
Greengairs
Longriggend
Calderbank
Condorrat
Annathill
Mollinsburn
Glenboig
Riggend
Brackenhurst
Stand
Airdriehill
Plains
Gartness
Glenmavis
Airdrie
Craigneuk
Chapelhall
Coatdyke
COATBRIDGE
Calderbank
Bargeddie
Newhouse
Holytown
Newarthill
Carfin
Cleland
New Stevenson
Mossend
Bellshill
Motherwell
Wishaw
Craigneuk
Cleekhimin
Newpark
Tannochside
Uddingston
Bothwell
Shields
Netherton
Overtown
Ashgill
Dalserf
Larkhall
Allanton
Ferniegair
Eddlewood
Quarter
Millheugh
Limekilnburn
HAMILTON
Meikle Earnock
Laighstonehall
Auchentibber
High Blantyre
Blantyre
Fleminton
Newton
Baillieston
Easterhouse
Garnkirk
Gartcosh
Moodiesburn
Muirhead
Waterside
Stepps
Millerston
Gartloch
Barlanark
Queenslie
Shettleston
Carmyle
EAST KILBRIDE
Leigh Knoweglass
Kirkintilloch
Lenzie
Auchinloch
Lumloch
Torrance
Springburn
Bishopbriggs
Cadder
Bardowie
Balmore
Rutherglen
Cambuslang
Nerston
Carmunnock
Thorntonhall
Cathcart
Clarkston
Busby
Sheddens
Jackton
Eaglesham
Auldhouse
GLASGOW
Maryhill
Milngavie
Hillfoot
Bearsden
Temple
Drumchapel
Anniesland
Scotstoun
Partick
Govan
Pollokshields
Pollokshaws
Giffnock
Thornliebank
Newton Mearns
Mearnskirk
Waterfoot
Nitshill
Hillington
Yoker
CLYDEBANK
Renfrew
PAISLEY
Barrhead
Gateside
Neilston
Netherplace
Craigton
Dodside
Long Loch
Bennan Loch
Gabroc Hill
Duntocher
Faifley
Hardgate
Parkhall
Dalmuir
Old Kilpatrick
Craigend
Erskine
Inchinnan
Caplaw
Foxbar
Earn Water
M8
M73
M74
M80
M77
M898
A8
A80
A82
A726
A736
A737
A749
A724
A725
A721
A723
A73
A71
A72
A77
A803
A807
A879
A810
B8048
B803
B804
B812
B765
B766
B767
B769
B773
B762
B757
B822
B8049
B815

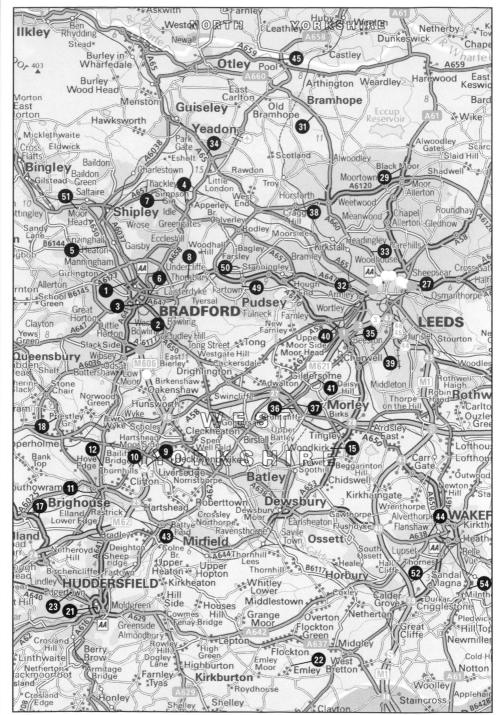

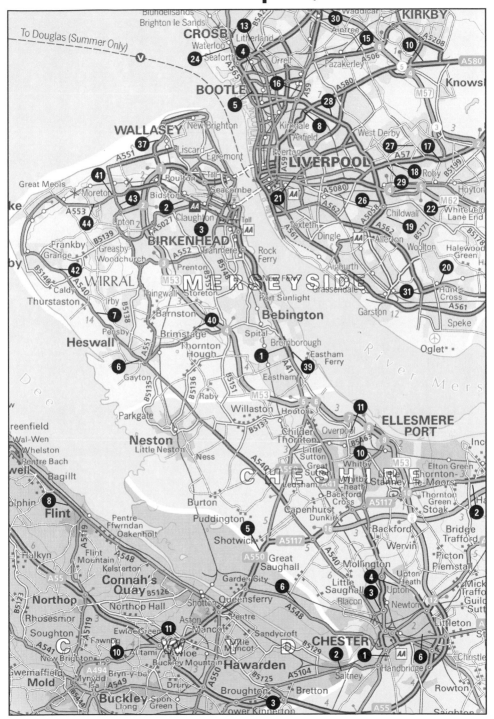

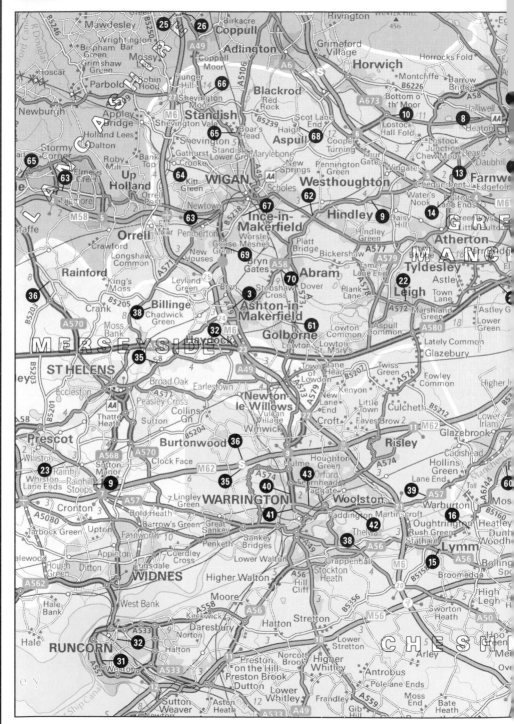

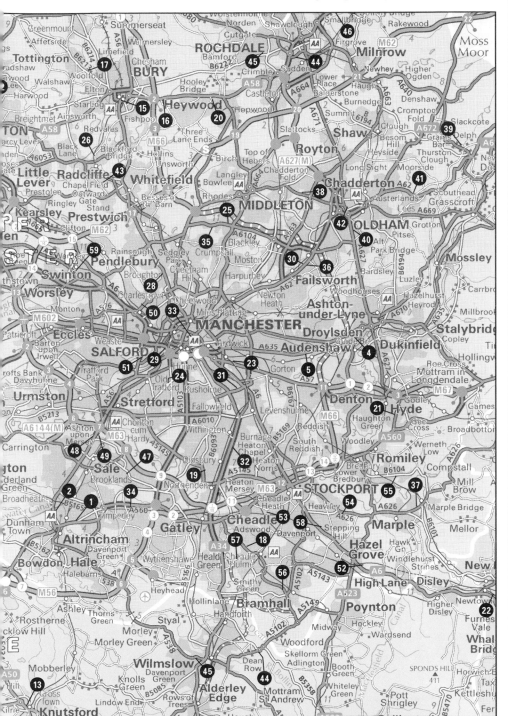

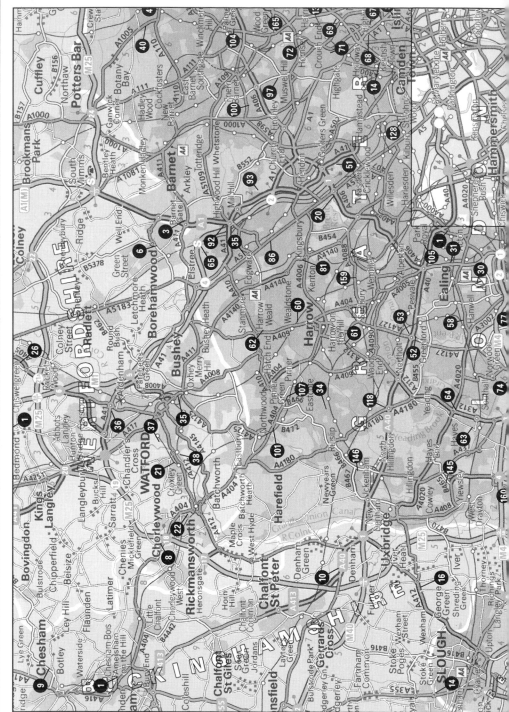

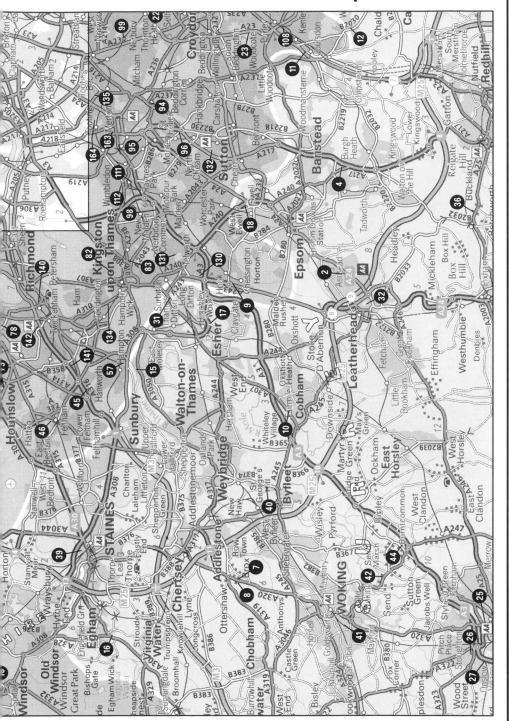

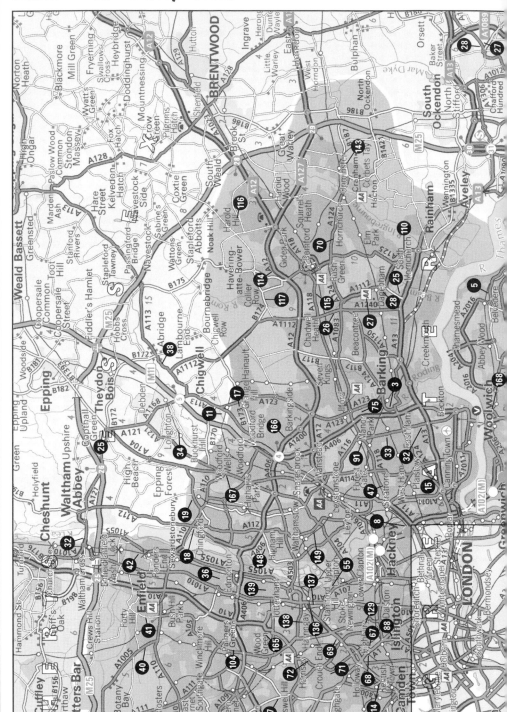

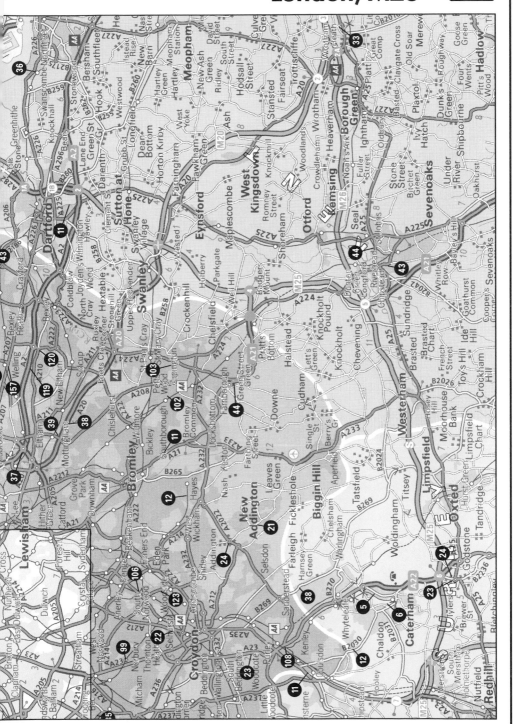

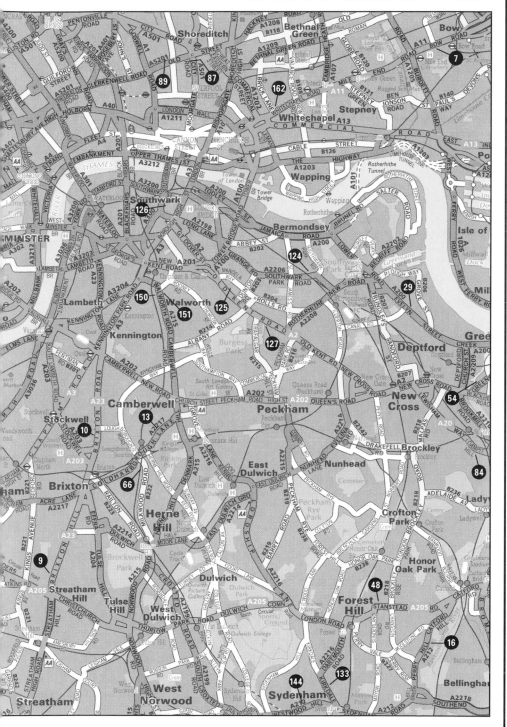

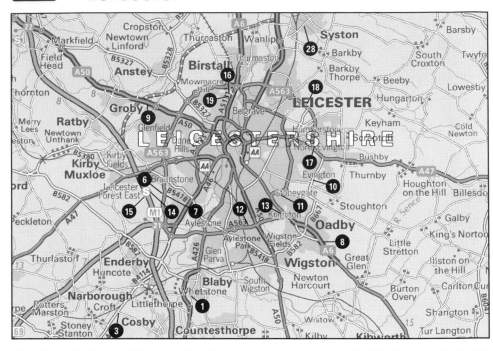

Medway Towns

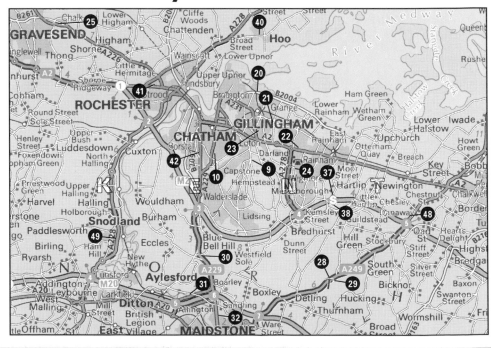

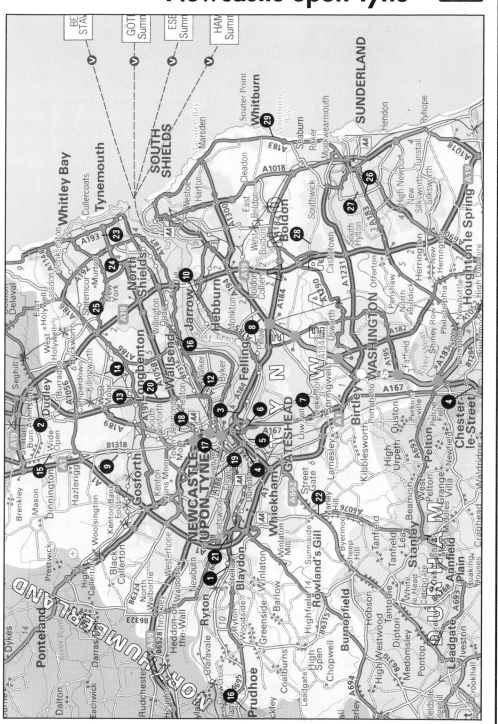

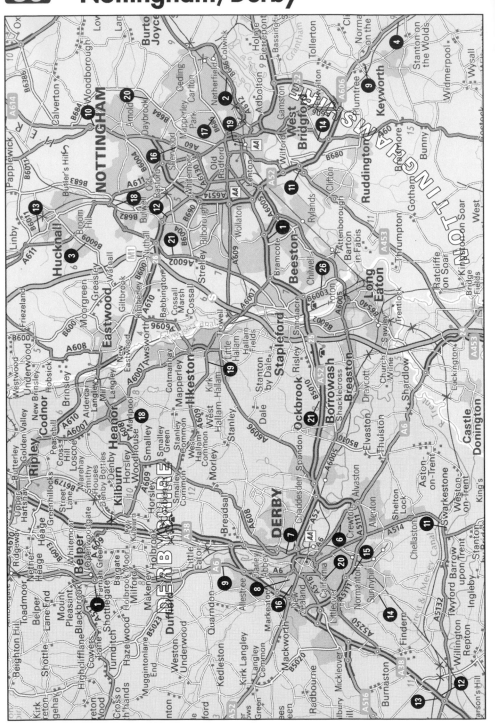

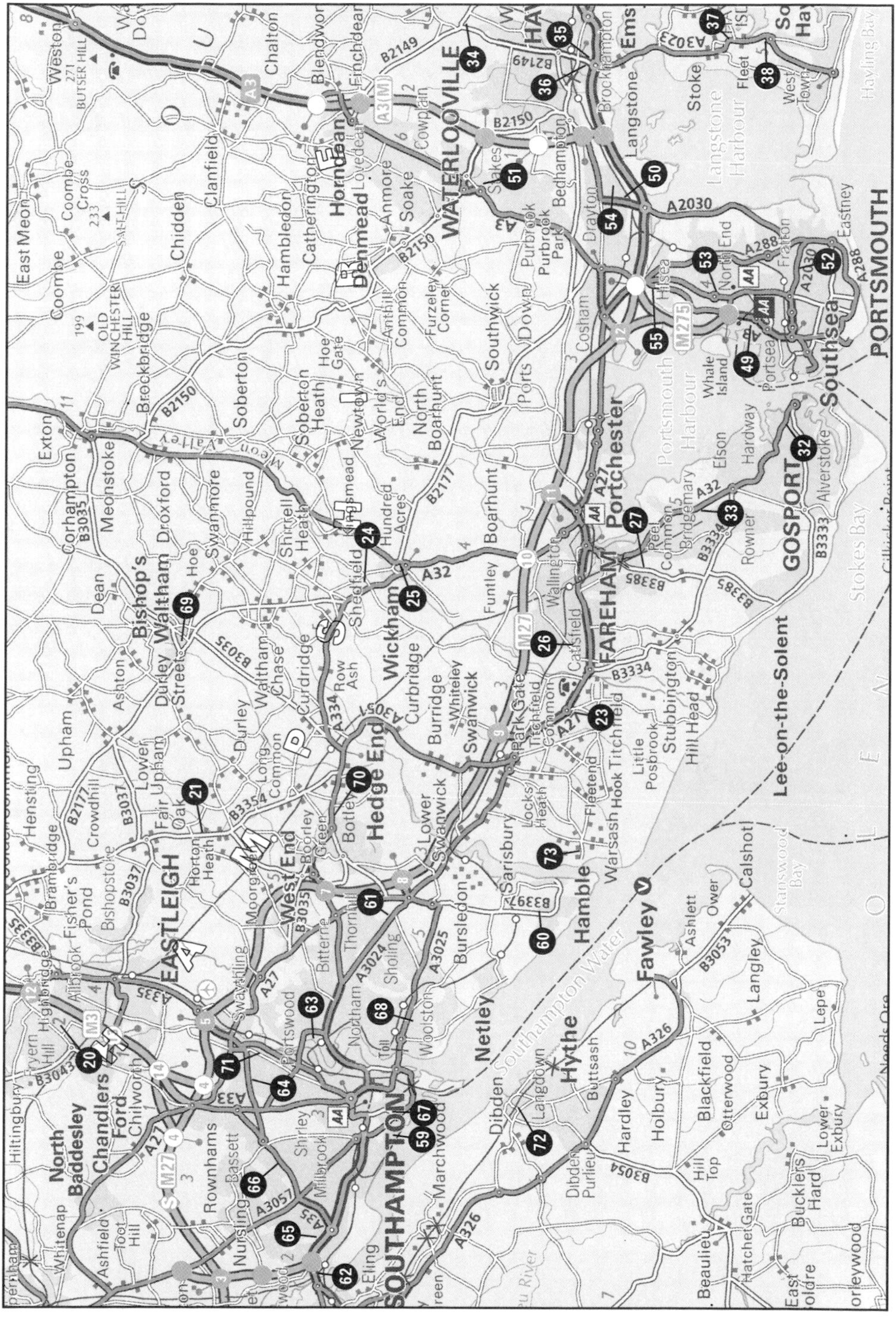

SOUTHAMPTON
PORTSMOUTH
EASTLEIGH
FAREHAM
GOSPORT
WATERLOOVILLE
Southsea
Portchester
Bishop's Waltham
Wickham
Hedge End
West End
Horndean
Denmead
Lee-on-the-Solent
Hamble
Netley
Hythe
Fawley
Chandlers Ford
North Baddesley
Botley
Swanwick
Sarisbury
Warsash
Titchfield
Stubbington
Hill Head
Calshot
Langley
Exbury
Beaulieu
Bucklers Hard
Hardley
Holbury
Blackfield
Dibden
Dibden Purlieu
Marchwood
Eling
Nursling
Rownhams
Bassett
Chilworth
Shirley
Millbrook
Portswood
Swaythling
Bitterne
Sholing
Woolston
Thornhill
Bursledon
Cosham
Drayton
Bedhampton
Havant
Emsworth
Langstone
Stoke
Hayling Bay
Langstone Harbour
Portsmouth Harbour
Whale Island
Portsea
Eastney
Fratton
North End
Hilsea
Alverstoke
Stokes Bay
Southampton Water
Rowner
Bridgemary
Elson
Hardway
Wallington
Funtley
Boarhunt
North Boarhunt
Southwick
Purbrook
Cowplain
Catherington
Clanfield
Chalton
Blendworth
Hambledon
Soberton
Soberton Heath
Droxford
Meonstoke
Exton
Corhampton
East Meon
Upham
Durley
Swanmore
Shedfield
Curdridge
Hook
Fleetend
Locks Heath
Park Gate
Whiteley
Burridge
Horton Heath
Fair Oak
Bishopstoke
Fisher's Pond
Allbrook
Highbridge
Hiltingbury
Ashfield
Totton
M27
M3
M275
A3(M)
A27
A32
A3
A33
A35
A326
A334
A3024
A3025
A3057
A2030
A288
B2150
B2177
B3035
B3037
B3354
B3334
B3385
B3333
B3397
B3053
B3054

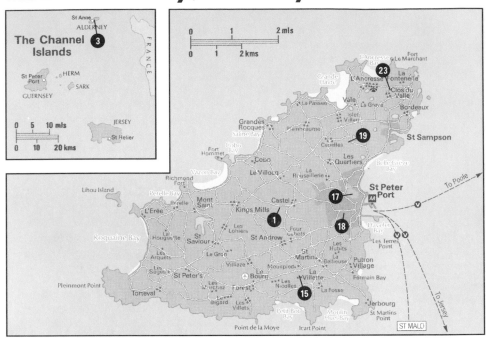

Jersey

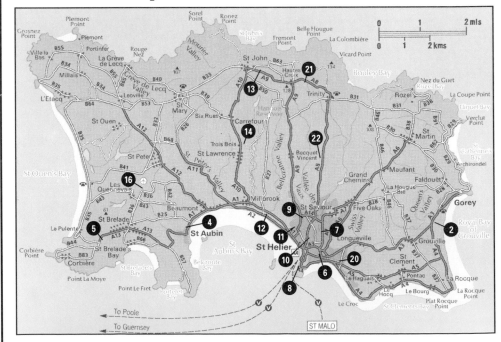

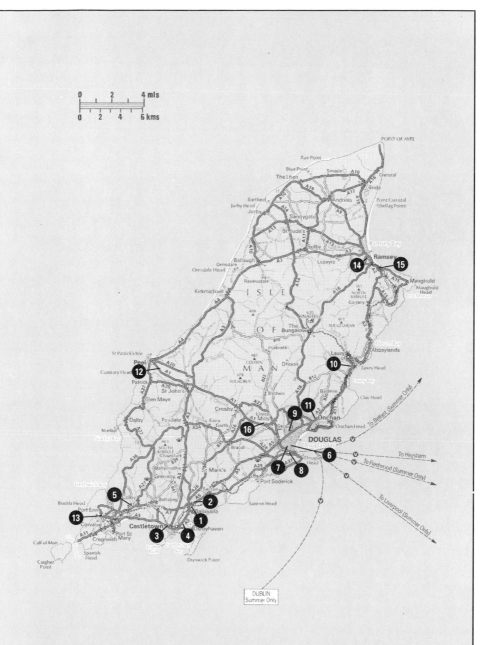

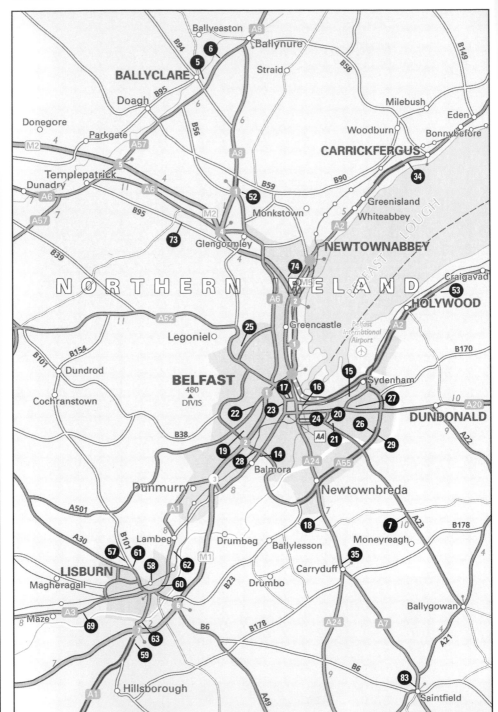

Index to place names

Each entry in the index is followed by the atlas page number and then two letters denoting the 100km grid square. The last two figures refer to the west-east and south-north numbered grid lines.

For example   Whitchurch 30 SJ54

Turn to page 30. The major national grid square we are looking at is SJ. The figure '5' is found along the bottom of the page and the second figure '4' is found along the lefthand side of the page. Whitchurch can be found within the intersecting square.

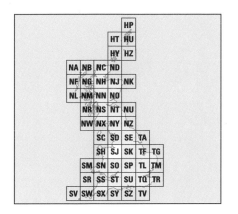

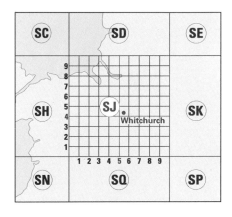

Place	Page	Ref
Appin	55	NM94
Appleby-in-Westmorland	39	NY62
Applecross	59	NG74
Appledore	6	SS43
Appleton-le-Moors	41	SE78
Arbroath	53	NO64
Archiestown	61	NJ24
Archirondel	9	JS00
Ardarroch	59	NG84
Ardbeg	50	NR44
Ardelve	59	NG82
Arden	51	NS38
Ardentinny	51	NS18
Ardersier	61	NH75
Ardfern	51	NM80
Ardgour	55	NN06
Ardingly	12	TQ32
Ardleigh	19	TM02
Ardlui	51	NN31
Ardlussa	50	NR68
Ardrishaig	51	NR88
Ardrossan	46	NS24
Ardtainaig	52	NN63
Arduaine	51	NM80
Ardvasar	54	NG60
Ardwell	42	NX14
Arinagour	50	NM25
Arisaig	54	NM68
Armadale	47	NS96
Armathwaite	44	NY54
Arncliffe	39	SD97
Arnol	64	NB34
Arnprior	52	NS69
Arnside	39	SD47
Arrochar	51	NN20
Arundel	11	TQ00
Ascog	51	NS16
Ascot	17	SU96
Ash	11	SU85
Ash	13	TR25
Ashbourne	31	SK14
Ashburton	8	SX77
Ashbury	16	SU28
Ashby-de-la-Zouche	31	SK31
Ashby Parva	24	SP58
Ashford	17	TQ07
Ashford	13	TR04
Ashford-in-the-Water	31	SK16
Ashington	45	NZ28
Ashington	11	TQ11
Ashtead	17	TQ15
Ashton Keynes	15	SU09
Ashton-in-Makerfield	34	SJ59
Ashton-under-Lyne	35	SJ99
Askam-in-Furness	38	SD27
Askern	36	SE51
Askrigg	39	SD99
Aspatria	43	NY14
Aspley Guise	25	SP93
Aspull	34	SD60
Aston Clinton	16	SP81
Aston on Clun	23	SO38
Atherstone	24	SP39
Atherton	34	SD60
Attleborough	27	TM09
Auchencairn	43	NX75
Auchterarder	52	NN91
Auchterderran	53	NT29
Auchterhouse	53	NO33
Auchterless	62	NJ74
Auchtermuchty	53	NO21
Achtertyre	59	NG82
Audenshaw	35	SJ99
Audgirth	43	NX98
Audlem	30	SJ64
Aughton	34	SD30
Auldearn	61	NH95
Aultbea	59	NG88
Austwick	39	SD76
Avebury	15	SU17
Aveley	12	TQ57
Aviemore	56	NH81
Avon	10	SZ19
Avonbridge	47	NS97
Avonmouth	14	ST57
Axbridge	14	ST45
Axminster	8	SY29
Aylesbeare	8	SY09
Aylesbury	16	SP81
Aylesford	12	TQ75
Aylsham	27	TG12
Aynho	24	SP53
Ayr	47	NS32
Aysgarth	40	SE08
Ayton	49	NT96
Babbacombe	8	SX96
Backaland	67	HY53
Backwell	14	ST46
Bacton	27	TG33
Bacup	35	SD82
Badmington	15	ST78
Badminton	15	ST88
Bagby	40	SE48
Bagillt	29	SJ27
Baginton	24	SP37
Bagshot	16	SU96
Baguley	35	SJ89
Bagworth	31	SK40
Baillieston	47	NS66
Bainbridge	39	SD98
Bainton	36	SE95
Bakewell	31	SK26
Bala	29	SH93
Balallan	64	NB22
Balbeggie	53	NO12
Balblair	57	NH76
Baldersby	40	SE37
Balderton	32	SK85
Baldock	18	TL23
Baldrine	38	SC48
Balfour	67	HY41
Balfron	52	NS58
Balintore	61	NH87
Balivanich	64	NF75
Ballachulish	55	NN05
Ballantrae	42	NX08
Ballasalla	38	SC27
Ballater	57	NO39
Ballaugh	38	SC39
Ballinluig	52	NN95
Ballintuim	52	NO15
Balloch	51	NS38
Ballygrant	50	NR36
Balmacara	59	NG82
Balmaha	51	NS49
Balmedie	57	NJ91
Balquhidder	52	NN52
Balsall Common	24	SP27
Balsham	18	TL55
Baltasound	63	HP60
Bamburgh	49	NU13
Bamford	31	SK28
Bampton	39	NY51
Bampton	16	SP30
Bampton	7	SS92
Banavie	55	NN17
Banbury	24	SP44
Banchory	57	NO69
Banff	62	NJ66
Bangor	28	SH57
Bangor-on-Dee	30	SJ34
Bankfoot	52	NO03
Banks	34	SD32
Bannockburn	52	NS89
Banstead	12	TQ26
Banwell	14	ST35
Bar Hill	18	TL36
Barbon	39	SD68
Bardney	33	TF16
Bardon Mill	44	NY76
Bardsea	38	SD27
Barford	24	SP26
Barford St Martin	15	SU03
Bargoed	14	ST19
Bargrennan	42	NX37
Barham	13	TR24
Barking	18	TQ48
Barkingside	18	TQ48
Barlby	36	SE63
Barley	18	TL43
Barnby Moor	36	SE74
Barmouth	28	SH61
Barnard Castle	40	NZ01
Barnby Moor	32	SK68
Barnet	17	TQ29
Barnham Broom	27	TG00
Barnoldswick	35	SD84
Barnsley	35	SE30
Barnstaple	6	SS53
Barnton	48	NT17
Barr	42	NX29
Barregarrow	38	SC38
Barrhead	47	NS45
Barrhill	42	NX28
Barrow-in-Furness	38	SD16
Barry Island	7	ST16
Barry	7	ST16
Barton Mills	26	TL77
Barton	34	SD53
Barton Stacey	10	SU44
Barton on Sea	10	SZ29
Barton	18	TL45
Barton under Needwood	31	SK11
Barton upon Humber	37	TA02
Barton-le-Clay	25	TL03
Barvas	64	NB34
Basildon	18	TQ78
Basingstoke	11	SU65
Baslow	31	SK27
Bassenthwaite	44	NY23
Baston	33	TF11
Bath	15	ST76
Bathgate	48	NS96
Batley	35	SE22
Battle	12	TQ71
Baughurst	16	SU56
Baumber	33	TF27
Bawdeswell	27	TG02
Bawtry	36	SK69
Baycliff	38	SD27
Baydon	16	SU27
Beachley	17	ST59
Beaconsfield	17	SU99
Beadnell	49	NU22
Beaminster	9	ST40
Beare Green	11	TQ14
Bearsden	47	NS57
Beattock	43	NT00
Beaulieu	10	SU30
Beauly	60	NH54
Beaumaris	28	SH67
Beaumont	9	JS00
Bebington	29	SJ38
Beccles	27	TM49
Beckenham	17	TQ36
Beckhampton	15	SU06
Beckington	15	ST85
Becquet Vincent	9	JS00
Bedale	40	SE28
Beddgelert	28	SH54
Beddingham	12	TQ40
Bedford	25	TL04
Bedlington	45	NZ28
Bedlinog	14	SO00
Bedwas	14	ST18
Bedworth	24	SP38
Beeford	37	TA15
Beer	8	SY28
Beeston	30	SJ55
Beeston	32	SK53
Beetham	39	SD47
Beetley	27	TF91
Beith	47	NS35
Belbroughton	24	SO97
Belford	49	NU13
Bellingham	44	NY88
Bellochantuy	46	NR63
Bellshill	47	NS76
Belmont	63	HP50
Belmont	34	SD61
Belper	31	SK34
Belsay	45	NZ07
Belton	28	SE70
Bembridge	11	SZ68
Benderloch	54	NM93
Bentleet	12	TQ78
Benllech Bay	28	SH58
Benson	16	SU69
Bentley	36	SE50
Benwick	26	TL39
Bere Alston	5	SX46
Bere Ferrers	5	SX46
Bere Regis	9	SY89
Berkeley Road	15	SO70
Berkeley	15	ST69
Berkhamsted	17	SP90
Bernisdale	58	NG45
Berriedale	67	ND12
Berrow	14	ST25
Berrynarbor	6	SS54
Berwick	12	TQ50
Berwick-upon-Tweed	49	NT95
Bethersden	13	TQ94
Bethesda	28	SH66
Bettyhill	66	NC70
Betws-Y-Coed	29	SH75
Beulah	22	SN95
Beverley	37	TA03
Bewdley	23	SO77
Bexhill-on-Sea	12	TQ70
Bexley	12	TQ47
Bexleyheath	12	TQ47
Bibury	15	SP10
Bicester	16	SP52
Bickleigh	6	SS90
Biddenden	13	TQ83
Biddulph	30	SJ85
Bideford	6	SS42
Bidford-on-Avon	24	SP15
Bigbury-on-Sea	5	SX64
Biggar	48	NT03
Biggar	38	SD16
Biggin Hill	12	TQ45
Biggleswade	25	TL14
Bilbrook	7	ST04
Bilbrough	36	SE54
Bildeston	19	TL94
Billericay	18	TQ69
Billesley	24	SP15
Billinge	34	SD50
Billingham	40	NZ42
Billingshurst	11	TQ02
Bilston	24	SO99
Binbrook	37	TF29
Bingley	35	SE13
Birchgrove	21	SS79
Birchington	13	TR36
Birdlip	17	SO91
Birdwood	23	SO71
Birkenhead	34	SJ38

Index of Shell Service Stations

How to use this index

To help you find your way around the road maps we have individually coloured each **COUNTY.** Within each county we have individually numbered and located every **SHELL SERVICE STATION.** Cross reference this number with the **INDEX** below of Shell Service Stations by looking up the county, which is in alphabetical order, and then the number of the location. Alongside this number you will find the name, address and telephone number for each Shell Service Station followed by a range of **INFORMATION** most frequently requested by customers. This includes;

Road Number, where the Service Station is located on a major road

• **Telephone Number,** should you wish to contact the Service Station for more
information

• **Fuels available;**
4 = 4 Star Leaded petrol
U = Premium Unleaded petrol (min. 95 Octane)
S = Super Unleaded petrol (min. 98 Octane)
D = Diesel

• **Shell Cards accepted;**
G = Shell Gold Card
A = Shell Agency Card
E = euroShell Card

24 Hour, where the Service Station is open 24 hours a day for fuel
(shop opening hours may vary)

H.G.V., where refuelling facilities are available for vehicles up to 38 tons

SELECT, where there is a Select shop

Car Wash, where there is a full roll-over car wash available

Loc. Ref.	Shell Ref.	TOWN	NAME	ADDRESS	Road No.	Tel. No.	Fuel	Cards	24 hour	HGV	Select

AVON

Loc. Ref.	Shell Ref.	TOWN	NAME	ADDRESS	Road No.	Tel. No.	Fuel	
1	348318	BATH	A Richardson & Son	Sydney Wharf, Bathwick Hill BA2 4EF	A36	(0225) 466286	4UD	GAE
2	348321	BATH	Crescent Filling Station	23 Crescent Lane, Julian Road BA1 2PX		(0225) 429910	4USD	GAE
3	348971	BATH	Hartwells of Bath Ltd	Newbridge Road BA1 2PP	A4	(0225) 312774	4U	GAE
4	353363	BATH	Bence Ford	Marksbury BA2 9HN	A368	(0761) 470391	4USD	GAE
5	348262	BRISTOL	D C Banwell & Co	Unity Street, St Phillips BS2 OHN		(0272) 273222	4UD	GAE
6	348267	BRISTOL	Shiner Auto's	22 Church Road, Lawrence Hill BS5 9JB	A420	(0272) 556035	4UD	GA
7	348274	BRISTOL	Ridgeway Garage	Wells Road, Whitchurch BS14 9PD	A37	(0272) 832618	4USD	GAE
8	348277	BRISTOL	Brookside Self Serve	Bath Road, Brislington BS4 5AD	A4	(0272) 775516	4UD	GAE
9	348282	BRISTOL	Eastville Park – Shell	Muller Road, Eastville BS5 6PX	B4469	(0272) 525150	4USD	GAE
10	348287	BRISTOL	Longwell Green Self Serve	106 Bath Road, Longwell Green BS15 6DE	A431	(0272) 322317	4USD	GAE
11	348289	BRISTOL	Somerdale – Shell	Bath Road, Keynsham BS18 1TN	A4	(0272) 866681	4UD	GAE
12	348291	BRISTOL	Pensford Garage	Pensford BS18 4AR	A37	(0761) 490328	4UD	GAE
13	348294	BRISTOL	Wick Self Serve	81 London Road, Wick BS15 5SJ	A420	(0275) 822478	4UD	GAE
14	348298	BRISTOL	Kennings Hartcliffe Way	Hartcliffe Way BS3 5RP	A4174	(0272) 661429	4UD	GAE
15	348300	BRISTOL	Bridgwater Road S/Stn (Plev)	Bridgwater Road, Dundry BS18 8JP	A38	(0275) 392212	4USD	GAE
16	348302	BRISTOL	King William Self Serve	92-108 North Street, Bedminster BS3 1HF	B3120	(0272) 632646	4USD	GAE
17	348391	BRISTOL	Gordano Motorway Service Area	Gordano Service Area, Portbury BS20 9XG	M5	(0275) 375885	4USD	GAE
18	348561	BRISTOL	Berkley Vale Motors Ltd	Gloucester Road, Alveston BS12 2LJ	A38	(0454) 412207	4UD	GAE
19	348780	BRISTOL	Westminster Self Serve	Whitehall Road BS5 7BG	B4465	(0272) 517202	4USD	GAE
20	348818	BRISTOL	Cribbs Causeway Self Serve	Cribbs Causeway BS10 7TG	A4018	(0272) 500464	4USD	GAE
21	348864	BRISTOL	Wheelers Garage	141 High Street, Portishead BS20 9PY	B3124	(0272) 845454	4USD	GAE
22	348878	BRISTOL	Bedminster South F/Stn	174 Bedminster Road BS3 5NQ	A38	(0272) 669341	4UD	GAE
23	348882	BRISTOL	St Phillips Self Serve	Feeder Road BS2 OUB		(0272) 712294	4USD	GAE
24	348890	BRISTOL	Redland Self Serve	Hampton Road, Redland BS6 6JA		(0272) 735151	4USD	GAE
25	348942	BRISTOL	Aust Motorway Service Area	Aust Service Area, Severn Bridge BS12 3BH	M4	(0454) 632855	D	GAE
26	349021	BRISTOL	Downend – Shell	Badminton Road, Downend BS17 1AH	A432	(0272) 564116	4USD	GAE
27	349027	BRISTOL	Stanshawes S/Stn (Yate) Ltd	Westerleigh Road, Yate BS17 4BG		(0454) 318962	4UD	GAE
28	349083	BRISTOL	Hartcliffe Way Self Serve	Hartcliffe Way BS3 5RP	A4174	(0272) 662559	4USD	GAE
29	351931	BRISTOL	Redcatch Self Service	Redcatch Road BS4 2EP	B3122	(0272) 712248	4USD	GAE
30	532670	BRISTOL	Masters of Kingswood	Hanham Road, Kingswood BS15 2PR	B4046	(0272) 600074	4USD	GAE
31	539789	BRISTOL	Avonmouth Filling Station	Avonmouth Road, Avonmouth BS11 9LP	A4	(0272) 825921	4USD	GAE
32	348286	CHIPPENHAM	Pennsylvania Filling Station	Nr. Marshfield SN14 8LB	A46	(0225) 891460	4UD	GAE
33	348861	WESTON-SUPER-MARE	Ashcombe Self Serve	165 Locking Road BS23 3HE	A370	(0934) 415295	4USD	GAE
34	348967	WESTON-SUPER-MARE	Weston – Shell	92-94 New Bristol Road, Worle BS22 OAT	A370	(0934) 5141690	4USD	GAE

BEDFORDSHIRE

Loc. Ref.	Shell Ref.	TOWN	NAME	ADDRESS	Road No.	Tel. No.	Fuel	
1	356937	AMPTHILL	Ampthill – Shell	15 Bedford Street MK45 2LU	B530	(0525) 406024	4UD	GAE
2	353062	BEDFORD	Plough Self Serve	Ampthill Road MK42 9RA	A6	(0234) 343785	4UD	GAE
3	348949	BEDFORD	Greycourt Service Station	73 Bedford Road, Willington MK44 3PR	A603	(0234) 838852	4UD	GAE
4	355218	BIGGLESWADE	Station Road Filling Station	Station Road SG18 8AL		(0767) 312266	4UD	GAE
5	357100	BIGGLESWADE	Biggleswade South F/Stn	Great North Road SG18 9BE	A1	(0767) 312020	4USD	GAE
6	340154	DUNSTABLE	Oldhill Self Serve	55 London Road LU6 3DH	A5	(0582) 661988	4USD	GAE
7	357111	DUNSTABLE	Wilbury – Shell	Poynters Road LU6 4SN		(0582) 471706	4USD	GAE
8	357134	DUNSTABLE	Eastgate Self Serve	138 Church Street LU5 4HN	A505	(0582) 663451	4USD	GAE
9	357094	HITCHIN	Shillington Garage	84 High Road, Shillington SG5 3LP		(0462) 711247	4UD	GAE
10	353224	LEIGHTON BUZZARD	St Christophers – Shell	Leighton Road, Linslade LU7 7LG	A4146	(0525) 378112	4USD	GAE
11	355806	LUTON	Motorway Self-Serve	Castle Street LU1 3AL		(0582) 36076	4USD	GAE
12	356919	LUTON	Luton Airport – Shell	Eaton Green Road LU2 9HD		(0582) 402697	4USD	GAE
13	357136	LUTON	Sundon Road Filling Stn	166 Sundon Park Road LU3 3AD		(0582) 574789	4UD	GAE
14	356945	SANDY	Potton S/Stn	Biggleswade Road, Potton SG19 2LU	B1040	(0767) 260422	4USD	GAE
15	356955	SANDY	Tempsford S/Stn	43 Tempsford SG19 2AF	A1	(0767) 680432	4USD	GAE

BERKSHIRE

Loc. Ref.	Shell Ref.	TOWN	NAME	ADDRESS	Road No.	Tel. No.	Fuel	
1	308061	BRACKNELL	Europa – Shell	Bagshot Road RG12 3SE	A322	(0344) 426468	4USD	GAE
2	302836	CAMBERLEY	Sandhurst Garage	297 Yorktown Road, College Town GU15 4QA	A33	(0276) 35353	4USD	GAE
3	347707	HENLEY-ON-THAMES	Whitehill S/Stn	Remenham Hill, Remenham RG9 3EP	A423	(0491) 573430	4USD	GAE
4	308495	MAIDENHEAD	W R Hammant Ltd	The Garage, Woodlands Park Road SL6 3NH		(0628) 823211	4UD	GAE
5	347722	NEWBURY	Newbury – Shell	Bath Road, Speen RG13 1QT	A4	(0635) 40163	4USD	GAE
6	349077	NEWBURY	Membury Motorway Service East	M4 Service Area (East Bound), Lambourne RG16 7TU	M4	(0488) 71881	D	GAE
7	349081	NEWBURY	Membury Motorway Service West	M4 Service Area (West Bound), Lambourne RG16 7TU	M4	(0488) 71881	D	GAE
8	347700	READING	Fairfield – Shell	585 Basingstoke Road RG2 0HZ	A33	(0734) 312976	4USD	GAE
9	347703	READING	Oakstead of Reading	160 Basingstoke Road RG2 0HJ	A33	(0734) 312620	4USD	GAE

108

Loc. Ref.	Shell Ref.	TOWN	NAME	ADDRESS	Road No.	Tel. No.	Fuel	Cards	24 hour	HGV	Select	Car Wash
10	347715	READING	Norcot – Shell	856 Oxford Road RG3 1EL	A329	(0734) 452975	4USD	GAE				
11	347717	READING	Wargrave Motors Ltd	High Street, Wargrave-On-Thames RG10 8PU	A321	(0734) 402207	4U					
12	348956	READING	Weldale Motors Ltd	Chatham Street RG1 7JF	A329	(0734) 583322	UD	GAE				
13	384100	READING	City Shinfield	209-211 Shinfield Road RG2 8HB	A327	(0734) 869647	4US	GAE				
14	308131	SLOUGH	Farnham Road S/Stn	416 Farnham Road SL2 1JA	A355	(0753) 525953	4UD	GAE				
15	308135	WINDSOR	Windsor – Shell	Clarence Road SL4 5AE	B3024	(0753) 831177	USD	GAE				
16	308476	WINDSOR	Arthur Road Self Serve	72-74 Arthur Road SL4 1RX		(0753) 856841	4U	GAE				
17	347965	WOKINGHAM	Wokingham – Shell	115 London Road RG11 1YD	A329	(0734) 891297	4USD	GAE				

BORDERS

Loc. Ref.	Shell Ref.	TOWN	NAME	ADDRESS	Road No.	Tel. No.	Fuel	Cards	24 hour	HGV	Select	Car Wash
1	376193	COLDSTREAM	Coldstream Garage	High Street TD12 4AG	A697	(0890) 882159	4UD	GAE				
2	381001	COLDSTREAM	Orange Lane Garage	Orange Lane TD12 4LY	A697	(0890) 84267	4UD	GAE				
3	377619	HAWICK	Mosspaul Filling Station	Teviotdale TD9 0LP	A7	(0450) 85245		GAE				
4	380923	HAWICK	Bridge Street Filling Station	Bridge Street TD9 9BD	A7	(0450) 74074	4USD	GAE				
5	377607	JEDBURGH	Jed Service Station	89 Bongate TD8 6DU	A68	(08356) 2810	4USD	GAE				
6	380719	WEST LINTON	Manor Garage	Edinburgh Road EH46 7DR	A702	(0968) 60313	4UD	GAE				

BUCKINGHAMSHIRE

Loc. Ref.	Shell Ref.	TOWN	NAME	ADDRESS	Road No.	Tel. No.	Fuel	Cards	24 hour	HGV	Select	Car Wash
1	302612	AMERSHAM	Amersham S/Stn	40-42 Woodside Road HP6 6AJ	A416	(0494) 725607	4USD	GAE				
2	353213	AYLESBURY	Bicester Road – Shell	171 Bicester Road HP19 3BB	A418	(0296) 85485	4USD	GAE				
3	353229	AYLESBURY	London Road S/Stn	South Street, Wendover HP22 6DU	A413	(0296) 623085	4USD	GAE				
4	353232	AYLESBURY	Halton Service Station	Tring Road, Halton HP22 5PN	A4011	(0296) 623141	4UD	GAE				
5	353234	AYLESBURY	Blinking Owl F/Stn	Oxford Road, Dinton HP17 8TT	A418	(0296) 748622	4UD	GAE				
6	308076	BEACONSFIELD	Hughes of Beaconsfield Ltd	55 Station Road HP9 1QJ	B474	(0494) 672141	4USD	GAE				
7	353215	BLETCHLEY	Whaddon Way – Shell	Buckingham Road MK3 5JJ	B4034	(0908) 720244	4USD	GAE				
8	339697	BOURNE END	Cress Self Serve	Marlow Road SL8 5SE	A4155	(0628) 529194	4USD	GAE				
9	308449	CHESHAM	Plough Filling Station	1 Broad Street HP5 3EA	B4505	(0494) 783742	4UD	GAE				
10	308079	GERRARDS CROSS	Phoenix Motors Ltd	Oxford Road, Tatling End SL9 7AR	A40	(0753) 885156	4UD	GAE				
11	308075	HIGH WYCOMBE	Cressex – Shell	Marlow Road HP11 1TB		(0494) 463640	4USD	GAE				
12	308080	HIGH WYCOMBE	Pedestal Garage	504 West Wycombe Road HP12 4AH	A40	(0494) 532545	4USD	GAE				
13	308084	HIGH WYCOMBE	W & M Stevens	Pond Approach, Holmer Green HP15 6RQ		(0494) 713185	4USD	GAE				
14	308447	HIGH WYCOMBE	Hazlemere – Shell	Hazlemere Cross Roads, Hazlemere HP15 7LG	A404	(0494) 716174	4USD	GAE				
15	308469	HIGH WYCOMBE	Ridge Service station	Chinnor Road, Bledlow Ridge HP14 4AJ		(0240) 27420	4U	GAE				
16	302508	IVER	Timms Garage	Uxbridge Road SL0 0LR	A412	(0753) 655440	4USD	GAE				
17	276245	MILTON KEYNES	Leadenhall – Shell	Grafton Street, Leadenhall MK6 5AD		(0908) 694112	4USD	GAE				
18	353058	MILTON KEYNES	Stacey Bushes – Shell	H3 Monks Way, Stacey Bushes MK12 6HU	A422	(0908) 316890	4USD	GAE				
19	353078	MILTON KEYNES	Blakelands Self Serve	Monksway, Blakelands MK14 5JA	A422	(0908) 614238	4USD	GAE				
20	353272	MILTON KEYNES	City Tongwell	Monksway, Stacey Bushes MK15 8HR	A422	(0908) 618020	4USD	GAE				
21	299954	NEWPORT PAGNELL	Newport Pagnell MWSA (S)	M1 Motorway Southbound MK16 8DS	M1	(0908) 610593	4USD	GAE				
22	353218	NEWPORT PAGNELL	Newport Pagnell MWSA (N)	M1 Motorway Northbound MK16 8DS	M1	(0908) 216150	4USD	GAE				
23	353220	NEWPORT PAGNELL	North Bucks Motors	Wood Corner MK16 8JU	B526	(0908) 610057	4UD	GAE				
24	356940	OLNEY	Hilary Brock Ltd	High Street MK46 4DE	A509	(0234) 711250	4UD	GAE				
25	308132	SLOUGH	Kenning Self Serve	344 Bath Road SL1 6JA	A4	(06286) 64362	4USD	GAE				
26	353217	STONY STRATFORD	BMG Stoney Stratford	London Road MK11 1JQ		(0908) 565554	4UD	GAE				

CAMBRIDGESHIRE

Loc. Ref.	Shell Ref.	TOWN	NAME	ADDRESS	Road No.	Tel. No.	Fuel	Cards	24 hour	HGV	Select	Car Wash
1	302777	CAMBRIDGE	Hallens Self Serve	1 Milton Road CB4 1PP	A1309	(0223) 356225	4UD	GAE				
2	302781	CAMBRIDGE	Camboritum – Shell	149 Hills Road CB2 2RQ	A1307	(0223) 411075	4USD	GAE				
3	355801	CAMBRIDGE	Marshalls (Cambridge) Ltd	400 Newmarket Road CB5 8LH	A1303	(0223) 65111	4USD	GAE				
4	356912	CAMBRIDGE	Gibbet – Shell	St Neots Road, Caxton CB3 8PD	A45	(0954) 718829	4USD	GAE				
5	356913	CAMBRIDGE	Trumpington – Shell	High Street, Trumpington CB2 8SH	A1309	(0223) 845454	4USD	GAE				
6	356923	CAMBRIDGE	Fourwentways Self Serve	Fourwentways CB1 6AR	A11	(0223) 835677	4USD	GAE				
7	356924	CAMBRIDGE	Hallens of Cambridge Ltd	Union Lane, Chesterton CB4 1PP		(0223) 356225	4UD	GAE				
8	356925	CAMBRIDGE	E F G Moule	28 Cambridge Road, Sawston CB2 4QH		(0223) 833116	4UD	GAE				
9	356928	CAMBRIDGE	Teversham Corner F/Stn	Newmarket Road, Teversham CB5 8BH	A1303	(0220) 53232	4USD	GAE				
10	357103	CAMBRIDGE	Newnham Self Serve	Newnham Road CB3 9EY	A603	(0223) 359354	4USD	GAE				
11	302817	ELY	Crown Garage	1-5 High Street, Soham CB7 5HB		(0353) 720779	4U	GAE				
12	302827	HUNTINGDON	Huntingdon – Shell	Stukeley Road PE18 6HG	A141	(0480) 413013	4USD	GAE				
13	308490	HUNTINGDON	Fenstanton (905) – Shell	Cambridge Road A604, Fenstanton CB4 4JB	A604	(0954) 32028	4USD	GAE				
14	356864	HUNTINGDON	Abbots – Shell	Huntingdon Road, Hemingford Abbots PE18 9HQ	A604	(0480) 492262	4USD	GAE				
15	356869	HUNTINGDON	Cromwell Self Serve	Walden Road PE18 6AZ	B1043	(0480) 453102	4UD	GAE				
16	356893	HUNTINGDON	Burton Brothers	Bury Road, Ramsey PE17 1NE	B1040	(0487) 813545	4USD	GAE				
17	353066	PETERBOROUGH	Rainbow Filling Station	Paxton Road, Orton Goldhay PE2 0HF		(0733) 391248	4USD	GAE				
18	356887	PETERBOROUGH	Crawthorne Road S/S	Crawthorne Road PE1 4AA		(0733) 558279	4USD	GAE				

Loc. Ref.	Shell Ref.	TOWN	NAME	ADDRESS	Road No.	Tel. No.	Fuel	Cards	24 hour	HGV	Select
19	356890	PETERBOROUGH	Northmead – Shell	Lincoln Road, Walton PE1 3HA	A15	(0733) 75036	4USD	GAE			
20	356895	PETERBOROUGH	Wittering – Shell	Great North Road, Thornhaugh PE8 6HA	A1	(0780) 782255	4USD	GAE		■	
21	356897	PETERBOROUGH	Woodston STC	Oundle Road, Woodston PE2 9QP	A605	(0733) 558608	4USD	GAE			
22	357120	PETERBOROUGH	Westwood – Shell	Atherstone Avenue, Westwood PE3 6TT		(0733) 262086	4USD	GAE			
23	357125	PETERBOROUGH	Marshalls (of Peterborough)	7 Oundle Road PE2 9AA	A605	(0733) 66011	4USD	GAE			
24	356946	SANDY	Empsons Garage Ltd	Potton Road, Gamlingay SG19 3LW	B1040	(0767) 50236	4UD	GAE			
25	356867	ST IVES	Ramsey Road – Shell	Ramsey Road PE17 4RF	A1123	(0480) 466982	4USD	GAE			
26	356863	ST NEOTS	Buckden – Shell	Great North Road, Buckden PE18 9XF	A1	(0480) 811258	4USD	GAE			
27	356871	WISBECH	J.S. Holmes	High Road PE13 4RQ		(0945) 410243	4UD	GAE			

CENTRAL

Loc. Ref.	Shell Ref.	TOWN	NAME	ADDRESS	Road No.	Tel. No.	Fuel	Cards	24 hour	HGV	Select
1	380647	AIRTH	Kincardine Bridge – Shell	Kincardine Bridge Road FK2 8PH	A876	(0324) 831685	4USD	GAE		■	
2	381154	ALLOA	Alloa Motor Co Ltd	Hallpark Filling Station, Sauchie FK10 3NA	A908	(0259) 723912	4UD	GAE		■	
3	380495	BALFRON	WM Shearer & Co	Main Street G63 0RN	A875	(0360) 40464	4UD	GAE			
4	380638	BUCHLYVIE	West End Garage (Buchlyvie)	Main Street FK8 3LT	A811	(0360) 85228	4UD	GAE			
5	380585	CRAINLARICH	Clifton Filling Station	Tyndrum FK20 8RY	A82	(08384) 271	4UD	GAE			
6	380645	DENNYLOANHEAD	T Gillespie & Son	Park Garage, Longcroft FK4 1QY	A803	(0324) 812454	4UD	GAE			
7	380625	DOUNE	Deanston Filling Station	Stirling Road FK16 6AA	A84	(0786) 841061	4UD	GAE			
8	380516	DRYMEN	Mason Bros	The Square G63 0BL	A811	(0360) 60223	4UD	GAE			
9	380628	DUNBLANE	Duckburn Self Serve	Stirling Road FK15 9EY	B8033	(0786) 823536	4UD	GAE			
10	532324	DUNBLANE	Balhaldie – Shell	A9 Southbound FK15 0NB	A9	(0786) 825998	4USD	GAE		■	
11	380641	FALKIRK	Square Deal Motors	High Station Road FK1 5LW	B803	(0324) 34009	4UD	GA			
12	380649	FALKIRK	D Morrison & Sons Ltd	95 Glasgow Road, Camelon FK1 4JD	A803	(0324) 36504	4UD	GAE			
13	381038	FALKIRK	Gowanbank Self Serve	Grahams Road FK2 7BQ	B902	(0324) 35625	4UD	GAE			
14	380632	STIRLING	Borestone Self Serve	4 Borestone Crescent, St Ninians FK7 8BE	B8052	(0786) 464963	4USD	GAE			

CHANNEL ISLANDS

Loc. Ref.	Shell Ref.	TOWN	NAME	ADDRESS	Road No.	Tel. No.	Fuel	Cards	24 hour	HGV	Select
1	300175	CASTEL (GUERNSEY)	Thompson Motors	Rue De L'Eglise		(0481) 54383	4USD				
2	300195	GROUVILLE (JERSEY)	La Motte Ford Grouville	Gorey Coast Road JE3 9DA		(0534) 22262	4USD				
3	300173	ST ANNE (ALDERNEY)	Alderney Motors Ltd	Marais Square		(0481) 822727	4U				
4	300188	ST AUBIN (JERSEY)	Peterborough Garage	JE3 8BA		(0534) 41286	4USD				
5	300189	ST BRELADE (JERSEY)	La Moye Garage	JE3 8GQ		(0534) 42542	4USD				
6	300180	ST HELIER (JERSEY)	Park Garage	Hastings Road JE2 4PH		(0534) 20451	4UD				
7	300181	ST HELIER (JERSEY)	St Marks Garage	86 St Saviours Road JE2 4LA		(0534) 32327	4U				
8	300183	ST HELIER (JERSEY)	Southpier Shipyard	Southpier		(0534) 67750	4U				
9	300184	ST HELIER (JERSEY)	Curwoods Garage	46 Rouge Bouillon JE2 3ZA		(0534) 33122	4				
10	300185	ST HELIER (JERSEY)	De La Haye Motors Ltd	Grove Street JE2 4TU		(0534) 35429	4USD				
11	300186	ST HELIER (JERSEY)	Gordon Bisson (Motorcycles)	22 New St John's Road		(0534) 27897	4U				
12	300187	ST HELIER (JERSEY)	Brimichen Motors Ltd	First Tower JE2 3LX		(0534) 38377	4USD				
13	300192	ST JOHN (JERSEY)	Melbourne Garage	Route Des Issues JE3 4FA		(0534) 862709	4USD				
14	300191	ST LAWRENCE (JERSEY)	Mont Felard Garage	Three Oaks JE3 1FB		(0534) 863165	4UD				
15	300176	ST MARTIN (GUERNSEY)	La Villette Garage	La Villette		(0481) 37577	4U				
16	300190	ST PETER (JERSEY)	Falles Airport Garage	Airport Road JE3 7BQ		(0534) 45531	4USD				
17	300174	ST PETER PORT (GUERNSEY)	F. S. Leale	Mont Arrive		(0481) 722036	4S				
18	300177	ST PETER PORT (GUERNSEY)	Sarnia Car Hire	Stanley Road		(0481) 723933	4U				
19	300178	ST SAMPSON (GUERNSEY)	Baubigny Garage	Baubigny			4UD				
20	300182	ST SAVIOUR (JERSEY)	Victoria Garage	Victoria Road, Georgetown JE2 7QG		(NONE)	4UD				
21	300193	TRINITY (JERSEY)	Autocare	Hautes Croix JE3 5DS		(0534) 863059	4S				
22	300194	TRINITY (JERSEY)	Freelance	Augres Garage JE3 5JN		(0534) 861988	4USD				
23	300179	VALE (GUERNSEY)	Les Landes Garage	Les Landes		(0481) 45501	4UD				

CHESHIRE

Loc. Ref.	Shell Ref.	TOWN	NAME	ADDRESS	Road No.	Tel. No.	Fuel	Cards	24 hour	HGV	Select
1	299778	CHESTER	Handbridge Service Station	Queens Park Road CH4 7AD		(0244) 680158	4USD	GAE			
2	358539	CHESTER	Elton Green Service Station	Elton Green CH2 4LD	A5117	(0928) 25144	4UD	GAE			
3	358546	CHESTER	Abbots Park Self Serve	23 Liverpool Road CH2 1AU	A540	(0244) 374472	4USD	GAE			
4	358548	CHESTER	Upton Heath Motors Ltd	Long Lane CH2 1JF	A41	(0244) 390070	4USD	GAE			
5	358556	CHESTER	Woodbank STC	Welsh Road, Woodbank CH1 6HU	A550	(0244) 880055	4USD	GAE		■	
6	358767	CHESTER	Chester – Shell	Tarvin Road, Vickers Cross CH3 5NJ	A51	(0244) 316172	4USD	GAE			
7	357793	CONGLETON	Congleton – Shell	Clayton Bypass CW12 1LR	A34	(0260) 297638	4USD	GAE			
8	358608	CREWE	BS Morgan & Son	150 Main Road, Goostrey CW4 8JP		(0477) 532832	4UD	GAE			
9	358646	CREWE	West End Garage	523 West Street CW1 3PA		(0270) 589990	4UD	GAE			
10	357425	ELLESMERE PORT	M53 Ford	Rossmore Road L65 3BR	B5463	051-357 1221	4U	GAE		■	
11	358905	ELLESMERE PORT	Ellesmere Port – Shell	Whitby Road L65 6TF	B5132	051-355 4601	4USD	GAE			
12	394216	HOLMES CHAPEL	Greenoaks Service Station	Knutsford Road, Cranage CW4 8HJ	A50	(0477) 532984	4UD	GAE		■	

Loc. Ref.	Shell Ref.	TOWN	NAME	ADDRESS	Road No.	Tel. No.	Fuel	Cards	24 hour	HGV	Select	Car Wash
3	358563	KNUTSFORD	Knutsford – Shell	9 Toft Road WA16 0PF	A50	(0565) 621044	4USD	GAE				
4	358588	KNUTSFORD	Plumley Self Serve	Chester Road, Plumley WA16 0TZ	A556	056-572 2249	4USD	GAE				
15	358583	LYMM	Lymm – Shell	Higher Lane WA13 0BA	A56	(0925) 754468	4USD	GAE			■	
16	358593	LYMM	Rushgreen S/Stn	86 Rushgreen Road WA13 9PR	A6144	(0925) 752176	4USD	GAE				
17	358565	MACCLESFIELD	Broken Cross Self Serve	147 Broken Cross SK11 8TU	A537	(0625) 421534	4USD	GAE				
18	358567	MACCLESFIELD	Chelford Self Serve	Alderley Road, Chelford SK11 9AH	A537	(0625) 860077	4USD	GAE				
19	358645	MACCLESFIELD	Tytherington Self Serve	Manchester Road SK10 2JJ	A523	(0625) 421732	4USD	GAE				
20	358703	MALPAS	Barton Service Station	Barton SY14 7HF	A534	(0829) 271021	4USD	GAE				■
21	358601	NANTWICH	Mansion Service Station	Crewe Road CW5 5SF	A51	(0270) 623739	4USD	GAE				
22	358611	NANTWICH	Stapeley Service Station	18 London Road, Stapeley CW5 7JJ	A51	(0270) 626293	4UD	GAE			■	
23	358613	NANTWICH	Stuart Graham Ltd	Whitchurch Road, Aston CW5 8DB	A530	(0270) 780300	4UD	GAE				
24	358631	NANTWICH	Walgherton Garage	London Road, Walgherton CW5 7LA	A51	(0270) 841321	4UD	GAE				
25	299773	NORTHWICH	Knutsford M/Way Northbound	M6 Motorway Service Area, Knutsford WA16 0TJ	M6	(0565) 634167	D	GAE		■		
26	299774	NORTHWICH	Knutsford South Bound	M6 Motorway Service Area, Knutsford WA16 0TJ	M6	(0922) 415537	D	GAE				
27	358616	NORTHWICH	Sandiway – Shell	Toll Bar, Sandiway CW8 2PL	A556	(0606) 882121	4USD	GAE				
28	358617	NORTHWICH	Parkside Self Serve	485 London Road, Davenham CW9 8NA	A533	(0606) 40299	4USD	GAE				
29	358640	NORTHWICH	The Garage	1-11 Station Road CW9 5LR	A559	(0606) 46061	4USD	GAE				
30	530578	NORTHWICH	Lostock Garage	Manchester Road CW9 6LR	A556	(0606) 330066	4USD	GA				
31	358773	RUNCORN	Grangeside F/Stn Ltd	96 Weston Road, Weston WA7 4LL	A557	(0928) 572306	4UD	GAE				
32	358917	RUNCORN	Halton Brow Self Serve	Halton Brow, Halton WA7 2EQ		(09285) 64433	4USD	GAE				
33	357955	STOKE-ON-TRENT	Scholar Green Garage	133 Congleton Road, Scholar Green ST7 3HA	A34	(0782) 774310	4USD	GAE				
34	358642	STOKE-ON-TRENT	Radway Green S/Stn	Crewe Road, Alsager ST7 1AA	B5078	(0270) 872831	4USD	GAE				
35	299457	WARRINGTON	Burtonwood S/Area Westbound	M62 Motorway, Great Sankey WA5 3AX	M62	(0925) 51656	4USD	GAE		■		
36	358477	WARRINGTON	Burtonwood S/Area Eastbound	M62 Service Area, Great Sankey WA5 3AX	M62	(0925) 51656	4USD	GAE				
37	358535	WARRINGTON	Dunham Hill S/Stn	Dunham Hill, Helsby WA6 0NT	A56	(0244) 300304	4UD	GAE				
38	358572	WARRINGTON	Grappenhall Motor Co	194 Knutsford Road, Grappenhall WA4 2QJ	A50	(0925) 268444	4UD	GAE				
39	358579	WARRINGTON	Alan Taylor Ltd	The Bridge F/Stn, Rixton WA3 6HD	A57	061-775 8454	4UD	GAE				
40	358581	WARRINGTON	Longford Bridge – Shell	296 Winwick Road WA2 8HZ	A49	(0925) 411917	4USD	GAE				
41	358585	WARRINGTON	North End Filling Station	Winwick Street WA2 7TU	A49	(0925) 35068	4UD	GAE				
42	358597	WARRINGTON	Woolston S/Stn	43 Manchester Road, Woolston WA1 4AE	A57	(0925) 812246	4USD	GAE				
43	358730	WARRINGTON	Queens Self Serve	Orford Lane WA2 7BB	A574	(0925) 31806	4USD	GAE				
44	358569	WILMSLOW	Dean Row Self Serve	Adlington Road SK9 2LP	A5102	(0625) 529465	4USD	GAE				
45	358732	WILMSLOW	Fulshaw Self Serve	Hawthorne Street SK9 5EH	A538	(0625) 522829	4USD	GAE				
46	358603	WINSFORD	Dickinson Bros (Winsford) Ltd	Delamere Street, Over Square CW7 2LT	B5074	(0606) 592241	4USD	GAE				

CLEVELAND

Loc. Ref.	Shell Ref.	TOWN	NAME	ADDRESS	Road No.	Tel. No.	Fuel	Cards	24 hour	HGV	Select	Car Wash
1	366145	BILLINGHAM	Wolviston Road Garage	Wolviston Road TS22 5JF		(0642) 361291	4USD	GAE				■
2	366152	GUISBOROUGH	Newstead Self Serve	West End TS14 6RL	A171	(0287) 632732	4USD	GAE				
3	366159	HARTLEPOOL	Warren Self Serve	Eassington Road TS24 9AG	A179	(0429) 272872	4USD	GAE				
4	366272	HARTLEPOOL	Catcote Filling Station	Catcote Road TS25 4HL	B1277	(0429) 272128	4UD	GAE				■
5	366291	HARTLEPOOL	Hartlepool – Shell	Belle Vue Way TS25 1JZ	A689	(0429) 863554	4USD	GAE				
6	366021	MIDDLESBROUGH	Cannon Park Motors	Newport Road TS1 5JP	B6541	(0642) 249346	4USD	GAE				
7	366156	MIDDLESBROUGH	Oxford Road Self Serve	Oxford Road TS5 5DU	B1272	(0642) 820805	4USD	GAE				
8	366293	MIDDLESBROUGH	Park End Self Serve	Ormesby Road TS3 0NB		(0642) 322557	4USD	GAE				
9	366162	REDCAR	Trunk Road Self Serve	Trunk Road TS10 5BW	A1085	(0642) 472580	4USD	GAE				
10	362172	SALTBURN-BY-THE-SEA	Hazelgrove Filling Stn	Winsor Road TS12 1DQ	A174	(0287) 622048	4U	GAE				
11	366316	STOCKTON-ON-TEES	Summerville Hypermarket	Durham Road TS21 1BB	A177	(0642) 607418	4USD	GAE				■
12	366139	YARM	Yarm – Shell	Thirsk Road TS15 9LJ		(0642) 782344	4USD	GAE				

CLWYD

Loc. Ref.	Shell Ref.	TOWN	NAME	ADDRESS	Road No.	Tel. No.	Fuel	Cards	24 hour	HGV	Select	Car Wash
1	357760	ABERGELE	Expressway – Shell	Expressway, Llanddulas LL22 8HH		(0492) 512110	4USD	GAE				■
2	358504	CHESTER	Border – Shell	High Street, Saltney CH4 8BT	A5104	(0244) 671398	4USD	GAE				
3	358689	CHESTER	Gladstone – Shell	Main Road, Broughton CH4 0NR	A5104	(0244) 533050	4USD	GAE				
4	357439	COLWYN BAY	Gwynne's Auto Point	Conway Road, Mochdre LL28 5AL	A55	(0492) 466170	4USD	GAE				
5	358464	CORWEN	Glasfryn Garage	Cerrig-Y-Drudion LL21 0RY	A5	(0490) 82231	4UD	GA				
6	358747	DEESIDE	Smithy Service Station	Sealand Road CH5 2LQ	A548	(0244) 880283	4UD	GAE				
7	358506	DENBIGH	Castle View – Shell	Rhyl Road LL16 5SU	A525	(0745) 816522	4USD	GAE				
8	358911	FLINT	Coleshill F/Stn	Coast Road CH6 5RR	A548	(0352) 733717	4UD	GAE				
9	358500	MOLD	Loggerheads Garage	Llanferres LL13 0EH	A494	(0352) 85503	4UD	GAE				
10	384296	MOLD	Mold – Shell	Chester Road, New Brighton CH7 1XX	A494	(0352) 750417	4USD	GAE			■	
11	357790	NORTHOP	Northop – Shell	A55 Expressway CH7 6HF	A55	(0244) 550766	4UD	GAE				
12	358513	PRESTATYN	Pendre Garage	Gronant Road LL19 9DS		(0745) 852441	4UD	GAE				
13	358507	RHYL	Vale – Shell	Rhuddlan Road LL18 2PH	A525	(0745) 339227	4USD	GAE				■
14	358475	WREXHAM	Abermorddu Service Station	Mold Road, Abermorddu LL12 9BS	A541	(0978) 760447	4USD	GAE				
15	358482	WREXHAM	Newhaven Garage	Chester Road, Rossett LL12 0DG	B5445	(0244) 570492	4UD	GAE				
16	358487	WREXHAM	Johnstown Filling Station	Ruabon Road, Johnstown LL14 2SH	B5605	(0978) 843355	4USD	GAE				
17	358493	WREXHAM	C N Wason & Sons	Salop Road, Overton LL13 0EH	A528	(0978) 73240	4USD	GAE				
18	358662	WREXHAM	Parkwall Service Station	Mold Road, Gwersylt LL11 4AH	A541	(0978) 720198	4UD	GAE				

CORNWALL

Loc. Ref.	Shell Ref.	TOWN	NAME	ADDRESS	Road No.	Tel. No.	Fuel	Cards	24 hour	HGV	Select
1	348652	BODMIN	Camelot Garages Ltd	Valley Truckle, Camelford PL32 9RT	A39	(0840) 213217	4USD	GAE			
2	348671	BODMIN	Penlan Garage	Four Winds, Cardinham PL30 4HH	A30	(0208) 82231	4UD	GAE		•	
3	348673	BODMIN	St Kew Service Station	St Kew Highway PL30 3ED	A39	(0208) 84238	4USD	GAE			
4	348695	CALLINGTON	Pengelly Garage	Moss Side PL17 8AS	A390	(0579) 83249	4UD	GAE			
5	348596	CAMBORNE	Camborne – Shell	Treswithan Road TR14 7PB	A3047	(0209) 612027	4USD	GAE			
6	432975	CAMELFORD	Hallworthy Garage	Hallworthy PL32 9SH	A395	(08406) 501	4UD	GAE			
7	416714	DELABOLE	Rockland Garage	PL33 9BT	B3314	(0840) 213284	4USD	GA			
8	402342	FALMOUTH	Atlantic Services	Dracaena Avenue TR11 2ES	A39	(0326) 316562	4USD	GA			
9	348682	GUNNISLAKE	Pearces Service Station	Drakewalls PL18 9EE	A390	(0822) 832407	4UD	GAE			
10	348594	HAYLE	Atlantic Motors	101 Commercial Road TR27 4DF	B3301	(0736) 753247	4USD	GAE			
11	348620	HAYLE	Hayle – Shell	Carwin Rise (Loggans) TR27 5DG	A30	(0736) 753125	4USD	GAE		•	
12	348624	HELSTON	Riders Gges Ltd (Helston)	Sithney TR13 0AF	A394	(0326) 574111	4UD	GAE			
13	348659	LAUNCESTON	Prouts Garage Ltd	Okehampton Road PL15 9EW		(0566) 772171	4UD	GAE			
14	348678	LISKEARD	Addington Filling Station	Callington Road PL14 3HD	A390	(0579) 347840	4USD	GAE			
15	348822	LOOE	Polperro Park F/Stn	Polperro Road, Pelynt PL13 2JE	A387	(0503) 72416	4UD	GAE			
16	348902	LOOE	Riverbank Self Serve	Station Road PL13 1HN	A387	(0503) 263423	4USD	GAE			
17	431504	LOSTWITHIEL	Downend Garage & Motor Co.	Downend PL22 0RB	A390	(0208) 872363	4USD	GA			
18	348629	NEWQUAY	Braefel Filling Station	Hendra Croft, Rejerrah TR8 5QP	A3075	(0872) 573129	4USD	GAE			
19	348665	NEWQUAY	Globe Garage	East Road, Quintrell Downs TR8 4LQ	A392	(0637) 872410	4UD	GAE			
20	348667	NEWQUAY	Newquay – Shell	Hill Grove, Narrowcliffe TR7 3BQ		(0637) 872247	4USD	GAE			
21	353086	NEWQUAY	Westways Filling Station	Tregaswith, Newquay Road TR8 4JQ	A3059	(0637) 880150	4UD	GAE			
22	529938	NEWQUAY	Carland Cross – Shell	Carland Cross, Mitchell TR8 5AY	A30	(0872) 510747	4USD	GAE			
23	348618	PENZANCE	Penzance – Shell	The Cliff TR18 3NT		(0736) 67640	4UD	GAE			
24	383807	PENZANCE	Heamoor Garage	Heamoor TR18 3AH		(0736) 64055	4USD	GA			
25	386200	PENZANCE	Mayon Garage	1st & Last Filling Station, Sennen TR19 7AD	A30	(0736) 871203	4USD	GA			
26	348633	PERRANPORTH	Burrells Garage	Budnick Hill TR6 0BX	B3285	(0872) 572168	4UD	GAE			
27	348600	REDRUTH	Mount Ambrose Self Serve	Mount Ambrose TR15 1QZ	A3074	(0209) 212764	4UD	GAE			
28	348601	REDRUTH	Maynes Garage Ltd	Illogan Highway TR15 3EY	A3047	(0209) 215502	4USD	GAE			
29	348996	REDRUTH	North Country Filling Station	North Country TR16 4AA	B3300	(0209) 215877	4USD	GAE			
30	385719	REDRUTH	E Mitchell & Sons Ltd	Bridge Garage, Bridge TR16 4QG	B3300	(0209) 842230	4USD	GA			
31	348680	SALTASH	Caradon – Shell	Trerule Foot PL12 5BL	A38	(0752) 851663	4USD	GAE			
32	348796	SALTASH	Tamar S/Serve	New Road PL12 6HN		(0752) 846828	4USD	GAE			
33	348635	ST AGNES	Sevenmilestone Filling Station	Sevenmilestone TR5 0PF	B3277	(0872) 552592	4USD	GAE			
34	348611	ST IVES	Roach's Garages Ltd	Carbis Bay TR26 2LJ	A3074	(0736) 795188	4USD	GAE			
35	698251	ST MABYN	Longstone Filling Station	PL30 3BA	B3266	(0208) 84538	4USD	GA			
36	410949	ST TEATH	Allen Valley Garage	Knights Mill PL30 3JE	A39	(0208) 850270	4USD	GA			
37	348627	TRURO	Truro STC	Highertown TR1 3PY	A390	(0872) 40622	4USD	GAE			
38	348631	TRURO	Fal Garage	Tressilian TR2 4BA	A39	(0872) 52221	4USD	GAE			
39	348641	TRURO	Playing Place – Shell	Playing Place TR3 6HA	A39	(0872) 870060	4USD	GAE			
40	348644	TRURO	Vospers of Truro Ltd	Lemon Quay TR1 2LR		(0872) 73933	4UD	GAE			
41	348969	TRURO	Trafalgar – Shell	Tregolls Road TR1 1PU	A39	(0872) 76631	4USD	GAE			

CUMBRIA

Loc. Ref.	Shell Ref.	TOWN	NAME	ADDRESS	Road No.	Tel. No.	Fuel	Cards	24 hour	HGV	Select
1	357715	APPELBY-IN-WESTMORLAND	H Pigney & Son	Chapel Street CA16 6QR	B6260	(07683) 51240	4UD	GAE			
2	358318	ASKHAM IN FURNESS	Dalemount Filling Station	Ireleth Road LA16 7DL	A595	(0229) 62203	4UD	GAE			
3	358320	BARROW-IN-FURNESS	Lakeland – Shell	Abbey Road LA14 4HD	A590	(0229) 432474	4USD	GAE			
4	358752	BARROW-IN-FURNESS	Hadwins Low Road Garage	Ironworks Road LA14 2PG	A590	(0229) 430511	4UD	GAE			
5	357722	BRAMPTON	Low Row Service Station	A69 Low Row CA8 2JE	A69	(06977) 46344	4USD	GAE			
6	361913	BRAMPTON	Carlisle Road Garage	Carlisle Road CA8 1ST	A69	(06977) 2508	4UD	GAE			
7	358335	BROUGH	Mark Johns Motors	Kirkby Stephen CA17 0XX	A685	(07683) 712230	4USD	GAE			
8	358934	BROUGH	Stainmore Services	North Stainmore CA17 4EU	A66	(09304) 744	4USD	GAE			
9	357741	CARLISLE	Carlisle Nth Travellers Check	A74 Northbound, Todhills CA6 4HA	A74	(0228) 74355	4USD	GAE		•	
10	358316	CARLISLE	Valley End Motors	Silecroft, Millom LA18 5LR	A595	(0229) 772407	4UD	GAE			
11	361906	CARLISLE	Carlisle – Shell	Hardwicke Circus CA3 1JE	A7	(0228) 511213	4USD	GAE			
12	361908	CARLISLE	Golden Fleece Service Station	London Road, Carleton CA4 0AN	A6	(0228) 42766	4UD	GAE			
13	361915	CARLISLE	Petteril Bridge S/Serve	London Road CA1 2JU	A6	(0228) 23892	4USD	GAE			
14	361932	CARLISLE	Beckermet Service Garage	Brooklyn Place, Beckermet CA21 2XB	(094)	6841200	4UD	A			
15	358940	COCKERMOUTH	Fairfield Service Station	Station Road CA13 9PZ	A66	(0900) 861893	4USD	GAE			
16	398088	COCKERMOUTH	Derwent S/Stn (Toulsons)	CA13 0HH	A595	(0900) 68211	4USD	GAE			
17	361928	EGREMONT	Jubilee Garage (Egremont) Ltd	North Road CA22 2PR	A595	(0946) 820245	4USD	GAE			
18	361941	EGREMONT	Parkhouse Filling Station	North Road, Bigrigg CA22 2TL	A595	(0946) 810479	4USD	GAE			
19	358309	GRANGE-OVER-SANDS	Grange Motors Limited	Main Street LA11 6EE	B5277	(0539) 534237	4USD	GAE			
20	358341	KENDAL	Lound Road Garage	Lound Road LA9 7EG	A685	(0539) 723914	4UD	GAE			
21	358636	KENDAL	Appleby Road Service Station	Appleby Road LA9 6ES	A65	(0539) 722215	4USD	GAE			
22	361934	KESWICK	Fitz Park Self Serve	Penrith Road CA12 4HB	A591	(07687) 72386	4US	GAE			
23	358308	KIRBY IN FURNESS	Grizebeck Service Station	LA17 7XH	A595	(0229) 89259	4UD	GAE			
24	358331	KIRBY LONSDALE	Town End Garage	Casterton LA6 2RX	A683	(05242) 71421	4UD	GAE			
25	358321	MILLOM	Whartons Garage Ltd	Duke Street LA18 5BB	A5093	(0229) 773771	4USD	GAE			
26	358329	MILNTHORPE	Canal Garage	Crooklands LA7 7NX	A65	(04487) 401	4USD	GAE			
27	299484	PENRITH	Penrith Truck Stop	Penrith Industrial Estate CA11 9EH	A592	(0768) 66995	D	GAE		•	

	Shell Ref.	TOWN	NAME	ADDRESS	Road No.	Tel. No.	Fuel	Cards	24 hour	HGV	Select	Car Wash
									Facilities			
8	358338	PENRITH	T Simpson & Son	Main Street, Shap CA10 3LX	A6	(093) 16212	4UD	GAE				
9	358952	PENRITH	M6 Diesel Services	Tebay CA10 3SS	M6	(05874) 336	4UD				■	
0	361922	PENRITH	Penrith – Shell	Victoria Road CA11 8HU	A6	(0768) 65162	4USD	GAE				
1	720258	PENRITH	Mark Johns Motors	Ulswater Road CA11 0PG	A685	(0768) 64545	4USD	GAE				■
2	358303	ULVERSTON	Guy Smith (Newby Bridge Mtrs)	Newby Bridge LA12 8ND	A590	(0448) 31253	4USD	GAE				
3	358313	ULVERSTON	Hurley & Peaks Ltd	Greenodd LA12 7RE	A590	(0229) 861208	4UD	GAE				
4	358765	ULVERSTON	Ulverston – Shell	Oubas Hill LA12 7LA	A590	(0229) 52172	4USD	GAE				
5	361936	WHITEHAVEN	Solway Self Serve	Newtown CA28 7HU	B5345	(0946) 695765	4USD	GAE				
6	358325	WINDERMERE	Windermere Filling Station	Main Street LA23 1DX	A592	(05394) 47227	4UD	GAE				

DERBYSHIRE

	Shell Ref.	TOWN	NAME	ADDRESS	Road No.	Tel. No.	Fuel	Cards	24 hour	HGV	Select	Car Wash
	299833	BELPER	Belper Orangery Self Serve	Chapel Street DE56 1AR	A6	(0773) 828220	4USD	GAE				
	353312	CASTLE DONNINGTON	The Paddocks Donnington Park	The Paddock, Donnington Park DE7 2RP		(0332) 810048						
	357528	CHESTERFIELD	Spinning Wheel Filling Station	Sheffield Road, Sheepbridge S41 9EH	A61	(0246) 451772	4UD	GAE				■
	366186	CHESTERFIELD	Red House Service Station	Heath Road S44 5QS	A6175	(0246) 850329	4USD	GAE				
	366239	CHESTERFIELD	Graingers Service Station	Chesterfield Road, Holmewood S42 5TE	B6039	(0246) 850530	4UD	GAE				
	353069	DERBY	Navigation Self Serve	London Road, Alvaston DE24 8WA	A6	(0332) 752664	4USD	GAE				
	353343	DERBY	Whittle Way – Shell	Sir Frank Whittle Road DE21 4RX	A61	(0332) 294126	4USD	GAE				
	353350	DERBY	Clarence Road Service Station	241 Clarence Road DE3 6CU		(0332) 768076	4UD					
	355382	DERBY	Allestree Self Serve	Duffield Road, Allestree DE22 2DG	A6	(0332) 556300	4USD	GAE				
0	355388	DERBY	Doves Garage	High Street, Melbourne DE7 1GJ	B587	(0332) 862123	4USD	GAE				
1	355393	DERBY	Cottage Filling Station	Swarkestone DE7 1JB	A514	(0332) 700304	4USD	GAE				
2	355398	DERBY	Y Pas, Willington Services Sth	Willington Crossroads, Egginton DE65 6GY	A38	(0283) 703707	4USD	GAE				
3	355568	DERBY	Y Pas, Willington Services Nth	Willington Crossroads, Egginton DE65 6GY	A38	(0283) 703349	4USD	GAE				
4	355579	DERBY	Sunnyhill Service Station	Blagreaves Lane, Littleover DE23 7PT		(0332) 770855	4UD	GAE				
5	355589	DERBY	Ringroad Self Serve	Osmaston Park Road DE23 8WL	A5111	(0332) 766141	4USD	GAE				
6	355813	DERBY	Friargate – Shell	Ashbourne Road DE3 3AF	A52	(0332) 291501	4USD	GAE				
7	366242	DERBY	Somercotes Self Serve	Nottingham Road, Somercoates DE55 4JJ	B600	(0773) 602562	4USD	GAE				
8	527177	HEANOR	Service Station – Shell	127 Derby Road DE7 7QL	A608	(0773) 714410	4USD	GAE				
9	355376	ILKESTON	Nutbrook – Shell	Derby Road DE7 5FH	A609	(0602) 302885	4USD	GAE				
'0	355396	LITTLEOVER	Y Pas Omega	Burton Road DE3 6FQ	A5250	(0332) 766198	4UD	GAE				■
'1	355366	OCKBROOK	Ockbrook – Shell	Borrowash By-Pass DE72 3HN	A52	(0332) 280760	4UD	GAE				
'2	366219	STOCKPORT	Paragon Garage	Buxton Road, New Mills SK12 3JT	A6	(0663) 743486	4UD	GAE				

DEVON

	Shell Ref.	TOWN	NAME	ADDRESS	Road No.	Tel. No.	Fuel	Cards	24 hour	HGV	Select	Car Wash
	348371	AXMINSTER	Kilmington Cross Services	Kilmington EX13 7RX	A35	(0297) 35251	4USD	GAE				■
	531189	AXMINSTER	Hunters Lodge Garage Ltd	Charmouth Road EX13 5ST	A35	(0297) 32737	4UD	GAE				■
	348807	BARNSTAPLE	Fremington Service Station	Yelland Road, Fremington EX31 2NX	A39	(0271) 73896	4USD	GAE				
	308519	BIDEFORD	Northgate (Honda) Filling Stn	East-the-Water EX39 4AQ	A386	(0237) 476795	4UD	GAE				
	348457	BIDEFORD	Boards Garage	East The Water EX39 4BQ		(02374) 72292	4UD	GAE				
	348458	BIDEFORD	Raleigh Garage (Bideford) Ltd	Northam Road EX39 3NH	B3235	(0237) 472384	4U					■
	348881	BRAUNTON	Orchard Self Serve	Chaloners Road EX33 2ES	A361	(0271) 815200	4UD	GAE				
	348373	BUDLEIGH SALTERTON	Salterton Garage	6-10 High Street EX9 6LQ		(0395) 442277	4UD	GAE				
	348364	COLYTON	Colyford Filling Station	Swan Hill Road, Colyford EX13 6QQ	A3052	(0297) 552341	4UD	GAE				
0	348466	CREDITON	Crediton – Shell	Exeter Road EX17 3BN	A377	(0363) 777927	4USD	GAE				
1	348702	DARTMOUTH	Premier Garage	Dartmouth Road, Stoke Fleming TQ6 0RE	A379	(0803) 770324	4UD	GAE				
2	348473	DAWLISH	Marine Garage	Exeter Road EX7 0AQ	A379	(0626) 863298	4USD	GAE				
3	348369	EXETER	Little Copse Service Station	Bradninch EX5 4LD	B3181	(0392) 881224	4UD	GAE				■
4	348464	EXETER	Redlands Service Station	Exmouth Road, Clyst St Mary EX5 1AR	A376	(0392) 873040	4UD	GAE				
5	348470	EXETER	Countess Wear – Shell	399 Topsham Road, Countess Wear EX2 6HD	A379	(0392) 876652	4USD	GAE				
6	348472	EXETER	Cowley Road Self Serve	Cowley Bridge Road EX4 5AF	A377	(0392) 52208	4USD	GAE				
7	348477	EXETER	Polsloe Bridge Self Serve	282 Pinhoe Road EX4 7JQ	B3212	(0392) 215127	4UD	GAE				
8	348480	EXETER	Haldon Thatch Self Serve	Telegraph Hill, Kennford EX6 7XX	A380	(0392) 833238	4USD	GAE				
9	348481	EXETER	Oaklands Garage Ltd	Sidmouth Road, Aylesbeare EX5 2JJ	A3052	(0325) 232241	4USD	GAE				
0	348486	EXETER	Speedway Self Serve	63 Cowick Street EX4 1HW	A3212	(0392) 72269	4UD	GAE				
1	348487	EXETER	Speedway Garage	Tiverton Road, Rewe EX5 4DY	A396	(0392) 860298	4UD	GAE				
2	349017	EXETER	Kennford – Shell	A38, Kennford EX6 7UD	A38	(0392) 832487	4USD	GAE				■
3	348790	EXMOUTH	Exmouth – Shell	223 Exeter Road EX8 3DZ	A376	(0395) 272555	4USD	GAE				
4	348367	HONITON	Windmill Garage	Offwell EX14 9RP	A35	(0404) 831228	4USD	GAE				■
5	348828	HONITON	Fenny Bridges Garage	Fenny Bridges, Honiton Road EX14 8DF	A30	(0404) 850357	4UD	GAE				
6	541167	HONITON	Heathpark Service Station	Heathpark Industrial Estate EX14 8SF	A30	(0404) 47325	4USD	GAE				
7	266673	KINGSBRIDGE	Fir Tree Filling Station	Ashford, Aveton Gifford TQ7 4NF	A379	(0548) 550714	4UD	GAE				
8	348709	KINGSBRIDGE	Salcombe Road Garage Ltd	Salcombe Road, Malborough TQ7 3BX	A381	(0548) 561333	4UD	GAE				
9	433896	LAUNCESTON	Jacksons Garage	St Giles on the Heath PL15 9ST	A388	(0566) 772972	4USD	GAE				
0	348443	NEWTON ABBOT	Stover Self Serve	Exeter Road TQ12 6PP	A382	(0626) 64663	4USD	GAE				
1	348582	NEWTON ABBOT	Halfway Filling Stn	Torquay Road, Kingskerswell TQ12 5HG	A380	(0803) 872204	4USD	GAE				
2	348708	NEWTON ABBOT	Peartree Cross Self Serve	Ashburton TQ13 7RB	B3380	(0364) 52302	4UD	GAE				
3	400024	NEWTON ABBOT	Benedicts Bridge Garage	Liverton TQ12 6HQ		(0626) 821338	4UD	GAE				
4	281976	OKEHAMPTON	Okehampton – Shell	Sourton Cross EX20 4HH	A30	(0837) 55011	4USD	GAE				
5	347151	PAIGNTON	Riviera – Shell	376 Torquay Road TQ3 2DN	A3022	(0803) 664604	4USD	GAE				■
6	348577	PAIGNTON	Chenhalls Ltd	349-353 Totnes Road TQ4 7DF	A385	(0803) 558567	4UD	GAE				
7	347158	PLYMOUTH	Plymouth – Shell	Plymouth Road, Crabtree PL3 6EE	A374	(0752) 252025	4USD	GAE				■

Loc. Ref.	Shell Ref.	TOWN	NAME	ADDRESS	Road No.	Tel. No.	Fuel	Cards	24 hour	HGV	Select
38	348689	PLYMOUTH	Hartley – Shell	Mannamead Road PL3 5RF	A3064	(0752) 771474	4USD	GAE			
39	348692	PLYMOUTH	Swan National Rentals Ltd	Alexandra Road, Mutley PL4 7EL	B3214	(0752) 666145	4UD	GAE			
40	348697	PLYMOUTH	Lee Mill Services	Lee Mill, Nr Ivybridge PL21 9OE	A38	(0752) 690554	4UD	GAE			
41	348714	PLYMOUTH	Smithaleigh S/Stn	Smithaleigh PL7 5AX	A38	(0752) 893003	4UD	GAE			
42	348833	PLYMOUTH	Charles Roundabout Self Serve	Charles Church PL4 0AX	A374	(0752) 667111	4UD	GAE			
43	348834	PLYMOUTH	Vospers Motor House (Plym'h)	Millbay Road PL1 3LW		(0752) 668040	4UD	GAE			
44	348851	PLYMOUTH	Plympton – Shell	150 Plymouth Road, Plympton PL7 4NE B3416		(0752) 336716	4USD	GAE			
45	353289	PLYMOUTH	Plymouth & South Devon Co-Op	Transit Way PL3 3TW	B3413	(0752) 795929	4USD	GAE			
46	535503	PLYMOUTH	Warren Bros	4-6 Radford Park Road, Plymstock PL9 9DQ		(0752) 484028	4UD	GAE			
47	348360	SIDMOUTH	Sidmouth Self serve	Woolbrook Road EX10 9UU	A3052	(0395) 579624	4USD	GAE			
48	348363	SIDMOUTH	Newmans Raleigh Self Serve	Exmouth Road, Colaton Raleigh EX10 0LD	B3178	(03956) 8444	4UD	GAE			
49	349000	SIDMOUTH	Sidford Service Station	Sidford EX10 9PF	A3052	(0395) 514710	4UD	GAE			
50	348700	SOUTH BRENT	Carew Self Serve	A38 TQ10 9ER	A38	(0364) 72209	4USD	GAE			
51	348440	TEIGNMOUTH	County Garage (Teignmouth) Ltd	106 Bitton Park Road TQ14 9DD	A381	(0626) 772501	4UD	GAE			
52	348494	TIVERTON	Blundell's Self Serve	Station Road EX16 4LF	B3391	(0884) 258005	4USD	GAE			
53	353331	TIVERTON	Tiverton – Travellers check	Junction 27, M5 EX16 7HD	M5	(0884) 821353	4UD	GAE			
54	400022	TIVERTON	Horsdon Garage	Blundells Road EX16 4DE	B3391	(0884) 255762	4UD	GAE			
55	348584	TORQUAY	Lymington Garage	Moores Motors, 230 Lymington Road TQ1 4AR		(0803) 327369	4UD	GAE			
56	348461	TORRINGTON	Torrington Motors	New Street EX38 8BX	A386	(0805) 22361	4UD	GAE			
57	348588	TOTNES	Red Post Garage	Littlehempston TQ9 6NQ	A381	(0803) 812389	4UD	GAE			
58	348803	TOTNES	Dartline Filling Station	Station Road TQ9 5HW	A385	(0803) 863960	4UD	GAE			
59	348455	WINKLEIGH	Beacon Garage	Dolton EX19 8PS	B3220	(0805) 4240	4USD	GAE			

DORSET

Loc. Ref.	Shell Ref.	TOWN	NAME	ADDRESS	Road No.	Tel. No.	Fuel	Cards	24 hour	HGV	Select
1	347819	BLANDFORD FORUM	Ashley Wood Filling Station	Tarrant Keyneston DT11 9JJ	B3082	(0258) 452595	4UD	GAE			
2	347809	BOURNEMOUTH	Boscombe – Shell	980 Christchurch Road BH7 6DW	A35	(0202) 418613	4USD	GAE			
3	347843	BOURNEMOUTH	East Howe Self Serve	271 Kinson Road BH10 5HE		(0202) 573300	4UD	GAE			
4	347937	BOURNEMOUTH	Strouden Park S/S	498 Castle Lane BH8 9UD	A3060	(0202) 521073	4USD	GAE			
5	348340	BRIDPORT	Harbour Garages (Bridport) Ltd	West Bay DT6 5LB	B3162	(0308) 421777	4UD	GAE			
6	347912	CHRISTCHURCH	Christchurch Self Serve	58 Barrack Road BH23 1PQ	A35	(0202) 484673	4UD	GAE			
7	347936	CHRISTCHURCH	Somerford – Shell	1 Lyndhurst Road BH23 4SA	A35	(0425) 270006	4USD	GAE			
8	299993	DORCHESTER	Five Cross Filling Station	Crossways DT2 8BE	B3390	(0305) 852213	4UD	GAE			
9	347814	DORCHESTER	London Road Self Serve	31-33 London Road DT1 1NF	B3150	(0305) 266066	4USD	GAE			
10	347828	DORCHESTER	Weatherbury Garage	A35, Puddletown DT2 8SN	A35	(0305) 848211	4UD	GAE			
11	348887	DORCHESTER	Kings Road Self Serve	Kings Road DT1 1NJ	B352	(0305) 267338	4USD	GAE			
12	353091	DORCHESTER	Bride Valley Motors	Winterbourne Abbas DT2 9LU	A35	(0305) 889370	4USD	GAE			
13	348383	GILLINGHAM	Five Bridges Garage	West Stour SP8 5SE	A30	(0747) 838240	4USD	GAE			
14	347849	POOLE	Harveys Self Serve	355 Blandford Road, Hamworthy BH15 4JL	A350	(0202) 674308	4UD	GAE			
15	347851	POOLE	Newtown Self Serve	540 Ringwood Road BH12 4LY	A348	(0202) 732008	4USD	GAE			
16	347853	POOLE	Darbys – Shell	13-17 Waterloo Road BH17 7JX	A349	(0202) 658498	4UD	GAE			
17	347857	POOLE	Parkstone – Shell	266 Bournemouth Road BH14 9AN	A35	(0202) 740347	4USD	GAE			
18	348313	POOLE	Alexandra Park Self Serve	124/130 Ashley Road BH14 9BX	B3061	(0202) 740314	4UD	GAE			
19	348524	POOLE	Hamworthy – Shell	490 Blandford Road, Hamworthy BH16 5BN	A350	(0202) 621791	4USD	GAE			
20	308504	RINGWOOD	St. Leonards – Shell	Ringwood Road BH24 2NR	A31	(0425) 471370	4USD	GAE			
21	347867	SALISBURY	Yewtree Garage	Blandford Road, Woodyates SP5 4LN	A354	(0725) 552550	4UD	GAE			
22	348389	SHERBORNE	Cross Roads Garage	Yetminster DT9 6LF		(0935) 872239	4UD	GAE			
23	348390	SHERBORNE	F.W.B. Saunders Ltd	Digby Road DT9 3NN		(0935) 812436	4UD ·	GA			
24	384303	SHERBORNE	Youngs Garage	Yeovil Road DT9 4BQ	A30	(0935) 813350	4UD	GAE			
25	348387	STALBRIDGE	Ring Street Filling Station	DT10 2NQ	A357	(0963) 62496	4USD	GAE			
26	299936	STURMINSTER NEWTON	Bridge Garage	Bridge DT10 2BS	A357	(0258) 72373	4USD	GAE			
27	347821	SWANAGE	Foleys	Valley Road, Harmans Cross BH19 3DZ	A351	(0929) 480215	4UD	GAE			
28	347833	SWANAGE	Burts Motors	281 High Street BH19 2NJ	A351	(0929) 422877	4U	GAE			
29	348284	SWANAGE	Studland Service Station	Swanage Road, Studland BH19 3AE	B3351		4UD	GAE			
30	347845	VERWOOD	Manor Road Garage	90 Manor Road BH21 6EB	B3072	(0202) 822353	4UD	GAE			
31	347858	VERWOOD	Verwood Motors Ltd	Ringwood Road BH31 7AD	B3081	(0202) 825222	4UD	GAE			
32	347823	WAREHAM	Wareham Auto Point	North Street BH20 4AG	B3075	(0929) 552823	4UD	GAE			
33	347834	WAREHAM	Garrison Garage (Bovington)	King George V Road, Bovington Camp BH20 6JQ		(0929) 462757	4UD	GAE			
34	347836	WAREHAM	Wool & Bovington Motors Ltd	The Garage, Wool BH20 6EH	A352	(0929) 462248	4UD	GAE			
35	347817	WEYMOUTH	Overcombe Filling Station	Preston Road DT3 6PU	A353	(0305) 834172	4UD	GAE			
36	347825	WEYMOUTH	Weymouth – Shell	316-318 Dorchester Road DT3 5AR	A354	(0305) 815151	4UD	GAE			
37	347830	WEYMOUTH	C & A.C. Neal	63 Abbotsbury Road DT4 0AQ	B3157	(0305) 785725	4UD	GAE			
38	348985	WEYMOUTH	Buxton – Shell	Buxton Road DT4 9PJ	A354	(0305) 777429	4USD	GAE			
39	347174	WIMBORNE	Simon Hartwell Ltd	236-240 Ringwood Road, Ferndown BH22 9AR	A31	(0202) 893589	4U	GAE			
40	347841	WIMBORNE	Dibbens Garage	West Street BH21 1JU	B3073	(0202) 882261	4UD	GAE			
41	347847	WIMBORNE	Three Cross Garage	Ringwood Road, Three Legged Cross BH21 6RD	B3072	(0202) 825255	4UD	GAE			
42	347860	WIMBORNE	Little Canford Garage	98 Wimborne Road West BH21 2DS	B3073	(0202) 883243	4UD	GAE			

DUMFRIES & GALLOWAY

Loc. Ref.	Shell Ref.	TOWN	NAME	ADDRESS	Road No.	Tel. No.	Fuel	Cards	24 hour	HGV	Select
1	381179	CASTLE DOUGLAS	Crown Garage	King Street DG7 2LB	A745	(0556) 2038	4USD	GAE			
2	377626	DUMFRIES	Collin – Shell	Annan Road DG1 3SE	A75	(0387) 75613	4USD	GAE			
3	380770	DUMFRIES	Tweedies Motors Ltd	81/83 Whitesands DG1 2RX		(0387) 53161	4UD	GAE			
4	380995	DUMFRIES	Border Cars – Shell	130/132 Terregles Street DG2 9DX		(0387) 67835	4USD	GAE			

Loc. Ref.	Shell Ref.	TOWN	NAME	ADDRESS	Road No.	Tel. No.	Fuel	Cards	24 hour	HGV	Select	Car Wash
5	380779	GLENLUCE	Glenluce Filling Station	78 Main Street DG8 0PS	A751	(0581) 3217	4UD	GAE				
6	380784	KIRKCUDBRIGHT	Beaconsfield Garage	Beaconsfield Place DG6 4DP	A755	(0557) 30558	4UD	GAE				
7	380768	LOCKERBIE	Townfoot Garage	Main Street DG1 2PB	B723	(05762) 3240	4USD	GAE				
8	287250	MOFFAT	Coatesgate Filling Station	Coatesgate, Beattock DG10 9SL	A74	(06833) 669	4USD	GAE		●		
9	380761	MOFFAT	Colvin Garage	High Street DG10 9HG	A701	(0683) 20147	4USD	GAE				
10	380786	NEWTON STEWART	Galloway Motor Co Ltd	Creebridge Garage DG8 6NP		(0671) 3603	4UD	GAE				
11	380766	SANQUHAR	Burnside Filling Station	Glasgow Road DG4 6BZ	A76	(0659) 50328	4UD	GAE				
12	380781	STRANRAER	Mirrey Self Serve	Stoneykirk Road DG9 7BU	A77	(0776) 3120	4USD	GAE				

DURHAM

Loc. Ref.	Shell Ref.	TOWN	NAME	ADDRESS	Road No.	Tel. No.	Fuel	Cards	24 hour	HGV	Select	Car Wash
1	366129	BARNARD CASTLE	The Garage	Catherstone DL12 9PH	B6277	(0833) 50492	4U					
2	362225	BISHOP AUCKLAND	Milford Garage	South Church DL14 5SY	B6282	(0388) 774545	4USD	GAE				●
3	366135	BISHOP AUCKLAND	West End Filling Station	Stanhope DL13 2NL	A689	(0388) 528414	4UD	GAE				
4	366092	CHESTER-LE-STREET	Chester-Le-Street T.C	Park Road South DH3 3LS	A167	091-387 1127	4USD	GAE				
5	366131	CROOK	Oates Garage	Hunwick Lane, Willington DL15 0HY	A690	(0388) 746666	4U	GAE				
6	366165	DARLINGTON	Darlington North – Shell	396/8 North Road DL1 3BH	A167	(0325) 381266	4USD	GAE				
7	366175	DARLINGTON	Darlington South – Shell	Carmel Road South DL3 8DQ	A67	(0325) 466613	4USD	GAE				
8	366180	DARLINGTON	Woodland Road Self Serve	Woodland Road DL3 9NQ	A68	(0325) 466044	4USD	GAE				
9	366249	DARLINGTON	Parkgate Filling Stn	Parkgate DL1 1RZ	B6280	(0325) 355600	4USD	GAE				
10	366111	DURHAM	Newbridge Self Serve	Great North Road, Nevilles Cross DH1 1AU	A167	091-386 7561	4USD	GAE				
11	366127	DURHAM	Aycliffe – Shell	Durham Road, Aycliffe Village DL5 6LL	A167	(0325) 301871	4USD	GAE				
12	366226	DURHAM	Durham – Shell	Durham Road, Belmont DH1 1LU	A690	091-386 4315	4USD	GAE				●
13	366154	PETERLEE	Newtown Self Serve	Yoden Way SR8 1AR	B1320	091-586 2415	4USD	GAE				
14	398135	PETERLEE	Warwick Garages Limited	Shotton Road SR8 2JA		091-518 0088	4USD	GAE				
15	366377	SEAHAM	Easington East – Shell	Hawthorn SR7 8SS	A19	091-527 2933	4USD	GAE				●
16	366379	SEAHAM	Easington West – Shell	Hawthorn SR7 8SS	A19	091-527 0473	4USD	GAE				
17	532852	WITTON GILBERT	Witton Garage	Front Street DH7 6TQ	A691	091-371 0238	4USD	GAE				

DYFED

Loc. Ref.	Shell Ref.	TOWN	NAME	ADDRESS	Road No.	Tel. No.	Fuel	Cards	24 hour	HGV	Select	Car Wash
1	348798	ABERAERON	Aeron Coast (Holidays) Ltd	Caravan Park North Road SA46 0JF	A487	(0545) 570649	4UD	GAE				
2	287199	ABERYSTWYTH	Dewi Garage	Capel Dewi SY23 3HR	A4159	(0970) 828389	4UD	GA				
3	299466	ABERYSTWYTH	Hillcrest Garage	New Cross SY23 4LY	B4340	(0974) 3503	4UD	GAE				
4	299467	ABERYSTWYTH	Davmor Garage	Talybont SY24 5HE	A487	(0970) 832278	4USD	GAE				
5	299468	ABERYSTWYTH	Exchange Service Station	Capel Bangor SY23 3LT	A44	(0970) 84268	4UD	GAE				
6	299613	ABERYSTWYTH	Rhydypennau Garage	Bow Street SY24 5AA	A487	(0970) 828221	4USD	GAE				
7	299992	ABERYSTWYTH	Erwyd Garage	Ponterwyd SY23 3LA	A44	(0970) 85664	4USD	GAE				
8	348753	ABERYSTWYTH	Aberystwyth Self Serve	Mill Street SY23 1HZ	A487	(0970) 615244	4UD	GAE				
9	348755	ABERYSTWYTH	Southgate Stores	Penparcau SY23 1RR	A487	(0970) 612603	4U	GAE				●
10	537349	ABERYSTWYTH	Pit Stop S/Stn	Trefechan SY23 1BE	A487	(0970) 624106	4UD	GAE				
11	299860	AMMANFORD	Central Garage	Glanamman SA18 1DR	A474	(0269) 822210	4UD	GAE				
12	282789	CARDIGAN	Davies Motors Ltd	Aberystwyth Road SA43 1NA	A487	(0239) 621222	4USD	GA				
13	299868	CARDIGAN	Gogerddan Garage	Tanygroes SA43 2HP	A487	(0239) 810414	4USD	GA				
14	348762	CARDIGAN	Express Garage	Llechryd SA43 2NR	A484	(0239) 87502	4USD	GA				
15	287043	CARMARTHEN	Waun y Groes Filling Station	Llangain SA33 5AN		(0267) 83250	4UD					
16	287492	CARMARTHEN	H.D. Griffiths Stores	Talog SA33 6NY		(0944) 484200	4U					
17	348741	CARMARTHEN	Tanerdy Garage	Tanerdy SA31 2EY	A40	(0267) 236203	4USD	GAE				
18	348745	CARMARTHEN	Carmarthen Road Self Serve	St Clears SA33 4NA	A40	(0994) 230153	4USD	GAE		●		
19	299465	CLYNDERWEN	Central Garage	Maenclochog SA66 7LA	B4313	(0437) 532298	4UD	GAE				
20	299465	CLYNDERWEN	Tyssul Garage	Glandy Cross SA66 7XA	A478	(0994) 419230	4UD	GAE				
21	348782	EGLWYSWRW	Penfro Filling Station	SA41 3TA	A487	(0239) 79618	4UD	GAE				
22	299464	GOODWICK	Duffryn Garage	SA62 6NX	A487	(0348) 872212	4UD	GAE				
23	348776	HAVERFORDWEST	Ridgeway Filling Station	Fishguard Road SA62 4BT	A40	(0437) 762228	4USD	GAE				
24	348778	HAVERFORDWEST	Newgale Filling Station	Newgale SA62 6AS	A487	(0437) 721398	4UD	GAE		●		
25	348773	KILGETTY	Cross Roads Garage	Begelly SA68 0YH	A478	(0834) 812276	4UD	GAE				
26	348757	LAMPETER	D D Evans & Sons	North Road SA48 7JA	A482	(0570) 422549	4UD	GAE				
27	348761	LAMPETER	Ystrad Service Station	Felinfach SA48 8AE	A482	(0570) 470384	4UD	GAE				
28	348721	LLANDEILO	Manordeilo Garage	Manordeilo SA19 7BN	A40	(0550) 777374	4UD	GAE				
29	299991	LLANDYSSUL	Bargoed Garage	Saron SA44 5EB	A484	(0559) 370335	4USD	GAE				
30	348764	LLANDYSSUL	Valley Services (Llandyssul)	Pencader Road, Pontwelly SA44 4AE	B4336	(0559) 362288	4UD	GAE				
31	349472	LLANELLI	Sandy Road Filling Station	Sandy Road SA15 4DP	A484	(0554) 751238	4UD	GAE				
32	349013	LLANELLI	North Dock Service Station	Cambrian Street SA15 2LE	B4309	(0554) 775530	4UD					
33	287696	LLANON	Maeshug Garage	Cross Inn SY23 5ND	B4337	(0974) 272630	4UD	GA				
34	299265	LLANON	Whitehall Garage	SY23 5HE	A487	(0974) 202217	4U	GA				
35	278894	LLANRHYSTYD	Llanrhystud Garage	SY23 5HA	A487	(0974) 202311	4USD	GAE				
36	299471	LLANWRDA	Checkpoint Filling Station	Harford SA19 8DT	A482	(0558) 5338	4UD	GA		●		
37	353283	MACHYNLLETH	Clettwr Cafe & F/Stn	Treirddol SY20 8PN	A487	(0970) 832255	4USD	GA				
38	299990	NEWCASTLE EMLYN	Maesycoed Stores	Beulah SA38 9QE	B4333	(0239) 810776	4UD	GA				
39	348788	NEWCASTLE EMLYN	Pensarnau Filling Station	Pentrecagel SA38 9HS	A484	(0559) 370781	4USD	GAE				
40	348769	PEMBROKE	Pembroke Auto Parts	104 Main Street SA71 4HN	A4075	(0646) 685894	4UD	GAE				●
41	434071	PENNAR	Pennar Filling Station	Treowen Road SA72 6DY	B4322	(0646) 685200	4UD	GAE				
42	299869	SAGESTON	Newhouse Garage	SA70 8SG	A477	(0646) 651321	4UD	GAE				
43	348770	TENBY	Gatehouse Service Station	Deer Park Road SA70 7LE	A4139	(0834) 843941	4UD	GAE				

Loc. Ref.	Shell Ref.	TOWN	NAME	ADDRESS	Road No.	Tel. No.	Fuel	Cards
44	299469	YSTRAD MEURIG	Derwen Service Station	Pontrhydfendigaid SY25 6EE	B4343	(0974) 5219	4UD	GA

EAST SUSSEX

Loc. Ref.	Shell Ref.	TOWN	NAME	ADDRESS	Road No.	Tel. No.	Fuel	Cards
1	308361	BATTLE	Stiles Garage (Battle) Ltd	2 Upperlake TN33 0AN	A2100	(0424) 773155	4UD	GAE
2	308505	BEXHILL-ON-SEA	Mount Pleasant Service Station	Ninfield Road, Sidley TN39 5JG	A269	(0424) 892056	4UD	GAE
3	302656	BRIGHTON	Superdrive Mtr Cntrs Ltd	62/66 Station Road, Portslade BN4 1DF	A259	(0273) 420085	4UD	GAE
4	308254	BRIGHTON	City Preston Park – Shell	193 Preston Road, Preston Park BN1 6SA	A23	(0273) 541386	4USD	GAE
5	299998	CROWBOROUGH	Caffyns Crowborough	Beacon Road TN6 1AN	A26	(0892) 652777	4USD	GAE
6	308111	CROWBOROUGH	DBS Crowborough	Crowborough Hill TN6 2EG	B2100	(0892) 652175	4UD	GAE
7	308165	EASTBOURNE	Seaside – Shell	520 Seaside BN23 6NJ	A259	(0323) 732638	4USD	GAE
8	308477	EASTBOURNE	Caffyns Plc (Upperton)	7 Upperton Road BN21 1ER	A22	(0323) 720191	4UD	GAE
9	308354	HAILSHAM	Caffyns Plc Hailsham	49 London Road BN27 3BX		(0323) 847056	4UD	GAE
10	308439	HASTINGS	Redlake Filling Station	Rye Road, Ore TN35 5DA	A259	(0424) 439269	4UD	GAE
11	308148	HAYWARDS HEATH	Baldocks Garage	Ditchling Road, Wivelsfield RH17 7RF	B2112	(0444) 84521	4UD	GAE
12	308349	HERSTMONCEAUX	Geo Collins (Engineers) Ltd	Buckwell Hill BN27 4JU	A271	(0323) 832211	4UD	GAE
13	308249	HOVE	First Avenue Garage	56 First Avenue BN3 2FF	A259	(0273) 735093	4U	GAE
14	308163	LEWES	Ringmer Motor Works	Lewes Road, Ringmer BN8 5EU	B2192	(0273) 812427	4UD	GAE
15	308156	NEWHAVEN	Brighton Mtl & Wellington F St	1 South Coast Road, Peacehaven BN9 8SY	A259	(0273) 583736	4UD	GAE
16	308161	NEWHAVEN	Peacehaven – Shell	180 South Coast Road, Peacehaven BN9 8JJ	A259	(0273) 588362	4USD	GAE
17	302510	POLEGATE	Dittons Rd F/Stn	Dittons Road BN26 6JB	A27	(0323) 482693	4USD	GAE
18	308152	SEAFORD	Kemp Brother Garage	14 Steyne Road BN25 1HT		(0323) 892469	4U	GAE
19	302474	UCKFIELD	Old Forge – Shell	High Street TN22 1AP	B2102	(0825) 769184	4USD	GAE
20	302853	WADHURST	Burnt Ash Garage	Durgates TN5 6PP	B2099	(0892) 882143	4UD	GAE

ESSEX

Loc. Ref.	Shell Ref.	TOWN	NAME	ADDRESS	Road No.	Tel. No.	Fuel	Cards
1	302109	BASILDON	Laindon – Shell	Southend Arterial Road, Laindon SS15 6EG	A127	(0268) 541127	4USD	GAE
2	340558	BISHOP'S STORTFORD	G.W.H.M. Barker & Sons	High Street, Elsenham CM22 6DD	B1051	(0279) 812364	4UD	GAE
3	340574	BRAINTREE	Whitecourt Self Serve	London Road CM7 8QG	A131	(0376) 330260	4UD	GAE
4	340615	BRAINTREE	Rayne Road Self-Serve	Rayne Road CM7 7QS	B1256	(0376) 346639	4USD	GAE
5	340599	BURNHAM-ON-CROUCH	Crouch Engineering Co	Station Road CM0 8HQ	B1010	(0621) 782130	4UD	GAE
6	302480	CHELMSFORD	Latchingdon Self Serve	The Street, Latchingdon CM3 6JP	B1010	(0621) 741848	4UD	GAE
7	340576	CHELMSFORD	Broomfield F/Stn	Main Road, Broomfield CM1 1SS	B1008	(0245) 440615	4USD	GAE
8	340581	CHELMSFORD	Premier Filling Station	Main Road, Boreham CM2 0HU	B1137	(0245) 467380	4UD	GAE
9	340619	CHELMSFORD	St Johns Service Station	Moulsham Street CM2 0JE		(0245) 258308	4UD	GAE
10	469173	CHELMSFORD	Hanningfield Service Station	Main A130, East Hanningfield CM3 8EE	A130	(0245) 400430	4UD	GAE
11	302102	CHIGWELL	North City SAAB	177 High Road IG7 6NX	A113	081-500 4144	4US	GAE
12	340601	CLACTON-ON-SEA	Kims Service Station	Main Road, Weeley Heath CO16 9ED	A133	(0255) 830334	4USD	GAE
13	540701	CLACTON-ON-SEA	Old Road – Shell	Old Road CO15 1HX	A133	(0255) 473266	4USD	GAE
14	299997	COLCHESTER	Marks Tey Garage	London Road, Marks Tey CO6 1EB	A12	(0206) 210266	4UD	GAE
15	302416	COLCHESTER	Old Forge Filling Station	41A Kingsland Road, West Mersea CO5 8RA	B1025	(0206) 382840	4USD	GAE
16	308245	COLCHESTER	Allstop – Shell	A12 Northbound, Langham CO4 5NQ	A12	(0206) 231321	4USD	GAE
17	308486	COLCHESTER	Birchwood – Shell	A12 Southbound, Dedham CO7 6HU	A12	(0206) 322895	4USD	GAE
18	340147	COLCHESTER	Magnolia – Shell	246 Shrub End Road CO3 4SA	B1022	(0206) 576276	4USD	GAE
19	340150	COLCHESTER	Tiptree – Shell	Maypole Road, Tiptree CO5 0EH	B1022	(0621) 815525	4USD	GAE
20	340565	COLCHESTER	Cols Tey Garage	London Road, Copford CO6 1BL	B1408	(0206) 211109	4UD	GAE
21	340567	COLCHESTER	Colchester Service Station	60 East Hill CO1 2QZ		(0206) 867522	4USD	GAE
22	340587	COLCHESTER	Sextons – Shell	Coggeshall Road, Marks Tey CO6 1LT	A120	(0206) 212003	4USD	GAE
23	340590	COLCHESTER	Corner – Shell	Main Road, Little Bentley CO7 8RX	A133	(0206) 251508	4USD	GAE
24	535693	COLCHESTER	Ardleigh – Shell	Colchester Road, Ardleigh CO7 7PA	A137	(0206) 230561	4USD	GAE
25	302588	EPPING	Epping – Shell	High Road CM16 5HW	B1393	(0992) 814952	4USD	GAE
26	386223	EPPING	Neales Garage	Thornwood Common CM16 6LZ	B1393	(0992) 572017	4USD	GAE
27	302119	GRAYS	Daneholes – Shell	Stanford Road RM16 4XS	A1013	(0375) 379290	4USD	GAE
28	302122	GRAYS	Grays Thurrock Motors	72-84 Orsett Road RM17 5EL		(0375) 375333	4UD	GAE
29	302103	HARLOW	Harlow – Shell	Potter Street, By-Pass CM17 9NP	A414	(0279) 414010	4USD	GAE
30	302107	HARLOW	Potter Street Service Station	Potter Street CM17 9AQ		(0279) 422611	4UD	GAE
31	435298	HARWICH	Parkeston – Shell	Main Road, Parkeston Quay CO12 4SY	A120	(0255) 241790	4USD	GAE
32	302099	INGATESTONE	Ingatestone Motors	High Street CM4 0AT		(0277) 353020	4USD	GAE
33	340579	INGATESTONE	Margaretting Filling Station	Main Road, Margaretting CM4 0AT	B1002	(0277) 352023	4UD	GAE
34	302375	LOUGHTON	Valley Service Station	1 Valley Hill IG10 3AA		081-508 1787	4UD	GAE
35	340569	MALDON	Palmers Garage	West Street, Tollesbury CM9 8RJ	B1023	(0621) 869200	4UD	GAE
36	302139	RAYLEIGH	Arterial – Shell	A127 Arterial Road SS6 7UP	A127	(0268) 746220	4USD	GAE
37	302142	RAYLEIGH	Rayleigh – Shell	High Road SS6 7SL	A129	(0268) 773554	4USD	GAE
38	302776	ROMFORD	Abridge – Shell	London Road, Abridge RM4 1XL	A113	(0992) 813247	4USD	GAE
39	340616	SIBLE HEDINGHAM	Hedingham – Shell	Swan Street CO9 3HP	A604	(0787) 60672	4USD	GAE
40	302137	SOUTHEND-ON-SEA	Broadway Service Station	201 The Broadway, Thorpe Bay SS1 3EX		(0702) 582548	4UD	GAE
41	302145	SOUTHEND-ON-SEA	Milton Self Serve	175 London Road SS1 1PW	A13	(0702) 351543	4USD	GAE
42	302147	SOUTHEND-ON-SEA	Sovereign – Shell	96-118 Prince Avenue SS2 6PL	A127	(0702) 347894	4USD	GAE
43	302438	SOUTHEND-ON-SEA	Porters Grange Self Serve	200 Queensway SS1 2LU	B1016	(0702) 463407	4USD	GAE
44	302501	SOUTHEND-ON-SEA	F C Jenkins	54 High Street, Shoeburyness SS3 9AP		(0702) 292791	4UD	GAE
45	302521	SOUTHEND-ON-SEA	Bournes Green Filling Stn	Shoebury Road SS1 3RS	A13	(0702) 587032	4US	GAE
46	302121	STANFORD-LE-HOPE	Bell Corner Service Station	London Road, Fobbing SS17 0LE	A13	(0268) 553773	4USD	GAE
47	302490	WITHAM	Doe Motors Ltd	Colchester Road CM8 3BL	B1389	(0376) 512925	4USD	GAE

Loc. Ref.	Shell Ref.	TOWN	NAME	ADDRESS	Road No.	Tel. No.	Fuel	Cards	24 hour	HGV	Select	Car Wash

FIFE

Loc. Ref.	Shell Ref.	TOWN	NAME	ADDRESS	Road No.	Tel. No.	Fuel	Cards	24 hour	HGV	Select	Car Wash
1	380604	ANSTRUTHER	Pitkierie Garage	St Andrews Road KY10 3JX	B9131	(0333) 310229	4UD	GAE				
2	381025	BURNTISLAND	Kirkton Filling Station	Aberdour Road KY3 0EL	A921	(0592) 873453	4UD	GAE				■
3	380617	CERES	Loch Garage	St Andrews Road KY15 5QQ	B939	(0334) 82236		GAE				
4	380621	COWDENBEATH	Beath Garage	4 High Street KY4 9NA	A909	(0383) 512455	4USD	GAE				
5	381019	CUPAR	Eastbridge Filling Station	Eastbridge KY15 4JL	A91	(0334) 55177	4UD	GAE				■
6	381017	GLENROTHES	Glenrothes — Shell	Leslie Road KY7 5PS	A911	(0592) 750894	4USD	GAE				
7	380606	KINGLASSIE	A Cockborn & Sons	The Garage KY5 0XF	B921	(0592) 82206	4UD	GAE				
8	380612	KIRKCALDY	Kirkcaldy — Shell	Hendry Road KY2 5DS		(0592) 641793	4USD	GAE				■
9	380608	LADYBANK	J B Dall Ltd	The Garage, Commercial Road KY7 7JS	B938	(0337) 30402	4UD	GA				
10	380610	LESLIE	H & H Gordon	Bankplace Garage, Kinross Road KY6 3LD	A911	(0592) 620202	4UD	GAE				
11	380973	LEVEN	Bawbee — Shell	Bawbee Brig KY8 3AN	A955	(0333) 423522	4USD	GAE				■
12	376185	METHILHILL	Auld Toll Garage	Sea Road KY8 2DJ	A955	(0592) 715233	4UD	GAE				
13	380894	ROSYTH	Camdean — Shell	Admiralty Road KY11 2BN	A985	(0383) 418398	4USD	GAE				■
14	381047	ST ANDREWS	Greyfriars Self Serve	Bridge Street KY16 9EX	A915	(0334) 72494	4USD	GAE				

GLOUCESTERSHIRE

Loc. Ref.	Shell Ref.	TOWN	NAME	ADDRESS	Road No.	Tel. No.	Fuel	Cards	24 hour	HGV	Select	Car Wash
1	348512	CHELTENHAM	Cheltenham — Shell	352/356 Gloucester Road GL51 7AY	A40	(0242) 224490	4USD	GAE				
2	348571	CHELTENHAM	Langton Self Serve	Montpelier Terrace GL50 1XE	A40	(0242) 523763	4UD	GAE				
3	348872	CHELTENHAM	Waghornes Self Serve	Shurdington Road GL53 0HY	A46	(0242) 513100	4USD	GAE				
4	348897	DURSLEY	Mill Garage	Draycott, Cam GL11 5DH	A4135	(0453) 543681	4USD	GAE				
5	348507	GLOUCESTER	City Crosshands — Shell	Cross Roads, Brockworth GL3 4PL	A417	(0452) 862507	4USD	GAE				
6	348519	GLOUCESTER	Barnwood Self Serve	Hucclecote Road, Barnwood GL4 7HA	A38	(0452) 616621	4USD	GAE				
7	348565	GLOUCESTER	Tuffley — Shell	Cole Avenue GL2 6ER	A38	(0452) 500947	4USD	GAE				
8	348983	GLOUCESTER	Beacon Self Serve	Painswick Road, Matson GL4 9BT	B4073	(0452) 303255	4USD	GAE				
9	348895	HUCCLECOTE	Ermin Way Self Serve	Barnwood By Pass GL3 3TZ	A417	(0452) 617321	4USD	GAE				
10	380975	STONEHOUSE	Gordons (Stroud) Ltd	Ebley Road GL10 2LH	A419	(0453) 822130	4UD	GAE				
11	353287	STROUD	Oldbury Services	Westend Roundabout, Stonehouse GL10 3SJ	A419	(0453) 828688	4USD	GAE				
12	299994	TETBURY	Northfield Garage	London Road GL8 8HN	A433	(0666) 502473	4USD	GAE				

GRAMPIAN

Loc. Ref.	Shell Ref.	TOWN	NAME	ADDRESS	Road No.	Tel. No.	Fuel	Cards	24 hour	HGV	Select	Car Wash
1	377595	ABERDEEN	C J Autos	Potterton Service Station, Potterton AB23 8UY	B999	(03584) 3828	4UD	GAE				
2	380413	ABERDEEN	Ashfield Filling Station	School Road, Kintore AB5 0UX	A96	(0467) 32203	4UD	GAE				■
3	380438	ABERDEEN	Campbell & Sellar F/Stn	10 Fountainhall Road AB9 2XL	A978	(0224) 641155	4USD	GAE				
4	380440	ABERDEEN	Holburn Self Serve	180 Holburn Street AB1 6DA		(0224) 574911	4UD	GAE				■
5	380442	ABERDEEN	Propeller — Shell	Inverurie Road, Bucksburn AB2 9BB	A96		4UD	GAE				
6	380444	ABERDEEN	Dee Bridge Service Station	4 Leggart Terrace AB1 5TX	B9077	(0224) 872728	4UD	GAE				■
7	380446	ABERDEEN	Market Self Serve	240 Market Street AB1 2PR	A956	(0224) 591966	4UD	GAE				
8	380450	ABERDEEN	Don — Shell	792 King Street AB2 1XN	A956	(0224) 276308	4USD	GAE				
9	380455	ABERDEEN	Cocket Hat North Self Serve	North Anderson Drive AB2 6DD	A92	(0224) 693358	4UD	GAE				
10	380457	ABERDEEN	Cocket Hat — Shell	North Anderson Drive AB2 6DW	A92	(0224) 311626	4USD	GAE				
11	380463	ABERDEEN	Wellington — Shell	Wellington Road AB1 4JX	A956	(0224) 871815	4USD	GAE				
12	380975	ABERDEEN	Gordon — Shell	785 Great Northern Road AB2 2BT	A96	(0224) 663868	4USD	GAE				
13	380453	ABOYNE	Dinnet Service Station	Ballater Road, Dinnet AB34 5LN	A93	(03398) 85261	4UD	GAE				
14	380459	ABOYNE	Kincardine O'Neil F/Stn	Kincardine O'Neil AB34 5AE	A93	(03398) 84237	4UD	GAE				
15	377599	ALFORD	Lonenwell Service Station	AB33 8ED	A944	(09755) 62215	4USD	GAE				
16	376191	BANCHORY	Crathes Garage	Stonehaven Road, Crathes AB31 3JD	A957	(03044) 528	4U	GAE				
17	381131	BANCHORY	Tor-Na-Coille Filling Station	Inchmarlo Road AB31 3RR	A93	(03302) 2217	4UD	GAE				
18	377605	BANFF	Keilhill Filling Station	King Edward AB45 3LT	A947	(02616) 491	4UD	GAE				
19	380405	BANFF	North Road Filling Station	Regent Street, Keith AB55 3ED	A96	(05422) 7811	4USD	GAE				■
20	380950	BANFF	Reidhaven Filling Station	6 Reidhaven Street AB45 1DU	A98	(0261) 812560	4UD	GAE				
21	380395	BUCKIE	Dawsons Garage	9-11 Harbour Street AB56 1LP	A942	(0542) 31288	4UD	GAE				
22	380401	BUCKIE	Cathcart Garage	14 West Carthcart Street AB56 1PN	A990	(0542) 32500	4U	GAE				
23	380420	ECHT	Echt Filling Station	Skene, AB32 6UL	B9119	(03306) 542	4UD	GAE				
24	380948	ELGIN	Lhanbryde Filling Station	Lhanbryde IV30 3NZ	A96	(0343) 842636	4USD	GAE				
25	381040	ELGIN	Bridge of Tyock F/Stn	East Road IV30 1XU	A96	(0343) 547650	4UD	GAE				
26	380393	FORRES	Garrow Brothers	36 Toolbooth Street IV36 0PH	B9010	(0309) 672375	4UD	GAE				
27	380397	FORRES	Brodie Service Station	Brodie IV36 0TD	A96	(03094) 262	4UD	GAE				
28	380403	FORRES	Pedigreed Cars	Bogton Place IV36 0LL	B9010	(0309) 672555	4USD	GAE				
29	380410	FRASERBURGH	Watermill Filling Station	Banff Road AB43 4ED	A98	(0346) 518225	4UD	GAE				
30	397133	FRASERBURGH	Kessock Service Station	South Road AB43 5TJ	A92	(0346) 510066	4UD	GAE				
31	377614	INSCH	Commercial Garage	South Road AB52 6XN	B9002	(0464) 20037	4UD	GAE				
32	380415	INVERURIE	The Filling Station Kemnay	Station Road, Kemnay AB5 9NB	B993	(0467) 42072	4UD	GAE				

Loc. Ref.	Shell Ref.	TOWN	NAME	ADDRESS	Road No.	Tel. No.	Fuel	Cards	24 hour	HGV	Select
33	380427	INVERURIE	Pinewood Self Serve	Port Elphinstone Road AB5 9UX	B993	(0467) 21497	4USD	GAE			
34	380431	INVERURIE	Pitcaple Filling Station	Pitcaple AB51 9HJ	A96	(0467) 681612	4UD	GAE			
35	380559	LAURENCEKIRK	Hantons Garage Ltd	25 High Street AB30 1AA	A937	(0561) 377303	4UD	GAE			
36	434683	LOSSIEMOUTH	Ian Watt (Garage) Ltd	The Square IV31 6DD	B9040	(0343) 812064	4UD	GAE			
37	543004	MONTROSE	St Cyrus Filling Station	Roadside, St Cyrus DD10 0BA	A92	(0674) 85333	4USD	GAE			
38	380423	OLDMELDRUM	Meldrum Motors	Spring Garden AB51 0AA	A947	(0651) 872247	4UD	GAE			
39	380424	OLDMELDRUM	Meldrum Motors	3 Market Square AB51 0AA	A920	(0651) 872247	4U	GAE			
40	380425	PETERHEAD	Newlands Garage	Fordyce Terrace, New Deer AB53 6TD	A981	(07713) 280	4UD	GAE			
41	380434	PETERHEAD	Clyne Autos	St Fergus AB42 7DD	A952	(0779) 838258	4UD	GAE			
42	434017	PETERHEAD	Victoria Garage	Victoria Road, Maud AB42 8NP	B9106	(07714) 234	4UD	GAE			
43	536978	PETERHEAD	Grange Garage	West Road AB42 7JE	A950	(0779) 78777	4UD	GAE			
44	380989	PORTSOY	Durnhill Filling Station	Aird Street AB4 2RD	A98	(0261) 42431	4USD	GAE			
45	376170	STONEHAVEN	Arduthie Motors	Auchenblae Road AB3 2NH		(0569) 62989	4UD	GAE			
46	381006	TURRIFF	Turriff Service Station	Station Road AB53 7ER	A947	(0888) 63449	4USD	GAE			

GREATER LONDON

Loc. Ref.	Shell Ref.	TOWN	NAME	ADDRESS	Road No.	Tel. No.	Fuel	Cards	24 hour	HGV	Select
1	302276	ACTON	Lawrences Western Avenue	Western Avenue, Corner Rosebank Way W3 6UD	A40	081-992 3758	4USD	GAE			
2	302019	BALHAM	Balham – Shell	67-93 Balham Hill SW12 9DP	A24	081-675 7877	4USD	GAE			
3	308497	BARKING	Barking City – Shell	London Road IG11 8BU	A124	081-594 0287	4USD	GAE			
4	302378	BAYSWATER	Hertford S/Stn (Normand)	104-5 Bayswater Road W2 3HJ	A40	071-723 3334	4U	GAE			
5	302171	BELVEDERE	Queensland Self Serve	199-201 Lower Road DA17 6DQ	A2016	(03224) 46127	4UD	GAE			
6	302168	BLACKHEATH	Shooters Hill – Shell	165 Shooters Hill Road SE3 8UQ	A207	081-293 5993	4USD	GAE			
7	302072	BOW	City Bow Road (67)	24-26 Bow Road E3 4LN	A11	081-980 8556	4USD	GAE			
8	302629	BOW	Old Ford – Shell	445-453 Wick Lane E3 2TB	B119	081-983 3990	4USD	GAE			
9	302476	BRIXTON	New Park Self Serve	230-242 Brixton Hill SW2 1HF	A23	081-674 1277	4USD	GAE			
10	537963	BRIXTON	Brixton Service Station	330 Brixton Road SW9	A23	081-533 4168	4USD	GAE			
11	302379	BROMLEY	Bromley Stc	116 Hastings Road BR2 8NA	A21	081-462 4574	4USD	GAE			
12	302388	BROMLEY	City Hayes (37)	1-3 Station Approach, Hayes BR2 7EQ	B251	081-462 6796	4UD	GAE			
13	302388	CAMBERWELL	Camberwell Self Serve	98-102 Coldharbour Lane SE5 9PU	A2217	071-274 8115	4USD	GAE			
14	302056	CAMDEN	Clarendon Filling Station	85 Camden Road NW1 9EY	A503	071-485 6667	4USD	GAE			
15	302065	CANNING TOWN	Park Garage	387 Newham Way E16 4ED	A13	071-476 1134	4USD	GAE			
16	302561	CATFORD	Perry Hill S/S	87-91 Perry Hill SE6 4LJ	A212	081-291 9119	4UD	GAE			
17	302098	CHIGWELL	Bald Hind Garage	124 Manor Road IG7 5PP	A123	081-500 9001	4USD	GAE			
18	302077	CHINGFORD	Ching Self Serve	53 Sewardstone Road E4 1AA	A112	081-524 1411	4USD	GAE			
19	302088	CHINGFORD	Forest Service Station	174/180 Station Road E4 6AN	A1069	081-524 8855	4USD	GAE			
20	302355	CRICKLEWOOD	Staples Corner – Shell	721 North Circular Road NW2 7AB	A406	081-452 1388	USD	GAE			
21	302157	CROYDON	Parkway – Shell	Parkway, New Addington CR0 0LA		(0689) 849916	4USD	GAE			
22	302446	CROYDON	Gloster – Shell	117 Whitehorse Road CR0 2LG	A212	081-684 7262	4USD	GAE			
23	302570	CROYDON	Purley Self Serve	698 Purley Way CR0 4RS	A23	081-688 7360	4USD	GAE			
24	302586	CROYDON	Addington – Shell	Kent Gateway, Addington CR0 5AR	A2022	(0689) 800067	4USD	GAE			
25	302128	DAGENHAM	Fords Self Serve	New Road RM10 9NB	A13	081-595 7109	4USD	GAE			
26	302129	DAGENHAM	Triptons – Shell	79 Whalebone Lane South RM8 1AJ	A1112	081-592 4442	4USD	GAE			
27	302632	DAGENHAM	Oxlow Lane Self Serve	Oxlow Lane RM9 5XJ		081-592 8835	4UD	GAE			
28	302893	DAGENHAM	Coronet Self Serve	Rainham Road South RM10 8YT	A1112	081-592 6110	4USD	GAE			
29	302173	DEPTFORD	Parkside – Shell	Evelyn Street SE8 5RJ	A206	081-692 5172	4USD	GAE			
30	302268	EALING	Pearlgge (Triangle Autos)	35/39 South Ealing Road W5 4QT	B455	081-567 5159	4UD	GAE			
31	302269	EALING	City Ealing – Shell	29-31 Hanger Lane, North Circular Road W5 3HJ	A406	081-566 8180	4USD	GAE			
32	302602	EAST HAM	East Ham Self Serve	194-200 High Street South E6 3RR	A112	081-472 0654	4USD	GAE			
33	308494	EAST HAM	High St North – Shell	410-419 High Street North E12 1JB	A117	081-552 4780	4USD	GAE			
34	302284	EASTCOTE	Field End Self Serve	313A Field End Road HA4 9NT		081-866 6947	4UD	GAE			
35	302307	EDGWARE	Fernhurst Filling Station	162-166 High Road HA8 7EL	A5	081-952 9862	4USD	GAE			
36	302452	EDMONTON	Lea Valley Service Station	500 Montagu Road N9 3AP		081-803 8311	4	GAE			
37	278024	ELTHAM	Wellhall Service Station	Well Hall Road SE9 5SX	A208	081-850 2693	4USD	GAE			
38	302175	ELTHAM	Sidcup STC	728 Sidcup Road SE9 3AJ	A20	081-857 7006	4USD	GAE			
39	302493	ELTHAM	City Mottingham	551 Sidcup Road SE9 3AF	A20	081-857 6262	4USD	GAE			
40	302346	ENFIELD	Lavender Hill Garage Ltd	The Ridgeway EN2 8JF	A1005	081-363 3456	4USD	GAE			
41	302574	ENFIELD	Baker Street Self-Serve	274 Baker Street EN1 3LF		081-363 1062	4USD	GAE			
42	398087	ENFIELD	Avenue Service Station	18 Brimsdown Avenue, Brimsdown EN3 5NZ		081-804 5686	4USD	GAE			
43	302572	ERITH	City Erith	North End Road DA8 3RF	A206	(0322) 335111	4USD	GAE			
44	302596	FARNBOROUGH	Farnborough Hill – Shell	Farnborough Way BR6 6DA	A21	(0689) 860669	4USD	GAE			
45	302600	FELTHAM	City Sunbury (Hanworth)	74 Twickenham Road, Hanworth TW13 6QR	A316	081-893 3598	4US	GAE			
46	302608	FELTHAM	City Feltham	Hounslow Road TW14 9AT	A466	081-890 4305	4UD	GAE			
47	302060	FOREST GATE	Francis Self Serve	176-180 Romford Road E7 9HY	A118	081-534 8835	4US	GAE			
48	302720	FOREST HILL	Forest Hill – Shell	163-165 Stanstead Road SE23 1HP	A205	081-291 9099	4USD	GAE			
49	302039	FULHAM	Atalanta Self Serve	79 New King's Road SW6 4SQ	A308	071-731 4343	4US	GAE			
50	302673	FULHAM	City Fulham	923-931 Fulham Road SW6 5HU	A304	071-735 1479	4USD	GAE			
51	302576	GOLDERS GREEN	Golders Green Self Serve	177 Golders Green Road NW11 9DA	A502	081-455 3390	4US	GAE			
52	302262	GREENFORD	Roundabout – Shell	Greenford Road UB6 9UA	A4127	081-575 7184	4USD	GAE			
53	537944	GREENFORD	Prompt Motors Ltd	Western Avenue UB6 8EU	A40	(0875) 782436	4USD	GAE			
54	302499	GREENWICH	Greenwich Self Serve	25-27 Greenwich High Road SE10 8JL	A206	081-694 8008	4USD	GAE			
55	302058	HACKNEY	Clapton Service Station	144/150 Upper Clapton Road E5 9JZ	A107	081-806 6400	4USD	GAE			
56	302040	HAMMERSMITH	Fulham Cross – Shell	222-224 Fulham Palace Road W6 6HP	A219	071-386 7339	4USD	GAE			
57	302260	HAMPTON	F A Yates Ltd	9 Tudor Road TW12 2NH		081-979 1120	4UD	GAE			
58	302627	HANWELL	Hanwell – Shell	6 Church Road W7 1DR		081-840 5216	4USD	GAE			
59	302007	HARROW	Westbourne Service Station	223 Harrow Road W2 5EH	A404	071-286 4116	4USD	GAE			
60	302280	HARROW	City Wealdstone	22 Station Road, Wealdstone HA1 2SL	A409	081-427 9706	4UD	GAE			
61	302286	HARROW	Midway Self Serve	50 Northolt Road HA2 0DW	A312	081-864 2834	4USD	GAE			
62	308195	HARROW WEALD	Peacock Service Station	High Road HA3 8BD	A409	081-863 5827	4UD	GAE			
63	302241	HAYES	Coldharbour Lane S/Stn	Coldharbour Lane UB3 3HA		081-573 5898	4UD	GAE			
64	302410	HAYES	Kusum Service Station	33-37 Uxbridge Road UB4 0JN	A4020	081-756 1505	4USD	GAE			

Loc. Ref.	Shell Ref.	TOWN	NAME	ADDRESS	Road No.	Tel. No.	Fuel	Cards	24 hour	HGV	Select	Car Wash
65	302528	HENDON	Scratchwood Service Area North	M1 Motorway (North Bound), Scratchwood NW7 3HB	M1	081-959 4514	4USD	GAE				
66	302167	HERNE HILL	Loughborough Self Serve	42 Hinton Road SE24 0HJ	B222	071-274 5800	4USD	GAE				
67	302017	HOLLOWAY	Holloway Service Station	104-116 Holloway Road N7 8JE	A1	071-700 5685	4USD	GAE				
68	302439	HOLLOWAY	Polytechnic Service Station	315 Holloway Road N7 6SU	A1	071-607 2493	4USD	GAE				
69	302519	HOLLOWAY	Finsbury Service Station	107-113 Seven Sisters Road N7 7QG	A503	071-272 7423	4UD	GAE				
70	302124	HORNCHURCH	Kilners Self Serve	193-197 Hornchurch Road RM12 4TF	A124	(0708) 446150	4UD	GAE				
71	302050	HORNSEY	Hornsey Rise — Shell	Hornsey Rise N19 3SH	A103	071-263 6027	4USD	GAE				
72	302400	HORNSEY	Hornsey Service Station	159 Tottenham Lane N8 9BT	A103	081-348 9342	4USD	GAE				
73	302424	HOUNSLOW	Hounslow Service Station	333/335 Bath Road TW3 3DH	A3006	081-570 0715	4USD	GAE				
74	302562	HOUNSLOW	City Heston	270 Heston Road, Heston TW5 0RG	A3005	081-577 0066	4USD	GAE				
75	302611	ILFORD	Ilford Lane Self Serve	200 Ilford Lane IG1 2LW	A123	081-553 1654	4USD	GAE				
76	302249	ISLEWORTH	Syon Hill — Shell	Great West Road TW7 5NU	A4	081-569 8695	4USD	GAE				
77	302251	ISLEWORTH	City Gillette Corner — Shell	Great West Road TW7 5NU	A4	081-569 7634	4USD	GAE				
78	302580	ISLEWORTH	City Isleworth (55)	493-497 London Road TW7 4DA	A315	081-560 8419	4USD	GAE				
79	302003	KENSINGTON	City Old Brompton Road (87)	106 Old Brompton Road SW7 3RA	A3218	071-373 4623	4US	GAE				
80	302048	KENSINGTON	City Kensington (54)	181/183 Warwick Road W14 4PU	A3220	071-370 1345	4U	GAE				
81	302812	KINGSBURY	City Kingsbury (71)	Kingsbury Circle NW9 9QT	A4006	081-204 5758	4USD	GAE				
82	302237	KINGSTON UPON THAMES	City Kingstonian (53)	160 Richmond Road KT2 5HD	A307	081-546 1663	4SD	GAE				
83	302658	KINGSTON UPON THAMES	Washington Self-Serve	144 London Road KT2 6QL	A308	081-546 4393	4UD	GAE				
84	302434	LEWISHAM	Lewisham S/S	97 Loampit Vale SE13 7TG	A20	081-692 4121	4USD	GAE				
85	302037	LONDON	Andrews Garage	1 Rushton Mews, St Marks Road W11 1RB		071-229 6415	4USD	GAE				
86	302288	LONDON	Pine Self Serve	421 Edgware Road, The Hyde NW9 0HS	A5	081-200 7303	4UD	GAE				
87	302387	LONDON	Old Street Service Station	198-208 Old Street EC1V 9BP	A5201	071-253 5036	4USD	GAE				
88	302471	LONDON	Upper Street — Shell	276 Upper Street N1 2TZ	A1	071-704 2246	4USD	GAE				
89	302606	LONDON	Central Street Self Serve	39-45 Central Street EC1V 8AB		071-253 6065	4USD	GAE				
90	302759	LONDON	Selfridges Garage	Edward Mews NW1A 1AB		071-629 1234	4US	GAE				
91	302070	MANOR PARK	Manor Self Serve	893-903 Romford Road E12 5JT	A118	081-514 2007	4USD	GAE				
92	302301	MILL HILL	Apex North — Shell	Apex Corner NW7 2JU	A1	081-959 8300	4UD	GAE				
93	302313	MILL HILL	Featherstone Garage	Bunns Lane NW7 2ES		081-959 2665	4UD	GAE				
94	534241	MITCHAM	Master of Mitcham	359 London Road CR4 4BF	A217	081-685 9990	4USD	GAE				
95	302234	MORDEN	Mann Egerton & Co Ltd	242 Morden Road SW19 3BZ	A24	081-542 8221	4SD	GAE				
96	302771	MORDEN	Master of Morden Ltd	100 Green Lane SM4 6ST	B278	081-685 9990	4UD	GAE				
97	302619	MUSWELL HILL	City Muswell Hill (20)	11 Colney Hatch Lane, Pages Lane N10 1QB	B550	081-883 1897	4UD	GAE				
98	302569	NEW MALDEN	Coombe Road Self-Serve	71-73 Coombe Road KT3 4QN	B283	081-942 3232	4SD	GAE				
99	302214	NORBURY	Norbury Service Station	1270 London Road SW16 4EA	A23	081-764 3205	4U	GAE				
100	302299	NORTH FINCHLEY	Woodhouse Service Station	236 Woodhouse Road N12 0RT	A1003	081-361 2580	4UD	GAE				
101	302290	NORTHWOOD	Northwood Self Serve	Pinner Road HA6 1DD	A404	(09274) 827584	4UD	GAE				
102	302183	ORPINGTON	Petts Wood — Shell	52 Queensway, Petts Wood BR5 1DH	A208	(0689) 896396	4USD	GAE				
103	302357	ORPINGTON	City St Mary Cray	Cray Avenue, St Mary Cray BR5 3PT	A224	(0689) 833839	4US	GAE				
104	302344	PALMERS GREEN	Palmers Green — Shell	148-150 Green Lanes N13 5UN	A105	081-886 7473	4USD	GAE				
105	302265	PARK ROYAL	Pronto Service Station	Coronation Road NW10 7PQ	B4492	081-965 7400	4UD	GAE				
106	302622	PENGE	Penge Self Serve	169-175 Croydon Road SE20 7TY	A213	081-659 6051	USD	GAE				
107	302292	PINNER GREEN	Pinner — Shell	Uxbridge Road HA5 2AF	A404	081-866 8062	4USD	GAE				
108	302150	PURLEY	Foxley Self Serve	14/16 Godstone Road CR2 2DB	A22	081-660 3486	4USD	GAE				
109	302771	PUTNEY	Putney — Shell	105 Lower Richmond Road SW15 1EU	B306	081-788 7082	4SD	GAE				
110	302548	RAINHAM	Rainham Self Serve	14 Rainham Road RM13 7RR	A125	(0708) 555154	4UD	GAE				
111	302202	RAYNES PARK	Arterial Self Serve	Bushey Road SW20 8BP	A298	081-542 8066	4SD	GAE				
112	302209	RAYNES PARK	Pepys Corner Self Serve	Worple Road SW20 8QT	B235	081-879 1136	4SD	GAE				
113	302263	ROEHAMPTON	Roehampton — Shell	237/239 Roehampton Lane SW15 4LB	A306	081-780 9989	4SD	GAE				
114	302105	ROMFORD	Rise Park (30) — Shell	Eastern Avenue East RM1 4SJ	A12	(0708) 735652	4USD	GAE				
115	302136	ROMFORD	Romford Self-serve	London Road RM7 9QD	A118	(0708) 727608	4USD	GAE				
116	302385	ROMFORD	Hilldene Service Station	Hilldene Avenue, Harold Hill RM3 8DL		(0708) 871631	4UD	GAE				
117	302583	ROMFORD	Collier Row — Shell	93-97 Collier Row Road RM5 2AU	B174	(0708) 734484	4USD	GAE				
118	302258	RUISLIP	Ruislip — Shell	West End Road HA4 6NF	A4180	081-841 6641	4USD	GAE				
119	302185	SIDCUP	Woodman Self Serve	Westwood Lane, Blackfen DA15 9PT	A210	081-850 6877	4UD	GAE				
120	302887	SIDCUP	Blendon — Shell	510 Blackfen Road, Blackfen DA15 9NT	A210	081-303 9115	4UD	GAE				
121	302005	SOUTH KENSINGTON	Queensgate S/Stn	1A Queen's Gate Mews SW7 5PN		071-372 5687	4U	GAE				
122	302021	SOUTH LAMBETH	Battersea (49) — Shell	326 Queenstown Road SW8 4LT	A3216	071-622 0328	4USD	GAE				
123	302159	SOUTH NORWOOD	Norwood — Shell	123-127 Portland Road SE25 4UN	A215	081-655 0018	4USD	GAE				
124	302023	SOUTHWARK	Southwark Park Service Station	297-309 Southwark Park Road SE16 2JN	A2206	071-237 3832	4USD	GAE				
125	302033	SOUTHWARK	Thomas A'Becket Self-Serve	233-247 Old Kent Road SE1 5LU	A2	071-237 4718	4USD	GAE				
126	302500	SOUTHWARK	Southwark Bridge S	101-103 Southwark Bridge Road SE1 0AX	A300	071-407 0894	4USD	GAE				
127	302545	SOUTHWARK	Old Kent Road S/S	430-432 Old Kent Road SE1 5AG	A2	071-232 2957	4USD	GAE				
128	302825	ST JOHN'S WOOD	Loudoun Road S/S	21A-23 Loudoun Road NW8 0NQ		071-624 4844	4US	GAE				
129	302066	STOKE NEWINGTON	Green Lanes Service Station	37 Green Lanes N16 9BS	A105	071-226 8811	4USD	GAE				
130	302216	SURBITON	Ace of Spades — Shell	Hook Rise North KT6 5AT	A3	081-974 1910	4USD	GAE				
131	308048	SURBITON	Raeburn Garage	Raeburn Avenue KT5 9EA		081-390 6388	4UD	GA				
132	302534	SUTTON	St Dunstans Hill Self Serve	95 St Dunstans Hill, Cheam SM1 2LW	A217	081-644 5434	4USD	GAE				
133	384866	SYDENHAM	Sydenham Motors	277 Kirkdale SE26 4QD		081-778 6187	4USD	GAE				
134	302635	TEDDINGTON	City Teddington (52)	220 Kingston Road TW11 9JF	A310	081-977 8002	4U	GAE				
135	302641	TOOTING	Amen Corner S/Serve	187-191 Mitcham Road SW17 9PG	A217	081-682 4929	4SD	GAE				
136	302086	TOTTENHAM	Marston S/S	734-736 Seven Sisters Road N15 1AA	A503	081-800 0679	4USD	GAE				
137	302404	TOTTENHAM	Tottenham Self Serve	103-109 High Road N15 6DL	A10	081-800 0349	4USD	GAE				
138	302633	TOTTENHAM	City St Annes Road	266 St Annes Road N15 5BN	B152	081-800 7390	4USD	GAE				
139	302823	TOTTENHAM	Wilsons Service Station	178 Lansdowne Road N17 9XX	B4060	081-808 4135	4USD	GAE				
140	302230	TWICKENHAM	Oak Lane Self Serve	Richmond Road TW1 3AB	A305	081-891 1880	4US	GAE				
141	302254	TWICKENHAM	Hospital Bridge Self Serve	Staines Road TW2 5JA	A305	081-894 1918	4USD	GAE				
142	302359	TWICKENHAM	Currie Motors (Twickenham) Ltd	161 Chertsey Road TW1 1EP	A316	081-892 0041	4UD	GAE				
143	302133	UPMINSTER	City Upminster (81)	168-170 St Mary's Lane RM14 3BS	B187	(0708) 220234	4UD	GAE				
144	302411	UPPER NORWOOD	Crystal Palace (96) — Shell	4 Crystal Palace Parade SE19 1UN	A212	081-766 6161	4USD	GAE				
145	302244	UXBRIDGE	Colham Green Garage	148 West Drayton Road UB8 3LJ	B465	(0895) 444122	4UD	GAE				
146	302294	UXBRIDGE	Swakeleys Self Serve — Shell	Long Lane, Ickenham UB10 8TB	B466	(08956) 34272	4USD	GAE				
147	302483	VICTORIA	City Victoria (76)	Ebury Street, Semley Place SW1 9QJ		071-730 1393	4USD	GAE				
148	302462	WALTHAMSTOW	Billet Road Service Stn	236-240 Billet Road E17 5DY	B179	081-523 1433	4UD	GAE				
149	385849	WALTHAMSTOW	Matzest Hoe Street	394 Hoe Street E17 9AA	A117	081-521 9433	4UD	GAE				
150	302030	WALWORTH	Walworth — Shell	120-138 Walworth Road North SE17 1SL	A215	071-703 9623	4UD	GAE				
151	302502	WALWORTH	City Walworth Rd Sth (48)	137-139 Walworth Road SE17 1JZ	A215	071-703 8348	4UD	GAE				
152	302042	WANDSWORTH	Trinity Cars Ltd	94 North Side, Wandsworth Common SW18 2QU	A3205	081-874 6812	4UD	GAE				

Loc. Ref.	Shell Ref.	TOWN	NAME	ADDRESS	Road No.	Tel. No.	Fuel	Cards
153	302045	WANDSWORTH	Riversdale Self Serve	289 Merton Road SW18 5JS	A218	081-870 1259	4US	GAE
154	302046	WANDSWORTH	Wandsworth Bridge S/S	8 Townmead Road SW6 2TY	A217	071-371 8328	4USD	GAE
155	302373	WANDSWORTH	Savoy Self Serve	262 York Road SW18 1TP	A3205	071-228 6068	4SD	GAE
156	384217	WANDSWORTH	Andrews Garage (No 3)	Armoury Way SW18 1HZ	A205	081-877 9818	4SD	GAE
157	302161	WELLING	Bellegrove – Shell	Bellegrove Road DA16 3RA	A207	081-304 9411	4USD	GAE
158	302172	WELLING	St Michaels Service Station	100 Upper Wickham Lane DA16 3HQ	A209	081-855 7011	4USD	GAE
159	302282	WEMBLEY	East Lane Filling Station	133-139 East Lane HA9 7PE	A4088	081-904 3217	4UD	GAE
160	302651	WEST DRAYTON	City Skyport	310 Bath Road, Harmondsworth UB7 0DG	A4	081-759 0764	4UD	GAE
161	302010	WESTMINSTER	City Embankment (88)	132 Grosvenor Road SW1V 3JY	A3212	071-834 8054	4US	GAE
162	302592	WHITECHAPEL	City Whitechapel Rd (28)	139-149 Whitechapel Road E1 1DT	A11	071-377 0071	4USD	GAE
163	302235	WIMBLEDON	South Wimbledon Self Serve	194 Merton Road SW19 1EQ	A219	081-543 5244	4SD	GAE
164	302663	WIMBLEDON	Plough Lane S/Serve	Plough Lane SW17 8HA	B235	081-946 1473	4SD	GAE
165	302096	WOOD GREEN	Roundway Service Station	1 The Roundway N17 7HA	A1080	081-808 2646	4UD	GAE
166	302083	WOODFORD GREEN	Woodford (22) – Shell	302 Southend Road IG8 8QH	A1400	081-551 9321	4USD	GAE
167	302884	WOODFORD GREEN	Victory S/Serve	High Road I 8 0RD	A104	081-505 3828	4USD	GAE
168	302584	WOOLWICH	City Woolwich (35)	125-129 High Street SE18 6DS	A206	081-854 6688	4USD	GAE

GREATER MANCHESTER

Loc. Ref.	Shell Ref.	TOWN	NAME	ADDRESS	Road No.	Tel. No.	Fuel	Cards
1	358081	ALTRINCHAM	Ringway – Shell	155 Stockport Road, Timperley WA15 7LT	A560	061-980 1311	4USD	GAE
2	358736	ALTRINCHAM	Timperley – Shell	282 Manchester Road, West Timperley WA14 5NB	A56	061-905 3025	4USD	GAE
3	358795	ASHTON-IN-MAKERFIELD	Eavesway Garage	201 Wigan Road WN4 9SN	A49	(0942) 727149	4USD	GAE
4	358739	ASHTON-UNDER-LYNE	Guide Bridge Self Serve	188 Stockport Road OL7 0NS	A6017	061-330 3632	4USD	GAE
5	358163	AUDENSHAW	Trough Self Serve	Audenshaw Road M34 5PJ	A635	061-370 8477	4USD	GAE
6	357820	BOLTON	Bolton STC	Kay Street BL1 7AT	A666	(0204) 27394	4USD	GAE
7	357821	BOLTON	Bridgeman Place Services Ltd	19 Bridgeman Place BL2 1DE	A579	(0204) 33310	4USD	GA
8	358113	BOLTON	Grafton Self Serve	Chorley Old Road BL1 5SX	B6226	(0204) 383924	4USD	GAE
9	358177	BOLTON	Southgrove Garage	Wigan Road, Westhoughton BL5 2AT	A58	(0942) 813404	4UD	GAE
10	358248	BOLTON	Beehive Garage	Chorley New Road, Lostock BL6 4LW	A673	(0204) 697645	4USD	GAE
11	358756	BOLTON	Trinity Self Serve	Thynne Street BL3 6BZ		(0204) 25351	4USD	GAE
12	358793	BOLTON	Crompton Way – Shell	Tonge Moor Road BL2 3BH	A58	(0204) 595531	4USD	GAE
13	358793	BOLTON	Beaumont Road Self Serve	Beaumont Road BL3 4RB	A58	(0204) 61726	4USD	GAE
14	384102	BOLTON	Newbrook – Shell	Newbrook Road, Over Hulton BL5 1GJ	A579	(0204) 651255	4USD	GAE
15	357474	BURY	Bury Rock – Shell	Rochdale Road BL9 7AX	A58	061-761 1129	4USD	GAE
16	357859	BURY	Heap Bridge Service Station	Bury New Road, Heap Bridge BL9 7HY	A58	061-761 7211	4USD	GAE
17	358127	BURY	Sunnymead Halt	Bury Road, Tottington BL8 3EU	B6213	(0204) 883265	4UD	GAE
18	358571	CHEADLE	Grange Self Serve	Cheadle Road, Cheadle Hulme SK8 5EU	A5149	061-485 3898	4USD	GAE
19	358053	DIDSBURY	Manor Park Self Serve	Wilmslow Road M20 8RH	A5145	061-445 3072	4USD	GAE
20	532321	HEYWOOD	Kempster Ford	Hardfield Garage, Hardfield Street OL10 1DL	A58	(0706) 369817	4UD	GAE
21	358043	HYDE	Hyde – STC	Dawson Road SK14 1QL	A560	061-367 8557	4USD	GAE
22	358179	LEIGH	Holden Road Service Station	Holden Road WN7 1HA	A572	(0942) 673530	4UD	GAE
23	357463	MANCHESTER	Hydro Self Serve	225/255 Hyde Road, West Gorton M12 5AB	A57	061-273 4043	4UD	GAE
24	358064	MANCHESTER	Jubilee Self Serve	Upper Chorlton Road, Brooks Bar M16 7RW	B5218	061-226 1440	4UD	GAE
25	358087	MANCHESTER	Avenue Self Serve	Rochdale Road, Higher Blackley M9 2QT	A664	061-795 8357	4USD	GAE
26	358119	MANCHESTER	Central Self Serve	Bury Road, Radcliffe M26 9UG	A605	061-723 2540	4USD	GAE
27	358131	MANCHESTER	Astley Self Serve	East Lancashire Road, Tyldesley M29 7HX	A580	(0942) 884099	4USD	GAE
28	358137	MANCHESTER	Hilton Park – Shell	Shell Hilton Park, Prestwick M25 8WP	A56	061-773 5203	4USD	GAE
29	358139	MANCHESTER	Castlefield STC	Dawson Street M3 4JZ	A57	061-832 3917	4USD	GAE
30	358153	MANCHESTER	Failsworth Self Serve	337 Oldham Road, Failsworth M35 0AN	A62	061-681 9293	4USD	GAE
31	358160	MANCHESTER	Southside Self Serve	Dickenson Road, Longsight M13 0YW	A6010	061-225 3447	4UD	GAE
32	358166	MANCHESTER	Kingsburn Self Serve	Kingsway, Burnage M19 1RD	A34	061-432 0116	4USD	GAE
33	358660	MANCHESTER	Ormond Street Garage	2-4 Lower Ormond Street M1 5QF		061-236 3847	4UD	GAE
34	358667	MANCHESTER	Baguley Self Serve	Altrincham Road M23 9AA	A560	061-946 0038	4USD	GAE
35	358686	MANCHESTER	Hillcrest Self Serve	Victoria Avenue, Higher Blackley M9 3WQ	A6104	061-740 3959	4USD	GA
36	392060	MANCHESTER	Shopping Giant	Sissons Street, Failsworth M35 0FN	A62	061-682 5016	4USD	GAE
37	395905	MARPLE	G.R. Yates	54 Stockport Road SK6 5AE	A626	061-427 8961	4USD	GAE
38	358090	OLDHAM	Chadderton Motor Co	838 Middleton Road West, Chadderton OL9 0PA	A669	061-633 2503	4UD	GAE
39	358092	OLDHAM	Denshaw Garage	Oldham Road, Denshaw OL3 5SP	A640	(0457) 874443	4UD	GAE
40	358097	OLDHAM	Alexandra Park – Shell	Park Road OL8 1DB	A627	061-627 5806	4USD	GAE
41	358109	OLDHAM	Two Counties – Shell	Huddersfield Road OL4 2HN	A62	061-628 3785	4USD	GAE
42	393780	OLDHAM	Normid Shopping Giant	Kings Square, Kings Street OL8 1ES	A62	061-624 5071	4USD	GAE
43	358145	RADCLIFFE	Stand Filling Station	Stand Lane M26 9JP		061-766 9676	4USD	GAE
44	358094	ROCHDALE	Eagle – Shell	Queensway OL11 1TJ	A664	(0706) 39289	4USD	GAE
45	358101	ROCHDALE	Marland Filling Station	Bolton Road OL11 4QX	B6222	(0706) 32857	4USD	GAE
46	358693	ROCHDALE	Ceylon Service Station	Yorkshire Street OL16 2DR	A58	(0706) 455346	4USD	GAE
47	358073	SALE	Cottage – Shell	375 Northenden Road M33 2PG	B5166	061-973 0534	4USD	GAE
48	358083	SALE	Sale – Shell	Cross Street M33 1JR	A56	061-905 1695	4USD	GAE
49	358085	SALE	Royal 2 Sale/Royal Self Serve	Cross Street M33 1BU	A56	061-973 5958	4UD	GAE
50	358132	SALFORD	Salford S/S	11-13 Cromwell Road M6 6SX	A576	061-745 7282	4USD	GAE
51	358785	SALFORD	Salford Quays Self Serve	Trafford Road M5 2AL	A5063	061-872 9284	4UD	GAE
52	358707	STOCKPORT	Hazel Filling Station	29 Buxton Road, Hazel Grove SK7 6AF	A6	061-483 8210	4UD	GAE
53	358045	STOCKPORT	Edgeley Road Self Serve	Edgeley Road SK3 9NG		061-477 8095	4USD	GAE
54	358051	STOCKPORT	Lisburne Garage Ltd	Lisburne Lane, Offerton SK2 5RJ		061-483 1332	4USD	GAE
55	358055	STOCKPORT	Romiley Garage	Compstall Road, Romiley SK6 4DE	B6104	061-430 2467	4UD	GAE
56	358595	STOCKPORT	Victoria Garage	Ack Lane, Bramhall SK7 1BB	A5149	061-439 4011	4U	GAE
57	358636	STOCKPORT	Cheadleway Self Serve	Turves Road, Cheadle Hulme SK8 6AW		061-486 0006	4USD	GAE
58	358930	STOCKPORT	Shellsport Centre	297/309 Buxton Road SK2 7NR	A6	061-483 3515	4USD	GAE
59	532697	SWINTON	Safeways Swinton	Swinton Hall Road M27	A6	061-728 4563	4USD	
60	358691	URMSTON	Partington Self Serve	Moss Lane, Partington M31 4EB	A6144	061-775 4540	4USD	GAE
61	358708	WARRINGTON	James Twist Ltd	151 Lowton Road, Golborne WA3 2HN	B5207	(0942) 728271	4UD	GAE
62	357437	WIGAN	United Co-Op Ltd	Cross Street, Hindley WN2 3AT	A577	(0942) 55256	4U	GA

Loc. Ref.	Shell Ref.	TOWN	NAME	ADDRESS	Road No.	Tel. No.	Fuel	Cards	24 hour	HGV	Select	Car Wash
63	357504	WIGAN	Park Service Station	Victoria Street, Newtown WN5 9BX	A571	(0942) 824027	4UD	GAE				
64	358235	WIGAN	Gathurst Service Station Ltd	Gathurst Lane, Shevington WN6 8HS	B5206	(0257) 255211	4UD	GAE				
65	358237	WIGAN	Boars Head Self Serve	Wigan Road, Standish WN6 0AD	A49	(0257) 425487	4USD	GAE				
66	358252	WIGAN	Langtree Garage	Preston Road, Standish WN6 0QG	A49	(0257) 422660	4UD	GAE				
67	358264	WIGAN	Poolstock Engineering Co Ltd	Poolstock Lane, Poolstock WN3 5EW	B5238	(0942) 35924	4UD	GAE				
68	358679	WIGAN	Culraven Filling Station	Haigh Road, Haigh WN2 1LD	B5239	(0942) 831274	4UD	GAE				
69	358754	WIGAN	Goose Green Self Serve	878 Warrington Road, Goose Green WN3 6XB	A49	(0942) 41227	4USD	GAE				
70	358860	WIGAN	Lily Lane Service Station	Lily Lane, Platt Bridge WN2 5LL	A58	(0942) 867601	4UD	GAE				

GWENT

Loc. Ref.	Shell Ref.	TOWN	NAME	ADDRESS	Road No.	Tel. No.	Fuel	Cards	24 hour	HGV	Select	Car Wash
1	348412	ABERGAVENNY	Aber Service Station	33-35 Brecon Road NP7 5UH	A40	(0873) 855875	4UD	GAE				
2	348843	ABERGAVENNY	Gilwern Self Serve	Aberbaiden, Gilwern NP7 0EF	A465	(0873) 830223	4USD	GAE			■	
3	348848	ABERGAVENNY	Boidenbrook Self Serve	Heads of the Valley Road, Gilwern NP7 0EF	A465	(0873) 831967	4USD	GAE			■	
4	434004	ABERGAVENNY	Brecon Road Service Station	Brecon Road NP7 7EL	A40	(0873) 854229	4UD	GAE				
5	348421	BLAINA	North Blaina Service Station	High Street NP3 3AN	A467	(0495) 290409	4UD	GAE				
6	348438	CHEPSTOW	Chepstow – Shell	Newport Road NP6 5YS	A48	(0291) 629382	4USD	GAE			■	
7	348410	CWMBRAN	Apollo Self Serve	Llantarnam Road, Llantarnam NP44 3BG		(0633) 860369	4USD	GAE				
8	348435	MONMOUTH	Dixton Self Serve	Dixton Road NP5 3PL	B4233	(0600) 716448	4UD	GAE				
9	348404	NEWPORT	Coleridge Self Serve	410 Chepstow Road NP9 8JH	A48	(0633) 281998	4USD	GAE				
10	348406	NEWPORT	Hanbury Garage	Uskside, Caerleon NP6 1AA	B4236	(0633) 420310	4UD	GAE				
11	348407	NEWPORT	Newport – Shell	1 Malpas Road NP9 5PA	A4042	(0633) 821414	4USD	GAE			■	
12	348859	NEWPORT	Highcross – Shell	High Cross Road, Rogerstone NP1 9AD	B4591	(0633) 892712	4USD	GAE				
13	299898	RAGLAN	Central Garage	High Street NP5 2DY		(0291) 690423	4UD	GAE				
14	348824	TREDEGAR	Tredegar Self Serve	Beaufort Road NP2 4XL	A4047	(0495) 252760	4UD	GAE				

GWYNEDD

Loc. Ref.	Shell Ref.	TOWN	NAME	ADDRESS	Road No.	Tel. No.	Fuel	Cards	24 hour	HGV	Select	Car Wash
1	358446	AMLWCH	Central Garage	Mona Street LL68 9AN	A5025	(0407) 830375	4UD	GAE				
2	358523	BALA	R A Roberts & G W Roberts	West End LL23 7AE	A494	(0678) 520210	4UD	GAE				
3	358734	BANGOR	Glanadda Filling Station	Caernarvon Road LL57 4SU	A4087	(0248) 364505	4UD	GAE				
4	358472	BETWS-Y-COED	Waterloo Bridge Self Serve	LL24 0AR	A5	(0690) 710305	4UD	GAE				
5	357977	BLAENAU FFESTINIOG	Prysor Filling Station	Cwmprysor Road, Trawsfynydd LL41 4TW	A4212	(0766) 87534	4USD	GAE				
6	357983	CAERNARFON	Dulyn Motors	Pen-y-Groes LL54 6NB	A487	(0286) 880218	4UD	GAE				
7	358455	CAERNARFON	Dinas Garage	Pwllheli Road, Llanwnda LL54 7YN	A487	(0286) 830277	4UD	GAE				
8	358457	CAERNARFON	Lleiod Garage	Llanberis Road LL55 2DF	A4086	(0286) 673249	4UD	GAE				
9	358727	CAERNARFON	Prince of Wales F/Stn	North Road LL55 1AR	A487	(0286) 673136	4UD	GAE				
10	358460	COLWYN BAY	Black Cat – Shell	Glan Conway LL28 5LE	A470	(0492) 581174	4USD	GAE			■	
11	358533	DOLCELLAU	Idris Service Station	Maes Caled LL40 1UE	A470	(0341) 422709	4UD	GAE				
12	358443	HOLYHEAD (ANGLESEY)	Service Station	Lon St Fraid, Trearddur Bay LL65 2YP	B4545	(0407) 860432	4UD	GAE				
13	209906	HOLYHEAD (ANGLESEY)	Dyffryn Service Station	London Road, Valley LL65 3DP	A5	(0407) 740658	4USD	GAE				
14	358451	HOLYHEAD (ANGLESEY)	Lands End Service Station	Victoria Road LL65 1UD	A5	(0407) 763660	4UD	GAE				
15	358474	LLANDUDNO	West Shore Garage	Herkomer Road LL30 2YZ		(0492) 877607	4UD	GAE				
16	357711	LLANERCHYMEDD	Bryntirion Garage	LL71 8DD	B5111	(0248) 470358	4UD	GAE				
17	299781	LLANFAIRFECHAN	Aber Falls Service Station	Aber LL33 0LD	A55	(0248) 680627	4UD	GAE				
18	357981	MENAI BRIDGE(ANGLESEY)	Four Crosses Service Station	Menai Bridge LL59 5RP	A5025	(0248) 716259	4UD	GAE				
19	358441	MENAI BRIDGE(ANGLESEY)	Britannia – Shell	LL59 5EB	A4080	(0248) 712373	4USD	GAE				
20	358453	PENMAENMAWR	Orme View Filling Station	Conway Road LL34 6UN	A55	(0492) 622741	4USD	GAE				
21	357971	PORTMADOG	Tremadoc Garage	Tremadog LL49 9RF	A498	(0766) 512662	4UD	GAE				
22	357996	PORTMADOG	Harbour Filling Station	High Street LL49 9NG	A487	(0766) 512716	4USD	GAE				
23	357979	PWLLHELI	Service Garage	Llanbedrog LL53 7TF	A499	(0758) 740249	4USD	GAE				
24	358717	PWLLHELI	Morfa Garage	Len Terfyn, Murfa Nefyn LL53 6AP	B4412	(0758) 720219	4UD	GAE				
25	358531	TALSARNAU	The Garage	LL47 6YB	A496	(0766) 770286	4UD	GA				

HAMPSHIRE

Loc. Ref.	Shell Ref.	TOWN	NAME	ADDRESS	Road No.	Tel. No.	Fuel	Cards	24 hour	HGV	Select	Car Wash
1	347790	ALRESFORD	Dean Self Serve	Winchester Road, Ropley SO24 0BG	A31	(0962) 773235	4USD	GAE				
2	298874	ALTON	Caffyns Ford	Ackender Road GU34 1JR		(0420) 83993	4USD	GA				
3	347736	ALTON	Holybourne Garage	Holybourne GU34 4HA	A31	(0420) 82288	4UD	G				
4	347787	ALTON	Chawton End Garage Ltd	Four Marks GU34 5HE	A31	(0420) 562354	4UD	GAE				
5	308125	ANDOVER	Portway – Shell	280 Weyhill Road SP10 3LS	B3402	(0264) 338663	4USD	GAE				
6	538558	ANDOVER	Enham Arch – Shell	A343 Newbury Road SP11 3TR	A343	(0264) 337368	4USD	GAE			■	
7	527864	ARLESFORD	New Cheriton Service Station	The Crossroads, New Cheriton SO24 0NQ	A272	(0962) 771234	4USD	GAE				
8	347793	BASINGSTOKE	City Pied Piper	Winchester Road RG22 6HW		(0256) 464875	4USD	GAE				
9	347796	BASINGSTOKE	Eastrop – Shell	Eastrop Roundabout RG21 1JJ		(0256) 465043	4USD	GAE				
10	347797	BASINGSTOKE	Buckskin – Shell	374 Worting Road RG22 5DZ	B3400	(0256) 330829	4USD	GAE			■	
11	347954	BASINGSTOKE	Jacksons (Basingstoke) Ltd	Lower Wote Street RG21 1HE		(0256) 473561	4USD	GAE				

Loc. Ref.	Shell Ref.	TOWN	NAME	ADDRESS	Road No.	Tel. No.	Fuel	Cards
12	348818	BASINGSTOKE	Fleet MWSA South	M3 Motorway (Southbound), Hartley Whitney RG27 8BN	M3	(0252) 627205	4USD	GAE
13	351932	BASINGSTOKE	Fleet MWSA (North)	M3 Motorway (Northbound), Hartley Whitney RG27 8BN	M3	(0252) 628539	4USD	GAE
14	347743	BORDON	Sleaford Self Serve	Sleaford GU35 0QP	A325	(0420) 472266	4USD	GAE
15	347915	BROCKENHURST	Gates Engineering Co Limited	Sway Road SO42 7SH		(0590) 23344	4UD	GAE
16	347939	CADHAM	Bramshaw Garage (Hampshire)	Bramshaw SO43 7JF	B3079	(0703) 813206	4U	GA
17	308500	CADHAM	Crossways Garage	Romsey Road SO1 0LN	A31	(0703) 812204	4UD	GAE
18	347910	CADHAM	Cadnam Garage	Southampton Road SO4 2NB	A336	(0703) 812159	4UD	GAE
19	349041	CAMBERLEY	Yateley Motors	Reading Road, Yateley GU17 7UH	A327	(0252) 874565	4USD	GAE
20	347878	EASTLEIGH	Chandlers Ford Self Serve	130 Winchester Road, Chandlers Ford SO5 2DS		(0703) 265056	4USD	GAE
21	347884	EASTLEIGH	Horton Heath Motors	Botley Road, Horton Heath SO5 7DN	B3354	(0703) 692260	4UD	GAE
22	308200	EMSWORTH	F.A. Collins & Sons	The Square, Westbourne PO10 8UE		(0243) 372628	4UD	GAE
23	347887	FAREHAM	Titchfield – Shell	Southampton Road, Titchfield PO14 4BB	A27	(0329) 844401	4USD	GAE
24	347890	FAREHAM	Redhill Service Station	Winchester Road, Wickham PO17 5HE	A334	(0329) 834131	4UD	GAE
25	347900	FAREHAM	Wickham Self Serve	Fareham Road, Wickham PO17 5BY	A32	(0329) 833110	4UD	GAE
26	347957	FAREHAM	Highlands – Shell	Highlands PO15 5PR		(0329) 842338	4USD	GAE
27	349064	FAREHAM	Paul Huxford (Fareham) Ltd	Newgate Lane PO14 1AL	B3385	(0329) 282811	4USD	GAE
28	347694	FARNBOROUGH	Tower Hill Garage	53 Cove Road GU14 0EL	B3014	(0252) 516856	4USD	GAE
29	349076	FARNBOROUGH	Henlys Ford (Farnborough)	Elles Road GU14 7QW		(0252) 544344	4UD	GAE
30	434122	FARNHAM	Frensham Service Station	Bucks Horn Oak GU10 4LT	A325	(0420) 23763	4UD	GAE
31	347692	FLEET	Station Garage	22 Fleet Road GU13 8QG	B3013	(0252) 616461	4US	GAE
32	302982	GOSPORT	Ferry Self Serve	Mumby Road PO12 1AA	A32	(0705) 586932	4UD	GAE
33	347896	GOSPORT	Solent – Shell	Fareham Road PO13 0XL	A32	(0329) 823501	4UD	GAE
34	347747	HAVANT	Whichers Gate Self Serve	Rowlands Castle PO9 6BB	B2149	(0705) 412144	4USD	GAE
35	347754	HAVANT	Havant Self Serve	Park Road South PO9 1HA	B2149	(0705) 483052	4US	GAE
36	347959	HAVANT	Langstone Self Serve	Park Road South PO9 1HB	B2149	(0705) 484102	4USD	GAE
37	302855	HAYLING ISLAND	Church Road Service Station	2/4 Church Road PO11 0NT	A3023	(0705) 462947	4UD	GAE
38	347752	HAYLING ISLAND	Hayling Motors Ltd	Hollow Lane PO11 9EY	A3023	(0705) 463800	4UD	GAE
39	347731	LIPHOOK	Liphook Garage Ltd	The Square GU30 7AG	B2131	(0428) 722955	4UD	GAE
40	542939	LIPHOOK	Liphook (North) – Shell	A3(T) North GU30 7TT	A3	(0428) 727626	4USD	GAE
41	542940	LIPHOOK	Liphook (South) – Shell	A3(T) South GU30 7TU	A3	(0428) 727626	4UD	GAE
42	347923	LYMINGTON	Meadens of Sway	Durnstown, Sway SO41 6AL	B3055	(0590) 682212	4UD	GA
43	347944	LYMINGTON	Leonards of Lymington	Undershore Road SO41 8SA		(0590) 673664	4UD	GAE
44	308115	NEW MILTON	New Milton Self Serve	51 Lymington Road BH25 6PR	A337	(0425) 611473	4USD	GAE
45	347921	NEW MILTON	Loaders Garage	St Johns Roads, Bashley BH25 5SA	B3058	(0425) 614722	4USD	GAE
46	302851	NEWBURY	West Kingsclere S/Stn	Newbury Road, Kingsclere RG15 8SP	A339	(0635) 297413	4UD	GAE
47	347720	NEWBURY	Murrays Service Station	R.A.&M.D. Butler, Ashford Hill RG15 8BQ	B3051	(0734) 813646	4UD	GA
48	349023	PETERSFIELD	M.V.F. Ltd	60 Winchester Road GU32 3PL	A272	(0730) 266241	4USD	GAE
49	302364	PORTSMOUTH	Victory – Shell	Kettering Terrace, Mile End PO2 7SB	A3	(0705) 823655	4USD	GAE
50	308066	PORTSMOUTH	Farlington – Shell	Eastern Road, Farlington PO6 1UW	A2030	(0705) 210760	4USD	GAE
51	347749	PORTSMOUTH	Waterlooville City – Shell	London Road, Waterlooville PO7 7AA	A3	(0705) 241968	4USD	GAE
52	347750	PORTSMOUTH	Fratton – Shell	Goldsmith Avenue PO4 8BH	A2030	(0705) 871817	4UD	GAE
53	347952	PORTSMOUTH	Northend Self Serve	170 London Road PO2 9BT	A2047	(0705) 696215	4UD	GAE
54	347967	PORTSMOUTH	Excel Service Station	Fitzherbert Road, Cosham PO6 1RU	A2147	(0705) 381799	4UD	GAE
55	650630	PORTSMOUTH	Bastion Self Serve	London Road, Hilsea PO2 9RP	A3	(0705) 660328	4UD	GAE
56	347946	RINGWOOD	Picket Post – Shell	Picket Post BH24 3HN	A31	(0425) 475911	4USD	GAE
57	348974	RINGWOOD	Forest Edge – Shell	A31, Picket Post BH24 3HN	A31	(0425) 476977	4USD	GAE
58	347783	ROMSEY	Timsbury Garage	Stockbridge Road, Timsbury SO51 0NE	A3057	(0794) 68254	4UD	GAE
59	302985	SOUTHAMPTON	Andrews (Shipside Services)	No 10 Gate, Western Docks SO9 1GA		(0703) 228001	4USD	GAE
60	347765	SOUTHAMPTON	Hamble Service Station	Hamble Lane, Hamble SO3 5JH	B3397	(0703) 454076	4UD	GAE
61	347769	SOUTHAMPTON	Acorn Self Serve	497 Burseldon Road, Sholing SO2 8NJ	A3024	(0703) 406620	4USD	GAE
62	347770	SOUTHAMPTON	E.G. Newman & Son Ltd	The Causeway, Redbridge SO1 0NP	A35	(0703) 865021	4UD	GAE
63	347773	SOUTHAMPTON	Cobden Bridge Self Serve	8/10 Cobden Avenue, Bitterne Park SO2 4FX	A3035	(0703) 555582	4UD	GAE
64	347775	SOUTHAMPTON	Langhorn Gate Self Serve	238 Burgess Road SO2 3AU	A35	(0703) 677717	4USD	GAE
65	347777	SOUTHAMPTON	Roselands – STC	Redbridge Road, Millbrook SO1 0LT	A35	(0703) 774345	4UD	GAE
66	347779	SOUTHAMPTON	Shirley – Shell	234 Winchester Road, Shirley SO1 2SB	A35	(0703) 776125	4USD	GAE
67	347780	SOUTHAMPTON	Tilbury (Southampton) Ltd	Western Esplanade SO9 5TX	A3024	(0703) 228951	4UD	GAE
68	347785	SOUTHAMPTON	Woolston Self Serve	170 Portsmouth Road, Woolston SO2 9AQ	A3025	(0703) 444995	4USD	GAE
69	347879	SOUTHAMPTON	Glider & Blue Mts Servs Ltd	Winchester Road, Bishops Waltham SO3 1DH	B2177	(0489) 892596	4USD	GAE
70	347902	SOUTHAMPTON	Sparchatts of Botley	Southampton Road, Botley SO3 2EU	A334		4USD	GAE
71	347962	SOUTHAMPTON	Swaythling – Shell	Thomas Lewis Way, Swaythling SO2 2JH	A335	(0703) 552572	4UD	GAE
72	348311	SOUTHAMPTON	Waterside – Shell	Southampton Road, Hythe SO4 5DA		(0703) 207042	4USD	GAE
73	432962	WARSASH	Roxby Garage	The Clock Tower SO3 9GQ		(0489) 572366	4U	GAE
74	308067	WINCHESTER	Sutton Scotney S/Area Nth Bnd	A34 Winchester-By-Pass, Sutton Scotney SO21 3JY	A34	(0962) 760622	4USD	GAE
75	308069	WINCHESTER	Sutton Scotney S/Area Sth Bnd	A34 Winchester-By-Pass, Sutton Scotney SO21 3JY	A34	(0962) 760622	4USD	GAE
76	347805	WINCHESTER	Ideal Garage	London Road, Micheldever SO21 3BS	A33	(0962) 774313	4UD	GAE
77	347894	WINCHESTER	Bereweeke Self Serve	A272 Stockbridge Road, Weeke SO22 5JG	A272	(0962) 842704	4USD	GAE
78	347949	WINCHESTER	Winnall – Shell	Easton Lane, The By-Pass SO23 7QJ	A33	(0962) 841421	4USD	GAE
79	434767	WINCHESTER	Yew Tree Service Station	Pitt Road, Hursley SO22 5GP	A3090	(0962) 854152	4USD	

HEREFORD & WORCESTER

Loc. Ref.	Shell Ref.	TOWN	NAME	ADDRESS	Road No.	Tel. No.	Fuel	Cards
1	355231	BROMSGROVE	Fairfield Garage	Fairfield B61 9LY	B4091	(0527) 73178	4USD	GAE
2	355232	BROMSGROVE	College Self Serve	116 Birmingham Road B61 0DF	A38	(0527) 36511	4USD	GAE
3	355524	BROMYARD	Top Garage (Bromyard) Ltd	Hereford Road HR7 4QU	A465	(0885) 483342	4USD	GAE
4	353431	HEREFORD	West Hereford S/Stn	Whitecross Road HR4 0DG	A438	(0432) 273298	4UD	GAE
5	355546	KIDDERMINSTER	Greenhill Service Station	Chester Road North DY10 2RS	A449	(0562) 824956	4USD	GAE
6	355526	LEOMINSTER	County Vehicles	52 Broad Street HR6 8DD	A49	(0568) 616465	4UD	GAE
7	355522	ROSS-ON-WYE	Daff-y-Nant Service Station	A40, Whitchurch HR9 6DW	A40	(0600) 890583	4USD	GAE
8	353425	ROSS-ON-WYE	Lea Garage	Lea HR9 7JZ	A40	(0989) 750295	4UD	GAE
9	340146	STOURBRIDGE	Cross Keys Garage	Kidderminster Road South DY9 0JL	A456	(0562) 882234	4USD	GAE
10	355523	TENBURY WELLS	Swan Garage	Worcester Road WR15 8AR	A456	(0584) 810466	4USD	GAE

Loc. Ref.	Shell Ref.	TOWN	NAME	ADDRESS	Road No.	Tel. No.	Fuel	Cards
11	077705	WORCESTER	Stoulton Motor Services Ltd	Stoulton WR7 4RD	A44	(0905) 840661	4USD	GAE
12	355266	WORCESTER	Redhill Filling Station	London Road WR5 2JJ	A44	(0905) 353777	4UD	GAE
13	355274	WORCESTER	Barneshall – Shell	Bath Road WR5 3ES	A38	(0905) 763856	4UD	GAE
14	355276	WORCESTER	Regal Garage	Upton on Severn WR8 0HU	A4104	(0684) 592316	4UD	GAE
15	355577	WORCESTER	Whinfield Service Station	Ombersley Road WR3 7HE	A449	(0905) 52242	4USD	GAE
16	435858	WORCESTER	Oakleigh Garage	Main Road, Hallow WR2 6NH	A443	(0905) 640294	4USD	GAE

HERTFORDSHIRE

Loc. Ref.	Shell Ref.	TOWN	NAME	ADDRESS	Road No.	Tel. No.	Fuel	Cards
1	302316	ABBOTS LANGLEY	Longhouse Filling Station	56 High Street, Bedmond WD5 0RH		(0923) 261538	4USD	GAE
2	356910	BALDOCK	Odsey Service Station	Baldock Road SG7 6SB	A505	(0462) 742252	4USD	GAE
3	302317	BARNET	City Stirling Corner (17)	Stirling Corner, Barnet By-Pass EN5 3TG	A1	081-449 9213	4USD	GAE
4	302465	BISHOP'S STORTFORD	Rye Street – Shell	Rye Street CM23 2HA	B1004	(0279) 653726	4USD	GAE
5	340560	BISHOP'S STORTFORD	Oaklands – Shell	1 Stansted Road CM23 2DR	B1383	(0279) 504702	4USD	GAE
6	302310	BOREHAMWOOD	Elstree Way – Shell	Elstree Way WD6 1LB	A5135	081-953 3969	4USD	GAE
7	340546	BUNTINGFORD	L.M. Bentley	Hare Street SG9 0EA	B1368	(0763) 289298	4USD	GAE
8	302377	CHORLEYWOOD	Chorleywood – Shell	Rickmansworth Road WD3 5SE	A404	(0923) 285651	4USD	GAE
9	302883	HATFIELD	Grays (Hatfield) Ltd	1 Great North Road AL9 5JA	A1000	(07072) 64366	4USD	GAE
10	302335	HEMEL HEMPSTEAD	Everest Way – Shell	Adeyfield Road HP2 4HZ		(0442) 232594	4USD	GAE
11	302429	HEMEL HEMPSTEAD	Apsley – Shell	14 London Road HP3 9SR	A41	(0442) 233904	4USD	GAE
12	302432	HEMEL HEMPSTEAD	Hemel Hempstead – Shell	Breakspear Way HP2 4TZ	A414	(0442) 245888	4USD	GAE
13	340554	HERTFORD	A E Abbiss Ltd	85-89 Railway Street SG14 1RT		(0992) 587777	4USD	GAE
14	340618	HERTFORD	Bengeo Service Centre	Bengeo Street SG14 3EY	B158	(0992) 581177	4USD	GAE
15	302332	HITCHIN	Walkers Garage	68A High Street, Kimpton SG4 8PT	B652	(0438) 832783	4UD	GAE
16	302495	HITCHIN	Burr Bros of Hitchin Limited	23 Old Park Road SG5 2JS	A600	(0462) 420333	4USD	GAE
17	340160	HITCHIN	Hitchin Self Serve	Bedford Road SG5 2TY	A600	(0462) 457579	4USD	GAE
18	356901	HITCHIN	Inter Counties Vehicles	86-88 High Street, Stotfold SG5 4LD	A507	(0462) 834833	4U	GAE
19	398116	HODDESDON	Fourways Service Station	Amwell Street EN11 9JL	A1170	(0992) 465141	4USD	GAE
20	302889	LETCHWORTH	Letchworth – Shell	Letchworth Gate SG6 2AZ	A6141	(0462) 482386	4USD	GAE
21	302321	RICKMANSWORTH	Croxley Green – Shell	185/187 Watford Road, Croxley Green WD3 3ED	A412	(0923) 241960	4USD	GAE
22	308189	RICKMANSWORTH	Rickmansworth S/Stn	Victoria Close WD3 4EQ	A404	(0923) 778787	4USD	GAE
23	280074	ROYSTON	Greenfield – Shell	Baldock Road SG8 9NN	A505	(0462) 743199	4USD	GAE
24	398136	ROYSTON	Earls Hill S/Stn – Shell	Baldock Street SG8 5QY		(0763) 247148	4USD	GAE
25	302328	ST ALBANS	Redbourn – Shell	Redbourn Road, Redbourn AL3 7AD	A5183	(0582) 794498	4USD	GAE
26	302338	ST ALBANS	Chiswell Self Serve	551 Watford Road AL2 3DE	A405	(0727) 830496	4USD	GAE
27	302566	ST ALBANS	Marshalswick – Shell	185 Marshalswick Lane AL1 4UY		(0727) 866385	4USD	GAE
28	302590	ST ALBANS	Smallford – Shell	608 Hatfield Road, Smallford AL4 0HP	A1057	(0727) 835185	4USD	GAE
29	308208	ST ALBANS	Flamstead Filling Station	London Road, Flamstead AL3 8HS	A5	(0582) 842098	4USD	GAE
30	340553	ST ALBANS	Watling Street Filling Station	London Road, Flamstead AL3 8HJ	A5	(0582) 842463	D	GAE
31	527554	TRING	Sears Garage Ltd	Grove Road HP23 5HA		(0442) 823306	4UD	GAE
32	302349	WALTHAM CROSS	Waltham Cross Self Serve	117 Eleanor Cross Road EN8 7NJ	A121	(0992) 711141	4UD	GAE
33	302390	WARE	Thundridge Garage	SG12 0SU	A10	(0920) 465951	4USD	GAE
34	340561	WARE	Baldock Street Garage	Baldock Street SG12 9DU	A1170	(0920) 465951	4USD	GAE
35	302323	WATFORD	High Street Service Station	258-262 Lower High Street WD1 2JJ	A411	(0923) 255522	4USD	GAE
36	302456	WATFORD	Sceptre – Shell	St Albans Road WD2 6AE	A41	(0923) 227381	4USD	GAE
37	385198	WATFORD	Hempstead Road	5-11 Hempstead Road WD1 3HB	A411	(0923) 248696	4US	GAE
38	433698	WATFORD	Watford Business Park	Greenhill Crescent WD1 8TF		(0923) 244455	4UD	GAE
39	340549	WELWYN GARDEN CITY	Garden City Service Station	Great North Road AL8 7TQ	B197	(07072) 64567	4USD	GAE
40	340610	WYMONDLEY	Wymondley Filling Station	Stevenage Road SG4 7JA		(0438) 353453	4UD	GAE

HIGHLAND

Loc. Ref.	Shell Ref.	TOWN	NAME	ADDRESS	Road No.	Tel. No.	Fuel	Cards
1	377635	ACHNASHEEN	Achnasheen Filling Station	IV22 2TE	A832	(0445) 88238	4UD	GAE
2	380873	ACHNASHEEN	Laide Post Office Stores	Laide IV22 2NB	A832	(0445) 731252	4UD	GAE
3	380918	ACHNASHEEN	Lochewe Service Station	Poolewe IV22 2JU	A832	(0445) 86239	4UD	GAE
4	381202	AVIEMORE	Aviemore Filling Station	Main Street PH22 1RH	B9152	(0479) 810514	4UD	GAE
5	380871	AVOCH	Burnside Garage	IV9 8QR	A832	(0381) 20355	4UD	GAE
6	539091	BALLINDALLOCH	Ballindalloch Shop	AB37 9AS	A95	(08072) 213	4UD	GAE
7	380375	BEAULY	Aird Motors & Eng Co Ltd	IV4 7BP	A862	(0463) 782266	4UD	GAE
8	380830	BONAR BRIDGE	Spinningdale Stores	Spinningdale IV24 3AD	A949	(0862) 88230	4UD	GAE
9	381042	BONAR BRIDGE	Sutherland Transport	North Road IV24 3AN	A836	(0549) 2465	4UD	GAE
10	299443	BRORA	Sutherland Arms Garage	Victoria Road KW9 6LN	A9	(0408) 621721	4UD	GAE
11	376199	CONON BRIDGE	Riverford Service Station	Riverford IV7 8AH	A862	(0349) 61361	4UD	GAE
12	380876	CONON BRIDGE	H & J Scott	The Garage, Poyntzfield IV7 8LV	B9163	(0381) 8210	4UD	GAE
13	52193	CROMARTY	Cromarty Stores	Bank Street IV11 8UY	A832	(0381) 7550	4UD	GAE
14	381083	DINGWALL	Gleaner Oils	Park Street IV15 9JH	A862	(0349) 64581	4UD	GAE
15	380826	DORNOCH	Evelix Service Station	Evelix IV25 3RE	A9	(0862) 810255	4UD	GAE
16	380891	DRUMNADROCHIT	West End Garage	IV3 6TZ	A831	(04562) 228	4UD	GAE
17	380814	DUNBEATH	Castlehill Filling Station	KW6 6EY	A9	(0593) 3212	4UD	GAE
18	434542	EVANTON	Skiach Services	Industrial Estate IV16 9XH	B817	(0349) 830888	4UD	GAE
19	380381	FORT AUGUSTUS	Glen Service Station	PH32 4DD	A82	(0320) 6365	4UD	GAE
20	380933	GLENCOE	Claymore Filling Station	PA39 4HP	A82	(08552) 308	4UD	GAE
21	380828	GOLSPIE	Sutherland Arms Garage	KW10 6RS	A9	(0408) 633411	4UD	GAE
22	380885	INVERGORDON	Royal Filling Station	High Street IV18 0ON	B817	(0349) 852128	4UD	GAE

Loc. Ref.	Shell Ref.	TOWN	NAME	ADDRESS	Road No.	Tel. No.	Fuel	Cards
23	377585	INVERNESS	Co-Op Superstore	Inshes IV1 2BB	B9006	(0463) 242525	4UD	GAE
24	380385	INVERNESS	Millburn Self Serve	Millburn Road IV2 3RA	B865	(0463) 230563	4USD	GAE
25	380388	INVERNESS	Ness Motors Ltd	16 Telford Street IV3 5LA	A862	(0463) 222848	4U	AE
26	380939	INVERNESS	Kingswell Self Serve	Old Perth Road IV2 3XH	B9006	(0463) 231458	4UD	GAE
27	381158	INVERNESS	Invercars Ltd	44 Harbour Road IV1 1UF	B865	(0463) 222841	4USD	GAE
28	380852	KINLOCHLEVEN	Kinlochleven Road Transport	Leven Road PA40 4RL	B863	(08554) 456	4UD	GAE
29	535143	KYLE OF LOCHALSH	Central Garage	IV40 8AG	A87	(0599) 4329	4UD	GAE
30	380834	LAIRG	Pittentrail Garage	Rogart IV28 3TU	A839	(0408) 641364	4UD	GAE
31	380838	LAIRG	Sutherland Transport	Main Street IV27 2DB	A836	(0549) 2465	4UD	GAE
32	400165	LAIRG	Inchnadamph Hotel	Loch Assynt IV27 4HL	A837	(057) 12202	4U	
33	380864	LOCHCARRON	Lochcarron Garage	IV54 8YS	A896	(0520) 2205	4UD	GAE
34	380866	MUNLOCHY	Munlochy Garage	IV8 8NE	A832	(0463) 81219	4UD	GAE
35	380386	NAIRN	P J Grant & Sons	Forres Road IV12 5NE	A96	(0667) 52243	4UD	GAE
36	397222	NAIRN	West End Service Station	Inverness Road IV12 4SG	A96	(0667) 52335	4USD	GAE
37	535100	ONICH	Onich Service Station	PH33 6RZ	A82	(08553) 276	4UD	GAE
38	380841	PORTREE	Dunvegan Garage	Dunvegan IV51 9HE	A850	(0470) 22234	4UD	GAE
39	380879	STRATHPEFFER	Smiths Garage	Contin IV14 9ES	A835	(0997) 421472	4UD	GAE
40	281711	TAIN	H Smith	The Stores, Fearn IV22 2JA	B9165	(0862) 832204	4U	
41	380378	TAIN	Fearn Service Station	Hill of Fearn, Fearn IV20 1TE	B9165	(0862) 832216	4UD	GAE
42	380887	TAIN	Tain Filling Station	Knockbreck Road IV19 1BW	B9174	(0862) 893622	4UD	GAE
43	330012	THURSO	Bridgend Filling Station	Bridgend KW14 8PP	A882	(0847) 64219	4UD	GAE
44	377611	THURSO	Castlevve Filling Station	Mey KW14 8XH	A836		4UD	
45	380820	THURSO	Bridge Street Garage	Bridge Street, Halkirk KW12 6XY	B874	(0847) 83278	4UD	GAE
46	380937	THURSO	Northern Motors	Coupar Square KW14 8AS	A882	(0847) 62778	4UD	GAE
47	380960	ULLAPOOL	Moss Garage	Moss Road IV26 2UN	A835	(0854) 612029	4UD	GAE
48	380966	ULLAPOOL	Lochbroom Filling Station	Garve Road IV26 2SX	A835	(0854) 612298	4UD	GAE
49	299445	WICK	Mowatts Garage	George Street KW1 4DG	A9	(0955) 2321	4UD	GAE
50	380822	WICK	Hastigrow Filling Station	Hastigrow, By Wick KW1 4T	B876	(0955) 84232	4UD	GA
51	380907	WICK	Lochshell Filling Station	Lochshell, By Wick KW1 4TB	A9	(0955) 3409	4UD	GAE
52	381157	WICK	Camps Filling Station	Shore Road KW1 4JH	A9	(0955) 5472	4U	GAE

HUMBERSIDE

Loc. Ref.	Shell Ref.	TOWN	NAME	ADDRESS	Road No.	Tel. No.	Fuel	Cards
1	365936	BEVERLEY	Canal Head Service Station	South Street, Leven HU17 5NY	A165	(0964) 542281	4USD	GAE
2	362202	BRIDLINGTON	Bridlington — Shell	Hilderthorpe Road YO15 3BH	A165	(0262) 400121	4USD	GAE
3	365917	BRIDLINGTON	Buckrose Motors Ltd	Flamborough Road YO15 2JQ	B1255	(0262) 672226	4UD	GAE
4	357721	BROUGH	Beacon — Shell	A63 Eastbound HU15 1SA	A63	(0430) 424446	4USD	GAE
5	365912	DRIFFIELD	Eling Transport	Station Garage, Middle Street South YO25 7PY	B1249	(0377) 42036	4UD	GAE
6	365920	DRIFFIELD	Kirkburn Filling Station	Kirkburn YO25 9EA	A163	(0377) 89225	4USD	GAE
7	534300	GOOLE	Glews Garage	Rawcliffe Road DN14 8TS	A614	(0405) 764525	4UD	GAE
8	357767	GRIMSBY	Grimsby — Shell	Moody Lane DN31 2SY	A180	(0472) 241214	4USD	GAE
9	366030	GRIMSBY	Toothill — Shell	Yarborough Road DN34 4EY	A1136	(0472) 241127	4USD	GAE
10	366360	GRIMSBY	Hartford Grimsby	Corporation Road DN31 1UH		(0472) 358941	4USD	GAE
11	535038	GRIMSBY	Victoria Street — Shell	Victoria Street DN31 1PF		(0472) 355313	4UD	GAE
12	363771	HULL	Saltend F/Stn	Hedon Road HU12 8EB	A1033	(0482) 896737	4USD	GAE
13	365929	HULL	Inglemire Self Serve	390 Cottingham Road HU6 8QE	B1233	(0482) 43474	4UD	GAE
14	365934	HULL	North Park Filling Station	Beverley Road HU6 7AD	A1079	(0482) 851139	4USD	GAE
15	365938	HULL	Portobello Self Serve	740 Holderness Road HU9 3JA	A165	(0482) 74284	4UD	GAE
16	366262	HULL	Riverside Filling Station	Hessle High Road HU4 7BG		(0482) 648665	4UD	GAE
17	536543	HULL	Stoneferry Service Station	Stoneferry Road HU8 8BZ		(0482) 225390	4USD	GAE
18	366252	NORTH FERRIBY	Grand Dale Self Serve	Main Road, Melton HU14 3HG	A63	(0482) 631210	4USD	GAE
19	366011	SCUNTHORPE	Brumby — Shell	Ashby Road DN16 2AQ	A159	(0724) 861192	4USD	GAE
20	366013	SCUNTHORPE	Roxby Road Garage	Roxby Road, Winterton DN15 9SX	A1077	(0724) 732260	4UD	GAE
21	366231	SCUNTHORPE	Grange Self Serve	Grange Lane South DN16 3BJ		(0724) 843968	4UD	GAE
22	366295	SCUNTHORPE	Westcliffe Self Serve	Burringham Cross Roads DN17 2BJ	B1450	(0724) 861229	4USD	GAE
23	534299	WILLERBY	Willerby — Shell	Beverley Road HU10 6AN		(0482) 657673	4USD	GAE

ISLE OF MAN

Loc. Ref.	Shell Ref.	TOWN	NAME	ADDRESS	Road No.	Tel. No.	Fuel	Cards
1	008713	BALLASALLA	Ballasalla Airport Garage			(0624) 822126	4UD	GAE
2	455020	BALLASALLA	Whitestone Garage	Douglas Road		(0624) 822884	4UD	GAE
3	629808	CASTLETOWN	Station Garage	Victoria Road		(0624) 823211	4UD	GAE
4	775702	CASTLETOWN	Airport Garage	Douglas Road		(0624) 822421	4UD	GAE
5	456706	COLBY	Colby Pump	Main Road		(0624) 833201	4UD	GAE
6	453303	DOUGLAS	Athol Garage	Hill Street		(0624) 674428	4UD	GAE
7	454104	DOUGLAS	E.B. Christians Bridge Garage			(0624) 673211	4UD	GAE
8	455602	DOUGLAS	Brown Bobby	Peel Road		(0624) 673342	4UD	GAE
9	769808	DOUGLAS	Bray Hill Filling Station	Bray Hill		(0624) 621181	4UD	GAE
10	459712	LAXEY	Fairy Filling Station	Pinfold Hill		(0624) 861541	4UD	GAE
11	778508	ONCHAN	Corkills Garage	Main Road		(0624) 611311	4UD	GAE
12	455215	PEEL	Market Garage	Athol Street		(0624) 842692	4UD	GAE
13	454306	PORT ERIN	Darnills	Station Road		(0624) 832247	4UD	GAE
14	455804	RAMSEY	Ray Motors	Parliament Square		(0624) 813000	4UD	GAE
15	778509	RAMSEY	Corner Filling Station	Waterloo Road		(0624) 813000	4UD	GAE

Loc. Ref.	Shell Ref.	TOWN	NAME	ADDRESS	Road No.	Tel. No.	Fuel	Cards
16	585426	UNION MILLS	Union Mills Garage	Main Road		(0624) 851240	4UD	GAE

ISLE OF WIGHT

Loc. Ref.	Shell Ref.	TOWN	NAME	ADDRESS	Road No.	Tel. No.	Fuel	Cards
1	999613	BEMBRIDGE	Hodge & Childs Ltd	Church Road PO35 5NA	B3395	(0983) 872121	4USD	A
2	999614	COWES	Northwood Garage	Newport Road PO31 8PG	A3020	(0983) 296031	4UD	GAE
3	999623	EAST COWES	York Avenue Garage	York Avenue PO32 6PH	A3021	(0983) 299205	4UD	GAE
4	999618	NEWPORT	Shalfleet Garage Co Ltd	Winchester Corner, Shalfleet PO30 4ND	A3054	(0983) 78307	4USD	GAE
5	999620	NEWPORT	Hale Common Filling Station	Hale Common, Arreton PO30 3AR	A3056	(0983) 865304	4UD	GAE
6	999619	RYDE	Staddlestones Garage	Ashey Road PO33 4BB		(0983) 62705	4UD	GAE
7	999622	RYDE	Wight Motors (Ryde) Ltd	Garfield Road PO33 2PR	A3054	(0983) 62281	4U	
8	999611	SANDOWN	Bartlett's Service Station	High Street, Newchurch PO36 0NF		(0983) 865338	4UD	GAE
9	999612	SANDOWN	Halfway Service Station	Green Lane PO36 9NL		(0983) 402441	4UD	GAE
10	302595	VENTNOR	Sandford Garage	Sandford PO38 3AL	A3020	(0983) 840211	4UD	GAE
11	999617	VENTNOR	Seamans Garage	Newport Road, Niton PO38 2DF		(0983) 730222	4UD	GAE
12	999621	VENTNOR	Victoria Street F/Stn	Victoria Street PO38 1ET	A3055	(0983) 852650	4UD	GAE
13	999632	VENTNOR	Rookley Autopoint	Main Road, Rookley PO38 3NG	A3020	(0983) 721045	4USD	GAE

KENT

Loc. Ref.	Shell Ref.	TOWN	NAME	ADDRESS	Road No.	Tel. No.	Fuel	Cards
1	308118	ASHFORD	Hilltop Garage	Canterbury Road, Charing TN27 0NL	A252	(0233) 713711	4UD	GAE
2	308317	ASHFORD	Ashford Self Serve	35 North Street TN24 8LQ	A292	(0233) 623152	4USD	GAE
3	308322	ASHFORD	Fairways Self Serve	Tutt Hill, Hothfield TN26 1AP	A20	(0233) 712234	4USD	GAE
4	308330	ASHFORD	Taylors Garage	Bridge Street, Wye TN25 5DS		(0233) 812331	4U	
5	302516	CANTERBURY	Ash Motor Company	Sandwich Road, Ash CT3 2AF	A257	(0304) 812627	4UD	GAE
6	308335	CANTERBURY	Arter Brothers	Folkestone Road, Barham CT4 6EX	A260	(0227) 831356	4UD	GAE
7	308340	CANTERBURY	Canterbury Motor Co Ltd	The Pavilion, Rhodaus Town CT1 2RH	A28	(0227) 780075	4USD	GAE
8	543046	CANTERBURY	Chilham Service Station	A28 Canterbury Road, Chilham CT4 8OZ	A28	(0227) 730116	4UD	GAE
9	302426	CHATHAM	Sherlodge Garage (Lordswood)	600 Lords Wood Lane, Lordswood ME5 8NJ		(0634) 861723	4USD	GAE
10	385833	CHATHAM	Magpie Service Centre	Magpie Hall Road ME4 5KJ		(0634) 813468	4UD	GAE
11	302595	DARTFORD	Hawley Self Serve	Hawley Road DA1 1PU	A225	(0322) 223101	4USD	GAE
12	308369	DEAL	Mill Service Station	Dover Road, Walmer CT14 8HB	A258	(0304) 372273	4UD	GAE
13	302460	DOVER	Western Docks Service Station	Snargate Street CT17 9BZ	A20	(0304) 203543	4USD	GAE
14	308058	DOVER	Priory — Shell	Folkestone Road CT17 9RU	A20	(0304) 214747	4USD	GAE
15	308381	EDENBRIDGE	Edenbridge — Shell	Mill Hill TN8 5DQ	B2026	(0732) 867767	4USD	GAE
16	308327	FAVERSHAM	Macknade — Shell	Canterbury Road ME13 8XA	A2	(0795) 530062	4USD	GAE
17	308336	FAVERSHAM	Lychgate — Shell	Thanet Way ME13 9EL	A299	(0227) 750595	4USD	GAE
18	308511	FAVERSHAM	Thanet Way — Shell	Thanet Way ME13 9EL	A299	(0227) 771147	4USD	GAE
19	308363	FOLKESTONE	Radnor Garage	Canterbury Road, Hawkinge CT18 7BN	A260	(0303) 892212	4USD	GAE
20	302192	GILLINGHAM	Auto Yachts Ltd	171 Pier Road ME7 1UA	B2004	(0634) 281333	4UD	GAE
21	302372	GILLINGHAM	Twydall Service Station	Goudhurst Road, Twydall ME8 6LQ		(0634) 231449	4UD	GAE
22	302551	GILLINGHAM	Rainham Mark — Shell	16 London Road, Rainham Mark ME8 6YX	A2	(0634) 230379	4USD	GAE
23	308343	GILLINGHAM	Park Self Serve	246-254 Nelson Road ME7 4NA		(0634) 854301	4USD	GAE
24	308329	GILLINGHAM	Sherlodge S/Stn — Shell	Hoath Lane, Wigmore ME8 0SW		(0634) 374444	4USD	GAE
25	302369	GRAVESEND	City Chalk (32)	Rochester Road, Chalk DA12 4TN	A226	(0474) 361030	4USD	GAE
26	308409	HAWKHURST	TG Waters, Four Throws Garage	Four Throws TN18 5ED	A268	(0580) 752399	4UD	GAE
27	308377	HYTHE	Caffyns Plc (Hythe)	East Street CT21 5ND	A259	(0303) 269335	4USD	GAE
28	308323	MAIDSTONE	Detling — Shell	Detling Hill Detling ME14 3HT	A249	(0622) 37690	4USD	GAE
29	308325	MAIDSTONE	Highland — Shell	Detling Hill, Detling ME14 3HT	A249	(0622) 39749	4USD	GAE
30	308392	MAIDSTONE	Cossington — Shell	Bluebell Hill, Aylesford ME20 7EZ	A229	(0634) 201281	4USD	GAE
31	308393	MAIDSTONE	Aylesford Motors	Forstal Road, Aylesford ME20 7AD		(0622) 718143	4UD	GAE
32	308395	MAIDSTONE	City Sandling Road	Sandling Road ME14 2RL		(0622) 758482	4USD	GAE
33	308397	MAIDSTONE	City Offham — Shell	London Road A20, West Malling ME19 6RB	A20	(0732) 842103	4USD	GAE
34	308347	MAIDSTONE	Tamarisk — Shell	Linton Road, Loose ME15 0AT	A229	(0622) 743864	4USD	GAE
35	308441	NEW ROMNEY	New Romney — Shell	High Street TN28 8AZ	A259	(0679) 66246	4USD	GAE
36	308106	NORTHFLEET	Northfleet — Shell	Eagle Way, Stonebridge Road DA11 9BJ	A226	(0474) 536364	4USD	GAE
37	308460	RAINHAM	Farthing Corner East Bound	M2 Motorway Service Area, Farthing Corner ME8 8PQ	M2	(0634) 377814	4USD	GAE
38	308461	RAINHAM	Farthing Corner West Bound	M2 Motorway Service Area, Farthing Corner ME8 8PQ	M2	(0634) 377814	4USD	GAE
39	308339	RAMSGATE	Royal Oak F/Stn	Canterbury Road East CT11 0LB	A253	(0843) 593035	4USD	GAE
40	302194	ROCHESTER	F.R. Bradford Ltd	Main Road, Hoo ME3 9AA		(0634) 250000	4UD	GAE
41	302198	ROCHESTER	Rochester — Shell	Watling Street, Strood ME2 3QL	A2	(0634) 721070	4USD	GAE
42	302200	ROCHESTER	City Way Self Serve	342 City Way ME1 2BJ	A229	(0634) 840990	4USD	GAE
43	308387	SEVENOAKS	Tubs Hill — Shell	London Road TN13 2JE	A224	(0732) 460562	4USD	GAE
44	308457	SEVENOAKS	City Seal — Shell	128 Seal Road TN14 5AY	A25	(0732) 743225	4USD	GAE
45	383576	SHEERNESS	Sheerness Self Serve	High Street ME12 1UX	A250	(0795) 580046	4USD	GAE
46	302195	SITTINGBOURNE	Swale Motors Limited	18 Canterbury Road ME10 4SD	A2	(0795) 470711	4UD	GAE
47	308318	SITTINGBOURNE	Ferrell & Baker Ltd	London Road, Teynham ME9 9QA	A2	(0795) 521286	4USD	GAE
48	383120	SITTINGBOURNE	Gleneagles Self Serve	Maidstone Road, Danaway ME9 7PT	A249	(0795) 842236	4USD	GAE
49	302193	SNODLAND	Ham Hill — Shell	Malling Road, Ham Hill ME6 5LB	A228	(0634) 242940	4USD	GAE
50	386551	SUTTON VALENCE	Braemar Service Stn	Headcorn Road, Hendon ME15 8BQ	A274	(0622) 843917	4UD	GAE
51	308423	TENTERDEN	Woodlands F/Stn & Cafe	Tenterden Road, Biddenden TN27 8BS	A262	(0580) 291473	4USD	GAE
52	308384	TONBRIDGE	Albion Garage	Albion Road, Marden TN12 9EA		(0622) 831278	4USD	GAE
53	308385	TONBRIDGE	City Tonbridge	54 Quarry Hill Road TN9 2SA	A26	(0732) 358547	4UD	GAE
54	308415	TONBRIDGE	Fairthorne Garage	Castle Hill TN12 7BP	A21	(0892) 822441	4UD	GAE

Loc. Ref.	Shell Ref.	TOWN	NAME	ADDRESS	Road No.	Tel. No.	Fuel	Cards	24 hour	HGV	Select	Car Wash
55	308444	TONBRIDGE	Shipbourne – Shell	Shipbourne Road TN10 3ED	A227	(0732) 367122	4USD	GAE			■	
56	302522	TUNBRIDGE WELLS	St Johns – Shell	37 St Johns Road TN4 9TP	A26	(0892) 511254	4USD	GAE				
57	308417	TUNBRIDGE WELLS	Southborough Self Serve	79 London Road, Southborough TN4 0NH	A26	(0892) 531688	4USD	GAE				■
58	308419	TUNBRIDGE WELLS	Spa Garage	Langton Road TN4 8XN	A264	(0892) 539466	4U	GAE				

LANCASHIRE

Loc. Ref.	Shell Ref.	TOWN	NAME	ADDRESS	Road No.	Tel. No.	Fuel	Cards	24 hour	HGV	Select	Car Wash
1	357499	ACCRINGTON	Rising Bridge – Shell	Blackburn Road, Rising Bridge BB5 2SB	A680	(0706) 218266	4USD	GAE				
2	358437	BACUP	R & G Matthews (Matthews Hge)	Rochdale Road OL13 9SE	A671	(0706) 873358	4UD	GAE				
3	537408	BARNOLDSWICK	Kelbrook Road S/Stn	Kelbrook Road BB8 5BX	B6383	(0282) 850144	4USD	GAE				
4	273818	BLACKBURN	Woodfield Garage	A&S Thomas, Clayton-Le-Dale BB2 7JA	A59	(0254) 812406	4UD	GAE				
5	357747	BLACKBURN	Jan's Self Serve	Accrington Road BB1 2AB	A679	(0254) 260581	4USD	GAE				■
6	358405	BLACKBURN	Devaspeed Ltd	Preston Old Road, Feniscowles BB2 5HZ	A674	(0254) 202324	4USD	GAE				
7	358711	BLACKBURN	Skewbridge Self Serve	Whalley New Road BB1 9SR	A666	(0254) 51844	4USD	GAE				■
8	434334	BLACKBURN	Naz Self Serve	Shadsworth Road BB1 2HS	B6130	(0254) 693484	4USD	GAE				■
9	278144	BLACKPOOL	Carleton Cross Roads Garages	2 Fleetwood Road, Poulton-Le-Fylde FY6 7NL	B5267	(0253) 899735	4USD	GAE				
10	357487	BLACKPOOL	Normid Blackpool	Cherry Tree Road FY4 4NS		(0253) 766384	4USD	GAE				
11	358389	BLACKPOOL	Blackpool – Shell	Preston Road FY3 9TN	A583	(0253) 791877	4USD	GAE				■
12	358391	BLACKPOOL	John Brimelows Garage	Hardhorn Road, Poulton-Le-Fylde FY6 7SS	B5269	(0253) 883525	4UD	GAE				
13	358393	BLACKPOOL	Singleton Cross Roads	Little Singleton FY6 8LX	A585	(0253) 882914	4UD	GAE				
14	358395	BLACKPOOL	Parkway Serve	Park Road FY3 9LA		(0253) 763333	4UD	GAE				
15	358399	BLACKPOOL	Woodheads GGES (Blackpool) Ltd	Squires Gate Lane FY4 1QP	B5262	(0253) 45544	4USD	GAE				
16	358402	BLACKPOOL	Blackpool North – Shell	Talbot Road FY1 3QX	A586	(0253) 294994	4USD	GAE				
17	357431	BURNLEY	Parkhill Petropoint	Padiham Road BB12 6TG	A671	(0282) 423892	4USD	GAE				
18	358429	BURNLEY	Colne Road Self Serve	Colne Road BB10 1EZ	A682	(0282) 839694	4USD	GAE				■
19	358346	CARNFORTH	Norjack Ltd	Scotland Road LA5 9JZ	A6	(0524) 732208	4UD	GAE				
20	358380	CARNFORTH	Pye Motors Limited	Yealand Conyers LA5 9RJ	A6	(0524) 732460	4UD	GAE				
21	358417	CARNFORTH	Warton Hall Garage	Warton LA5 9NJ		(0524) 732107	4UD	GAE				
22	358245	CHORLEY	Clayton Green Self Serve	Preston Road, Clayton-Le-Woods PR6 7JD	A6	(0772) 38170	4USD	GAE				■
23	358255	CHORLEY	Roemoor Garage (Eccleston) Ltd	Southport Road, Eccleston PR7 6ES	A581	(0257) 451211	4UD	GAE				
24	358258	CHORLEY	Bungalow Filling Station	Moor Road PR7 2NU	B5251	(02572) 62759	4USD	GAE				
25	358720	CHORLEY	Charnock Richard S/Area South	M6 Southbound PR7 5LR	M6	(0257) 791497	4USD	GAE				
26	358722	CHORLEY	Charnock Richard S/Area North	M6 Northbound PR7 5LR	M6	(0257) 791497	4USD	GAE				
27	358431	CLITHEROE	P Harrison & Co Ltd	Sawley Filling Stn, Chatburn	A59	(0200) 441482	4UD	GAE				
28	358432	CLITHEROE	Primrose Garage (Clitheroe)	Whalley Road BB7 1HU	A671	(0200) 23883	4USD	GAE				
29	363769	CLITHEROE	Leedhams Garage	Dunsop Bridge BB7 3BB		(02008) 237	4UD	GAE				
30	357520	DARWEN	T/A Savoy Self Serve	Blackburn Road BB3 1ET	A666	(0254) 705807	4USD	GAE				■
31	358387	FLEETWOOD	Westview – Shell	Hatfield Avenue FY7 7DZ	A587	(0253) 777855	4USD	GAE				■
32	358379	GARSTANG	Red Line Garage	J&K Dobson, Cabus PR3 1NL	A6	(0995) 602521	4USD	GAE				
33	358357	HEYSHAM	Heysham Motor Co Ltd	362 Heysham Road LA3 2BJ	A589	(0254) 51093	4USD	GAE				
34	299453	LANCASTER	Forton South Bound (M6)	M6 Southbound, Bay Horse LA2 9DU	M6	(0524) 791775	D	GAE				
35	299454	LANCASTER	Forton North Bound (M6)	M6 Northbound, Bay Horse LA2 9DU	M6	(0524) 791775	D	GAE				
36	358345	LANCASTER	Caton Road – Shell	Caton Road LA1 3PB	A683	(0524) 846667	4USD	GAE				■
37	358359	LANCASTER	Lunesdale Garage	G Lamb & Son Ltd, Hornby LA2 8JP	A683	(05242) 21219	4UD	GAE				
38	358788	LANCASTER	Pye Motors Ltd	Bulk Road LA1 1DN	A683	(0524) 63553	4UD	GAE				
39	358287	LYTHAM ST ANNES	Heyhouses Service Station	Heyhouses Lane FY8 3RQ	B5261	(0253) 726799	4USD	GAE				
40	358683	LYTHAM ST ANNES	Kiln Self Serve	Blackpool Road North FY8 3DE		(0253) 725750	4USD	GAE				■
41	358343	MORECAMBE	R & E Park (Morecambe) Ltd	431 Lancaster Road LA4 6NB	B532	(0524) 423010	4UD	GAE				
42	358349	MORECAMBE	Broadgate Garage	Middleton Road, Middleton LA3 3JJ		(0524) 52409	4UD	GAE				
43	358355	MORECAMBE	Fahys of Morecambe	Marine Road LA4 4DE	A589	(05242) 410134	4U	GAE				
44	358365	MORECAMBE	Regent Park – Shell	Regent Road LA4 4QY	A589	(0524) 411516	4USD	GAE				■
45	358367	MORECAMBE	Corner Garage – Shell	Thornton Road LA4 5NW	A589	(0524) 421001	4UD	GAE				
46	358885	MORECAMBE	Banbury Garage	Westgate LA3 3PL	B5273	(0524) 831163	4UD	GAE				
47	358270	ORMSKIRK	Dingle Belles	242 Southport Road L39 1LN	A570	(0695) 578432	4USD	GAE				
48	358239	PRESTON	Middleforth Self Serve	138 Leyland Road, Penwortham PR1 9QD	A582	(0772) 749941	4USD	GAE				
49	358243	PRESTON	Broadfield Garage	133 Leyland Lane, Leyland PR5 3HE	B5253	(0772) 422252	4USD	GAE				
50	358250	PRESTON	Howick Cross Self Serve	Liverpool Road, Penwortham PR1 0LY	A59	(0772) 749454	4USD	GAE				■
51	358254	PRESTON	Leyland – Shell	Wigan Road, Leyland PR5 2UD	A49	(0772) 421546	4USD	GAE				■
52	358266	PRESTON	Tarleton Service Station	Hesketh Lane, Tarleton PR4 6UD		(0772) 812358	4UD	GAE				
53	358285	PRESTON	Stonebridge Garage	Kestor Lane, Longridge PR3 3AE	B5269	(0772) 783298	4USD	GAE				
54	358291	PRESTON	Kinders Service Station	506-508 Garstang Road, Broughton PR3 5HE	A6	(0772) 863922	4USD	GAE				
55	358293	PRESTON	Leagate Self Serve	Blackpool Road, Leagate PR4 0XB	A583	(0772) 732321	4UD	GAE				■
56	358299	PRESTON	Station Road Garage	HA & J Armstrong, Kirkham PR4 2AS	B5259	(0772) 683239	4UD	GAE				
57	358301	PRESTON	Withy Trees Self Serve	Garstang Road, Fulwood PR2 3EB	A6	(0772) 749941	4USD	GAE				■
58	358351	PRESTON	Wyreside F/Stn	Garstang Road, St Michaels PR3 0TD	A586	(0995) 8631	4UD	GAE				
59	358363	PRESTON	New Holly Garage	Forton PR3 0BL	A6	(0524) 791424	4UD	GAE				
60	358385	PRESTON	Head Dyke Garage	Head Dyke Lane, Pilling PR3 6SD	A588	(0253) 790244	4UD	GAE				
61	358423	PRESTON	Windmill Garage	Preston New Road, Samlesbury BB2 7PU	A677	(0254) 812803	4USD	GAE				
62	393354	PRESTON	Westholme Garage	Fleetwood Road, Greenhalgh PR4 3HE	A585	(0253) 836321	4USD	GAE				
63	383709	ROSSENDALE	West End – Shell	Haslingden Road, Rawtenstall BB4 6QX	A682	(0706) 221192	4USD	GAE				■
64	358157	SKELMERSDALE	Whitemoss – Shell	Grimshaw Road WN8 8BL	B5312	061-773 5203	4USD	GAE				
65	358283	SKELMERSDALE	Old Town Self Serve	167 Blaguegate Lane WN8 8TY	A577	(0695) 22127	4USD	GAE				

LEICESTERSHIRE

Loc. Ref.	Shell Ref.	TOWN	NAME	ADDRESS	Road No.	Tel. No.	Fuel	Cards
1	355291	BLABY	Sunset Garage	Lutterworth Road LE8 3DX	A426	(0533) 771927	4USD	GAE
2	355293	BROUGHTON ASTLEY	Sutton Elms – Shell	Coventry Road LE9 6QD	B4114	(0455) 285545	4USD	GAE
3	355289	CROFT	Mayes Garage	Coventry Road LE9 6GP	B4114	(0455) 282213	4USD	GAE
4	355593	HINCKLEY	Hinckley – Shell	Burbage Road LE10 2TP	A5070	(0455) 610085	4USD	GAE
5	355285	KIBWORTH	Kibworth Service Station	Harborough Road LE8 ORB	A6	(0533) 792245	4UD	GAE
6	353324	LEICESTER	Meridian – Shell	Lubbesthorpe Way LE3 9XX	A563	(0533) 630023	4USD	GAE
7	353326	LEICESTER	Osiers – Shell	Lubbesthorpe Way LE3 2XD	A563	(0533) 630023	4USD	GAE
8	355295	LEICESTER	By Pass – Shell	Glen Road, Oadby LE2 4PE	A6	(0533) 713373	4USD	GAE
9	355416	LEICESTER	Branting Hill – Shell	Groby Road, Glenfield LE3 8GJ	A50	(0533) 311353	4USD	GAE
10	355427	LEICESTER	Spencefield Filling Station	Downing Drive, Evington LE5 6PD	B667	(0533) 419062	4UD	GAE
11	355428	LEICESTER	Castle Motor Co	Stoneygate Road, Castle Stoneygate LE2 2AF		(0533) 700521	4UD	GAE
12	355565	LEICESTER	Aberdale Road Self Serve	Aberdale Road LE2 6GB	A563	(0533) 884346	4UD	GAE
13	355584	LEICESTER	London Road	London Road, Oadby LE2 5DL	A6	(0533) 707058	4USD	GAE
14	355626	LEICESTER	Leicester Forest East S/Bound	M1 MWSA Southbound, Leicester Forest East LE3 3GB	M1	(0533) 386801	D	GAE
15	355628	LEICESTER	Leicester Forest East N/Bound	M1 MWSA (Northbound), Leicester Forest East LE3 3GB	M1	(0533) 386801	D	GAE
16	355643	LEICESTER	Conquest – Shell	Parker Drive LE4 0JF		(0533) 353505	4USD	GAE
17	355769	LEICESTER	Trocadero Self Serve	Uppingham Road LE5 2BE	A47	(0533) 769064	4USD	GAE
18	384293	LEICESTER	Hamilton – Shell	Thurmaston Lane LE5 0TE	A563	(0533) 461366	4USD	GAE
19	535322	LEICESTER	Abbey Lane Service Station	308 Abbey Lane LE4 2AB	A5131	(0533) 661900	4UD	GAE
20	353095	LOUGHBOROUGH	Epinal Way Self Serve	Epinal Way LE11 0QE	A6004	(0509) 214771	4USD	GAE
21	355554	LOUGHBOROUGH	Temple – Shell	Ashby Road LE11 3QU	A512	(0509) 232371	4USD	GAE
22	355344	LUTTERWORTH	Wycliffe Garage	Bitteswell Road LE17 4EZ	B577	(0455) 552177	4U	GAE
23	355634	LUTTERWORTH	St Marys Filling Station	Market Street LE17 4NE	A426	(0455) 552581	4USD	GAE
24	355407	MOUNTSORREL	Hill Top Garage	Leicester Road LE12 7DF		(0533) 302205	4UD	GAE
25	355339	NORTH KILWORTH	F Howkins & Son	Harborough Road LE17 6EP	A427	(0858) 880208	4USD	GAE
26	355409	OAKHAM	Adams & Sons Ltd	Morcott LE15 9DL	A47	(0572) 87215	4USD	GAE
27	355770	OAKHAM	Morcott S/Stn	Glaston Road, Morcott LE15 9DL	A47	(0572) 87663	4USD	GAE
28	355425	SYSTON	Syston Self Serve	1143 Melton Road LE7 8JS		(0533) 640950	4USD	GAE

LINCOLNSHIRE

Loc. Ref.	Shell Ref.	TOWN	NAME	ADDRESS	Road No.	Tel. No.	Fuel	Cards
1	357852	BOSTON	De Rodes Self Serve	East Heckington PE20 3QF	A17	(0205) 820307	4USD	GAE
2	362714	BOSTON	Mayflower Service Stn	London Road PE21 7HB	A16	(0205) 61177	4USD	GAE
3	363703	BOSTON	Boston – Shell	Sleaford Road PE21 8EH	A52	(0205) 359719	4USD	GAE
4	363708	BOSTON	Four Winds S/Stn	East Heckington PE20 3QF	A17	(0205) 820600	4USD	GAE
5	362184	GRANTHAM	Ancaster Road S/Stn	Willoughby Road, Ancaster NG32 3RT	A153	(0400) 30238	4UD	GAE
6	363372	GRANTHAM	Grantham – Shell	Brook Street NG31 6RU	A607	(0476) 64241	4USD	GAE
7	363376	GRANTHAM	The Garage Barkston	A607 Main Road, Barkston NG32 2NG	A607	(0400) 50488	4UD	GAE
8	366027	HORNCASTLE	The Laurels Service Station	Spilsby Road LN9 6NH	A158	(0507) 522533	4UD	GAE
9	366016	LINCOLN	Lincoln – Shell	Burton Road LN1 3ND	B1398	(0522) 546468	4USD	GAE
10	366337	LINCOLN	Hartford Motors (Lincs) Ltd	186 Wragby Road LN2 4PU	A158	(0522) 530101	4USD	GAE

LOTHIAN

Loc. Ref.	Shell Ref.	TOWN	NAME	ADDRESS	Road No.	Tel. No.	Fuel	Cards
1	380656	BATHGATE	Meadowpark Self Serve	13 Glasgow Road EH48 2AB	A89	(0506) 52281	4USD	GAE
2	380706	BONNYRIGG	J F Peden Ltd	Midfield Garage, 67-73 Polton Street EH19 3DQ	A6094	031-663 9191	4UD	GAE
3	376181	BROXBURN	Lex Rover Broxburn	West Main Street, Uphall EH52 5DW	A899	(0506) 853333	4UD	GAE
4	380709	DALKEITH	WM Stewart (Motors) Ltd	Newmills Road EH22 1DU	A6B	031-663 2272	4USD	GAE
5	380713	DANDERHALL	Danderhall Self Serve	Maulsford Avenue EH22 1PJ	A7	031-663 4054	4USD	GAE
6	381057	DUNBAR	Rigg Service Station	Edinburgh Road EH42 1DE	A1087	(0368) 62306	4UD	GAE
7	529396	EAST CALDER	GMC Sales (Ltd)	Unit 1, Calder Drive EH53 0ET	B7015	(0506) 880991	4UD	GAE
8	398092	EAST LINTON	Torness Motors	Dunbar Road EH40 3DE	A1	(0620) 860535	4USD	GAE
9	276346	EDINBURGH	Easter Road Service Station	372 Easter Road EH6 8JP		031-553 7299	4UD	GAE
10	299988	EDINBURGH	Dreghorn – Shell	Dreghorn Junction, City Bypass EH13 9QR	A720	031-441 6889	4USD	GAE
11	376162	EDINBURGH	Westfield Self Serve	Westfield Road EH11 2QT		031-346 2001	4USD	GAE
12	380661	EDINBURGH	Bowmac T.C. – Shell	19/21 Glasgow Road EH12 8HH	A8	031-334 4623	4USD	GAE
13	380664	EDINBURGH	Brandon Service Station	Buckstone Terrace EH10 6QQ	A702	031-445 4711	4USD	GAE
14	380666	EDINBURGH	Carrick Self Serve	Downie Terrace EH12 7AU	A8	031-334 3476	4USD	GAE
15	380668	EDINBURGH	Maybury – Shell	166 Glasgow Road EH12 8LS	A8	031-339 1867	4USD	GAE
16	380670	EDINBURGH	Circle – Shell	Crewe Toll EH4 2NT	A902	031-332 4372	4USD	GAE
17	380674	EDINBURGH	Inglis Green Self Serve	Inglis Green Road EH14 2ER		031-443 4497	4USD	GAE
18	380661	EDINBURGH	Leith Walk Self Serve	35-40 Haddington Place EH7 4AG		031-556 0141	4UD	GAE
19	380683	EDINBURGH	Maidencraig Garage Ltd	192 Queensferry Road EH4 2BN	A90	031-332 3636	4UD	GAE
20	380685	EDINBURGH	Abbeymount Self Serve	Montrose Terrace EH7 5DJ	A1	031-661 5593	4USD	GAE

Facilities

Loc. Ref.	Shell Ref.	TOWN	NAME	ADDRESS	Road No.	Tel. No.	Fuel	Cards
21	380686	EDINBURGH	Arnold Clark Autos	Lochrin Place, Tollcross EH3 9QW		031-229 8911	4UD	GAE
22	380696	EDINBURGH	Stenhouse – Shell	1 Stenhouse Road EH11 3LW	A71	031-455 7936	4USD	GAE
23	381021	EDINBURGH	Cragsview Self Serve	18 Gilmerton Road EH16 5UA	A7	031-664 2928	4UD	GAE
24	381211	EDINBURGH	Westerhailes Self Serve	50 Murrayburn Road EH14 2SN	B701	031-442 4194	4UD	GAE
25	380698	GOREBRIDGE	Newtonloan – Shell	Newtonloan Toll EH23 4LZ	A7	(0875) 22605	4USD	GAE
26	380954	GULLANE	Gullane Service Station	Main Street EH31 2AS	A198	(0620) 842243	4UD	GAE
27	380708	HADDINGTON	Ideal Garage	Hardgate EH41 3JN		(0620) 823287	4USD	GAE
28	381192	LIVINGSTON	Livingston Main – Shell	Howden West EH54 6AA		(0506) 414191	4USD	GAE
29	380702	MUSSELBURGH	Fisherrow – Shell	Edinburgh Road EH21 6DN	A199	031-665 3256	4UD	GAE
30	380652	NEWBRIDGE RATHO	Newbridge Self Serve	11 Edinburgh Road EH28 8SP	A89	031-333 3554	4UD	GAE
31	380700	PENICUIK	Angle Park Garage	128 John Street EH26 8NG	A703	(0968) 672947	4UD	GAE
32	380704	PENICUIK	AF Noble & Son	Milton Bridge Garage, Milton Bridge EH26 0NX	A703	(0968) 674482	4USD	GAE
33	377617	TRANENT	Co-Op Superstore F/Stn	High Street EH33 1LP	A199	(0875) 612127	4USD	GAE
34	380889	WEST CALDER	Polbeth Service Station	Chapelton EH55 8SD	A71	(0506) 872824	4USD	GAE

MERSEYSIDE

Loc. Ref.	Shell Ref.	TOWN	NAME	ADDRESS	Road No.	Tel. No.	Fuel	Cards
1	358540	BIRKENHEAD	Newhall Self Serve	1062 New Chester Road L42 2AD	A41	051-327 1426	4USD	GAE
2	358560	BIRKENHEAD	Wirralway Self Serve	413 Borough Road L42 0HA	A552	051-652 1921	4USD	GAE
3	358779	BIRKENHEAD	Hamilton Filling Station	Cleveland Street L41 3QB	A552	051-647 6493	4UD	GAE
4	358209	BOOTLE	Ryders Autoservices	215 Knowsley Road L20 4NW	A566	051-922 7585	4UD	GAE
5	398395	BOOTLE	Derby Road – Shell	100 Derby Road L20 1BP	A565	051-944 1813	4USD	GAE
6	358553	GAYTON	Gayton – Shell	Chester Road L60 3RY	A540	051-342 8495	4USD	GAE
7	358619	HESWALL	Quarry Service Station	Telegraph Road L60 6RN	A540	051-342 1660	4U	
8	357745	LIVERPOOL	Walton Village Motor Co	1-11 Haggerston Road, Walton L4 6TT	A580	051-525 7837	4UD	GAE
9	358181	LIVERPOOL	Rainhill Motors	Warrington Road, Rainhill L35 6PF	A57	051-426 4199	4UD	AE
10	358189	LIVERPOOL	East Lancs S/Stn	East Lancashire Road, Kirby L32 7QZ	A580	051-546 0580	4UD	GAE
11	358193	LIVERPOOL	Ince Blundell Self Serve	Formby by Pass, Hightown L38 1QA	A565	051-929 2706	4UD	GAE
12	358195	LIVERPOOL	Maghull Self Serve	Northway, Maghull L31 2HA	A59	051-526 3585	4USD	GAE
13	358197	LIVERPOOL	Sefton Self Serve	Hawthorne Road, Litherland L21 7PJ	A503	051-928 2724	4UD	GAE
14	358207	LIVERPOOL	Red Lion Garage	Liverpool Road North, Maghull L31 2HN	A5147	051-531 9087	4UD	GAE
15	358212	LIVERPOOL	Fazakerley STC	Longmoor Lane, Fazakerley L10 1LF	A506	051-530 1764	4USD	GAE
16	358214	LIVERPOOL	Park Self Serve	211 Rice Lane L9 1AQ	A59	051-525 6601	4UD	GAE
17	358215	LIVERPOOL	Cresent Service Station	Liverpool Road, Huyton L36 3RN	A57	051-480 4925	4USD	GAE
18	358217	LIVERPOOL	East Prescot Rd S/Stn	288/294 East Prescot Road L14 7NH	A57	051-228 3212	4UD	GAE
19	358219	LIVERPOOL	J A Fisher & Son Ltd	241 Woolton Road, Wavertree L16 8NA		051-722 1630	4UD	GAE
20	358229	LIVERPOOL	Hunts Cross STC	Hillfoot Avenue, Hunts Cross L26 1TA	A562	051-448 1015	4UD	GAE
21	358675	LIVERPOOL	St James Service Station	131-143 St James Street L1 5HA	A561	051-709 0520	4UD	GAE
22	358719	LIVERPOOL	Wheatlands Self Serve	Wheathill Road, Huyton L36 5US		051-487 3074	4UD	GAE
23	358725	LIVERPOOL	Rainhill STC	Warrington Road, Rainhill L35 9JB	A57	051-426 5887	4USD	GAE
24	358763	LIVERPOOL	Waterloo Service Station	Crosby Road, North L22 0LA	A565	051-928 6419	4USD	GAE
25	358772	LIVERPOOL	Mount Garage	The Mount, Melling L31 1AR	A506	051-546 5100	4USD	GAE
26	358858	LIVERPOOL	Childwall Self Serve	44/48 Queens Drive, Childwall L15 7NE	A5058	051-722 4011	4U	
27	358949	LIVERPOOL	Yew Tree Self Serve	Princess Drive L12 6QE		051-228 0634	4UD	GAE
28	882211	LIVERPOOL	Asda – Walton	Utting Avenue, Walton L4 9XU	A5058	051-256 7276	4USD	
29	882212	LIVERPOOL	Sainsburys – Knotty Ash	East Prescot Road, Knotty Ash L14 5PT	A57	051-252 0703		
30	882213	LIVERPOOL	Asda – Aintree	Ormskirk Road, Aintree L10 3LN		051-531 7778	4USD	
31	882214	LIVERPOOL	Asda – Hunts Cross	Speke Hall Road, Hunts Cross L24 9WF	A562	051-486 8010	4UD	
32	358170	NEWTON-LE-WILLOWS	Haydock Island – Shell	East Lancashire Road WA12 0HL	A580	(0925) 224241	4USD	GAE
33	357769	SOUTHPORT	Southport STC	3A Scarisbrick New Road PR8 5HN	A570	(0704) 536378	4USD	GAE
34	358279	SOUTHPORT	Reliance Self Serve	555 Liverpool Road, Ainsdale PR8 3BJ	A565	(0704) 74553	4USD	GAE
35	357762	ST HELENS	Caldo West End Road	West End Road WA11 0WL	A58	(0744) 30300	4UD	GAE
36	358188	ST HELENS	Central Garage	Ormskirk Road, Rainford WA11 8DD	B5203	(0744) 883454	4USD	GAE
37	358632	WALLASEY	Windsors (Wallasey) Ltd	Harrison Drive L45 3HP	A554	051-639 6181	4UD	GAE
38	358175	WIGAN	Billinge – Shell	Main Street, Billinge WN5 7PB	A571	(0744) 895731	4USD	GAE
39	358536	WIRRAL	Carlett Service Station	1201 New Chester Road, Eastham L62 0BZ	A41	051-327 5511	4USD	GAE
40	358543	WIRRAL	Threeways Garage	Clatterbridge Road L63 4JZ	A5137	051-334 8602	4U	
41	358558	WIRRAL	Upton Self Serve	Arrowe Park Road L49 0UE	A551	051-677 5098	4UD	GAE
42	358628	WIRRAL	Totteys Garage Ltd	Column Road L48 7EA	A540	051-625 6161	4UD	GAE
43	358886	WIRRAL	Arrowbrook Service Station	Arrowe Park Road L49 0UE	A551	051-648 6757	4UD	GAE
44	393877	WIRRAL	Grange Service Station	Hoylake Road, Moreton L46 6DG	A553	051-604 0393	4USD	GAE

MID GLAMORGAN

Loc. Ref.	Shell Ref.	TOWN	NAME	ADDRESS	Road No.	Tel. No.	Fuel	Cards
1	348414	ABERBARGOED	Duffryn Garage	New Road CF8 9BP	A469	(0443) 831959	4USD	GAE
2	348423	ABERDARE	Hirwaun Self Serve	Hirwaun Road, Hirwaun CF44 9HR	A4059	(0685) 811797	4UD	GAE
3	348800	ABERDARE	Golden Acres Self Serve	Park View Terrace, Abercwmboi CF44 6AA	B4275	(0443) 472380	4USD	GAE
4	348417	BLACKWOOD	Sirhowy Self Serve	Commercial Street, Pontllanfraith NP2 2JG	A472	(0495) 223344	4UD	GAE
5	347194	BRIDGEND	Sarn Park MWSA	M4 Motorway CF32 9RW	M4	(0656) 768521	4USD	GAE
6	348716	BRIDGEND	Pencoed Self Serve	11 Coychurch Road, Pencoed CF35 5NH		(0656) 860432	4USD	GAE
7	348719	BRIDGEND	Dunraven Self Serve	Tondu Road CF31 4JA	A4063	(0656) 650228	4USD	GAE
8	348830	BRIDGEND	Tremains Service Station	Tremains Road CF31 1TZ	A4061	(0656) 767950	4USD	GAE
9	348855	BRIDGEND	Porthcawl Road S/Sve	Porthcawl Road, South Cornelly CF33 4RG	A4229	(0656) 740039	4UD	GAE
10	348950	BRIDGEND	Crossing Service Station Ltd	Cemetery Road, Ogmore Vale CF32 7HR	A4061	(0656) 840454	4UD	GAE

Loc. Ref.	Shell Ref.	TOWN	NAME	ADDRESS	Road No.	Tel. No.	Fuel	Cards	24 hour	HGV	Select	Car Wash
11	348394	CAERPHILLY	Caerphilly Garages	Nantgarw Road CF8 1BW	A468	(0222) 861287	4UD	GAE				
12	348825	CAERPHILLY	Commercial Motors Ltd	Graig y Fedw, Abertridwr CF8 2AS	B4263	(0222) 830321	4UD	GAE				
13	348990	CAERPHILLY	Pontygwindy Self Serve	Pontygwindy Road CF8 3AD	A469	(0222) 865609	4UD	GAE				
14	348413	MERTHYR TYDFIL	Merthyr Self Serve	Pentrebach Road CF48 1YA	A470	(0685) 359669	4UD	GAE				
15	348884	MERTHYR TYDFIL	J Matthews & Son	Merthyr Tydfil Ind Estate, Dowlais CF48 2SR	A465	(0685) 384558	4UD	GAE				
16	348397	PENTRE	D G Weaver Motors Ltd	200 Gelli Road CF41 7LU	B4223	(0443) 435136	4UD	GAE				
17	348845	PORTH	Trebanog S/Stn	Trebanog Road CF39 9DT	A4277	(0443) 682109	4UD	GAE				
18	348396	TONYPANDY	Ivor Hael Garage	Salem Terrace CF40 2JJ	A4119	(0443) 432240	4UD	GAE				
19	348815	TONYPANDY	Tonypandy Self Serve	Tylacelyn Road, Penygraig CF40 1JS		(0443) 432397	4USD	GAE				
20	299473	YSTRAD MYNACH	Gwynns Garages Ltd	Caerphilly Road CF8 7XS	A469	(0443) 812112	4UD	GAE				

NORFOLK

Loc. Ref.	Shell Ref.	TOWN	NAME	ADDRESS	Road No.	Tel. No.	Fuel	Cards	24 hour	HGV	Select	Car Wash
1	302819	ATTLEBOROUGH	Besthorpe Filling Station	Attleborough by Pass, Besthorpe NR17 2LD	A11	(0953) 452441	4USD	GAE			•	
2	308480	ATTLEBOROUGH	Attleborough – Shell	A11 By-Pass, Besthorpe NR17 1PU	A11	(0953) 455550	4USD	GAE			•	
3	539228	BLAKENEY	Blakeney Garage	Morston Road NR27 7AY	A149	(0263) 741456	4UD	GAE				
4	357084	BRUNDALL	Manor Garage	The Street NR13 5JY		(0603) 713155	4UD	GAE				
5	357021	BUNGAY	Smiths Garage	Ditchingham NR35 2JQ	B1332	(0986) 892275	4U	GE				
6	432961	CROMER	R & B Autos	Prince of Wales Road NR27 9HA		(0263) 514858	4USD	GAE			•	
7	357075	DEREHAM	Superdrive Motoring Centre Ltd	Cowper Road NR19 2DA	B1135	(0362) 694215	4USD	GAE			•	
8	357026	DISS	Diss – Shell	Victoria Road IP22 3HF	A1066	(0379) 652833	4USD	GAE			•	
9	356880	DOWNHAM MARKET	Broomhill Self Serve	Broomhill PE38 9QY	B1507	(0366) 383579	4UD	GAE				
10	355633	FAKENHAM	Hillside – Shell	Creake Road NR21 9HT	A148	(0328) 855330	4USD	GAE			•	
11	355657	FAKENHAM	Sculthorpe Filling Station	Sculthorpe NR21 9QE	A148	(0328) 851300	4USD	GAE				
12	357071	FAKENHAM	Crossways Filling Station	Little Snoring NR21 0AX	A148	(0328) 878335	4UD	GAE				
13	357066	GREAT YARMOUTH	Jubilee STC	Caister Road NR30 4DL	A149	(0493) 842984	4USD	GAE			•	
14	357107	GREAT YARMOUTH	Orchard Self Serve	High Street, Caister-on-Sea NR30 5EP	A149	(0493) 377661	4UD	GAE				
15	308142	KING'S LYNN	Rainbow Filling Station	Grimston Road, South Wootton PE30 3PD	A148	(0553) 675469	4USD	GAE			•	
16	353040	KING'S LYNN	Gaywood – Shell	1-5 Lynn Road, Gaywood PE30 4PR	A1076	(0553) 763051	4USD	GAE			•	
17	356877	KING'S LYNN	Queensway S/Stn Ltd	Lynn Road (A47), West Bilney PE32 1HW	A47	(0553) 840505	4UD	GAE				
18	356883	KING'S LYNN	Dennis Marshall Ltd	Wisbech Road PE30 5JS		(0553) 771331	4UD	GAE				
19	357032	KING'S LYNN	E.W. English	Lynn Road, Stoke Ferry PE33 9SW	A134	(0366) 500254	4UD	GAE				
20	302711	NORWICH	Coltishall Island Filling Stn	High Street, Coltishall NR12 7DX	B1150	(0603) 737194	4USD	GAE			•	
21	302828	NORWICH	Cromer Road Filling Station	Cromer Road NR6 6NA	A140	(0603) 412390	4USD	GAE			•	
22	357002	NORWICH	Broadland Motor Co Ltd	Norwich Road, Wroxham NR12 8SL	A1151	(0603) 782961	4UD	GAE				
23	357004	NORWICH	Thunder Lane Garage Ltd	Thunder Lane, Thorpe NR7 0PX	B1140	(0603) 33848	4UD	GAE				
24	357009	NORWICH	Hales – Shell	Hales NR14 6SR	A146	(0508) 46288	4USD	GAE			•	
25	357014	NORWICH	Stratton Motor Co (Norfolk)	Ipswich Road, Long Stratton NR15 2XJ	A140	(0508) 30491	4UD	GAE				
26	357017	NORWICH	Harveys Autos (Hethersett) Ltd	Hethersett NR9 4DX		(0603) 810209	4USD	GAE				
27	357081	NORWICH	Ipswich Road – Shell	Ipswich Road NR4 6LA	A140	(0603) 507206	4USD	GAE			•	
28	357086	NORWICH	Rose Lane Filling Station	5-7 Prince of Wales Road NR1 1PN		(0603) 666593	4USD	GAE			•	
29	357090	NORWICH	Highfield Garage	Highfield Works, Swardeston NR14 8DW	B1113	(0508) 70341	4UD	GAE				
30	357092	NORWICH	Arlington Self Serve	84 Unthank Road NR2 2RW		(0603) 622975	4USD	GAE			•	
31	357113	NORWICH	Sweetbriar – Shell	Sweet Briar Road NR6 5AL	A47	(0603) 415952	4UD	GAE				
32	357123	NORWICH	Dereham Road Self Serve	60-62 Dereham Road, New Costessey NR5 0SY	A1074	(0603) 624091	4USD	GAE			•	
33	357130	NORWICH	Plumstead Road – Shell	Plumstead Road NR1 4LT	B1151	(0603) 300047	4UD	GAE				
34	357030	THETFORD	F Dye Ltd	Norwich Road, Watton IP25 6DD	B1108	(0953) 881506	4USD	GAE				
35	357041	THETFORD	Chase Filling Station	Norwich Road IP24 2HT	A1075	(0842) 766593	4USD	GAE				
36	356875	WISBECH	Marshalls of Wisbech Ltd	Norwich Road PE13 2AR	B198	(0945) 584342	4USD	GAE				

NORTH YORKSHIRE

Loc. Ref.	Shell Ref.	TOWN	NAME	ADDRESS	Road No.	Tel. No.	Fuel	Cards	24 hour	HGV	Select	Car Wash
1	365885	AUSTWICK	Harden Bridge Garage	Via Lancaster LA2 8AD	A65	(05242) 51309	4UD	GAE				
2	362230	BEDALE	Motel Leeming Filling Stn	Leeming Bar A1 DL8 1DT	A1	(0677) 422258	4USD	GAE			•	
3	363767	CARNFORTH	Three Peaks Service Station	New Road, Ingleton LA6 3DL	A65	(0527) 241770	4USD	GAE				
4	365955	EASINGWOLD	Easingwold Motors Ltd	Long Street YO6 3HZ	A19	(0347) 21694	4USD	GAE				
5	362204	HARROGATE	Jennyfield Self Serve	Ripon Road HG1 2BS	A61	(0423) 505141	4USD	GAE			•	
6	365858	HARROGATE	C. W. Abbott	The Garage, Dacre Banks HG3 4ED	B6451	(0423) 780293	4UD	GAE				
7	365864	HARROGATE	Oatlands Self Serve	91 Leeds Road HG2 8EY	A61	(0423) 871111	4USD	GAE			•	
8	365882	HARROGATE	High Harrogate Self Serve	Dragon Parade HG1 5DQ	A59	(0423) 522380	4USD	GAE			•	
9	365958	KIRKBYMOORSIDE	Ryedale Garages (1946) Ltd	Piercy End YO6 6DG	A170	(0751) 31434	4UD	GAE				
10	365859	KNARESBOROUGH	Goldsborough Filling Station	York Road HG5 0SS	A59	(0423) 867456	4UD	GAE				
11	357737	LEBBERSTON	Filey – Shell	Stonepit Lane, Book End YO11 3NX	A165	(0723) 581505	4USD	GAE			•	
12	363778	MALTON	Chapman (Norton) Ltd	Beverley Road, Norton YO17 9BU	B1248	(0653) 693303	4USD	GAE				
13	365945	MALTON	Norbury's of Malton Ltd	18 Church Street, Norton YO17 9HD	B1248	(0635) 695151	4UD	GAE				
14	539213	MALTON	Atkin Motor Engineers	Swinton YO17 0SL	B1257	(0653) 693610	4UD	GAE				
15	362264	NORTHALLERTON	Massingberd Group PLC	Massingberd Industrial Estate DL6 2PN	A167	(0609) 771011	4UD	GAE				
16	366168	NORTHALLERTON	Exelby Services Ltd	Londonderry Garage, Leeming Bar DL7 9NB	A1	(0677) 424287	4USD	GAE			•	
17	366170	NORTHALLERTON	Brompton Road Service Station	Brompton Road DL6 1DT	A684	(0609) 777299	4UD	GAE				
18	366182	RICHMOND	High Broom Moor Self Serve	Scotch Corner, Middleton Tyas DL10 6PB	A1	(0748) 850090	4USD	GAE			•	
19	366348	RICHMOND	S G Petch & K Snowdon Ltd	21-23 Victoria Road DL10 4AS	A6108	(0748) 825757	4USD	GAE				
20	363772	SCARBOROUGH	Arundale of Scarborough Ltd	Northway YO12 7AL	A165	(0723) 363533	4USD	GAE				
21	365914	SCARBOROUGH	Staxton Self Serve	Staxton YO12 4SB	A64	(0944) 70285	4USD	GAE			•	
22	398376	SCARBOROUGH	Manor Garage (East Ayton)	13/14 Main Street, East Ayton YO13 9HL	A170	(0723) 863146	4USD	GAE				

129

Loc. Ref.	Shell Ref.	TOWN	NAME	ADDRESS	Road No.	Tel. No.	Fuel	Cards
23	365927	SELBY	Hearthstone Filling Station	Hemingbrough YO8 7QG	A63	(0757) 638673	4UD	GAE
24	365887	SETTLE	Whitefriars Self Serve	9 Church Street BD24 9JD	B6479	(0729) 822995	4UD	GAE
25	363782	SKIPTON	Hambleton Garage	Bolton Abbey BD23 6AF	A59	(0756) 710230	4USD	GAE
26	384290	THIRSK	Busby Stoop Garage	Busby Stoop YO7 4EQ	A61	(0845) 587232	4USD	GAE
27	365954	WHITBY	Arundale of Whitby	Stakesby Garage, Castlepark YO21 3LG	B1460	(0947) 602841	4UD	GAE
28	365923	YORK	Ariel Self Serve	26/30 Hull Road YO1 3LP	A1079	(0904) 413316	4USD	GAE
29	365925	YORK	Trustees of H C F Fawcett	201 Acomb Road YO2 4HD	B1224	(0904) 798321	4USD	GAE
30	530757	YORK	Poppleton Garage	Boroughbridge Road YO2 6QD		(0904) 792651	4USD	GAE

NORTHAMPTONSHIRE

Loc. Ref.	Shell Ref.	TOWN	NAME	ADDRESS	Road No.	Tel. No.	Fuel	Cards
1	355350	BRACKLEY	Pimlico Self Serve	Syresham NN13 5TN	A43	(0280) 850257	4USD	GAE
2	355323	FLORE	P J Green	81 High Street NN7 4LW	A45	(0327) 40287	4USD	GAE
3	355559	HIGHAM FERRERS	Walnut Tree Service Station	North End NN9 8JB	A6	(0933) 56138	4USD	GAE
4	353103	NORTHAMPTON	Grose Eurocar	Boughton Green Road, Moulton Park NN3 1SG	A428	(0604) 494121	4USD	GAE
5	355330	NORTHAMPTON	Westbridge Mtrs (N'ton) Ltd	St James Road NN5 5HS	A508	(0604) 750600	4USD	GAE
6	355749	NORTHAMPTON	Northampton — Shell	London Road, Wootton NN4 0JN	A508	(0604) 761489	4USD	GAE
7	355412	PETERBOROUGH	Francis & Marshall	Benefield Road, Oundle PE8 4EX	A427	(0832) 273519	4UD	GAE
8	353361	RUSHDEN	Hamblins of Rushden	Northampton Road NN10 9AW	A4500	(0933) 53211	4USD	GAE
9	435373	THRAPSTON	Thrapston — Shell	A14 NN14 4UA	A14	(0832) 732952	4USD	GAE
10	353222	TOWCESTER	Paulerspury — Shell	Watling Street NN12 7LQ	A5	(0327) 33554	4USD	GAE
11	355283	WELLINGBOROUGH	Wellingborough — Shell	Finedon Road NN8 4AL	A510	(0933) 226853	4USD	GAE
12	355590	WELLINGBOROUGH	E Ward (Wellingborough) Ltd	Northampton Road NN8 3PP	A510	(0933) 440110	4USD	GAE

NORTHERN IRELAND

Loc. Ref.	Shell Ref.	TOWN	NAME	ADDRESS	Road No.	Tel. No.	Fuel	Cards
1	299448	AHOGHILL	R Gault	187 Largy Road BT42 2RH	B93	(0648) 50532	4USD	GAE
2	373194	ARDGLASS	Ardglass Service Station	5 Downpatrick Road BT30 7SF	A2	(0396) 841314	4UD	GAE
3	373196	ARMAGH	Martin Whittle Filling Station	132 Newry Road BT60 1ES	A28	(0861) 522232	4USD	GAE
4	299677	AUGHNACLOY	Aughnacloy Service Station	Caledon Road BT69 6AA	A28	(066252) 306	4UD	GAE
5	375349	BALLYCLARE	N Watt & Son	Ballynure Road BT39 9AG	B95	(09603) 52500	4USD	GAE
6	375412	BALLYCLARE	Milltown Service Station	91 Templepatrick Road BT39 9RQ		(09603) 52063	4UD	GAE
7	286915	BALLYGOWAN	JH Simpson	175 Moreyrea Road BT23 6BY	A23	(0238) 528337	4UD	
8	375352	BALLYMENA	J Gaston	284 Galgorm Road BT42 1JU	A42	(0266) 871422	4USD	GAE
9	299679	BALLYMONEY	Milltown Road Filling Station	Milltown Road BT53 6LE	B66	(02656) 62105	4UD	GAE
10	373137	BALLYNAHINCH	Mossvale Service Station	105 Belfast Road BT24 8EB	A24	(0234) 563434	4USD	GAE
11	299675	BANBRIDGE	Ballydown Service Station	124 Castlenellan Road BT32 4JF	A50	(08206) 62776	4USD	GAE
12	299451	BANGOR (CO DOWN)	Gransha Filling Station	Gransha Road BT20 4TL		(0247) 270276	4USD	GAE
13	375331	BANGOR (CO DOWN)	Bangor — Shell	139-141 Belfast Road BT20 3PP	A2	(0247) 463610	4USD	GAE
14	373184	BELFAST	Balmoral — Shell	2 Upper Lisburn Road	A1	(0232) 301540	4USD	GAE
15	299680	BELFAST	Connsbrook Filling Station	125-127 Connsbrook Avenue BT4 1JX		(0232) 653000	4UD	
16	373125	BELFAST	Bridge End Travellers Check	35/41 Bridge End BT5 4AA	A2	(0232) 452201	4USD	GAE
17	373133	BELFAST	Victoria Travellers Check	112/114 Gt. Victoria Street BT2 7BG	A1	(0232) 233374	4USD	GAE
18	373172	BELFAST	Cairnshill — Shell	221 Saintfield Road BT8 4HQ	A24	(0232) 401444	4USD	GAE
19	373198	BELFAST	Sinclairs Self Serve	204 Andersonstown Road BT11 9EB		(0232) 613209	4USD	GAE
20	375324	BELFAST	Edenvale Self Serve	226 Castlereagh Road BT5 5FZ	A23	(0232) 790592	4USD	GAE
21	375332	BELFAST	Bellsbridge — Shell	100 Ladas Drive BT6 9EH		(0232) 401131	4USD	GAE
22	375334	BELFAST	La Salle Filling Station	372 Falls Road BT12 6DG		(0232) 323946	4USD	GAE
23	375335	BELFAST	Durham St Filling Station	Durham Street BT12 4GD		(0232) 321490	4USD	GAE
24	375340	BELFAST	Ormeau Self Serve	126 Ormeau Road BT7 2EB		(0232) 234650	4USD	GAE
25	375348	BELFAST	Ballysillan Self Serve	156-158 Ballysillan Road BT14 7QR		(0232) 391249	4USD	GAE
26	375409	BELFAST	Shandon — Shell	211 Knock Road BT5 6QE	A55	(0232) 794571	4USD	GAE
27	375411	BELFAST	Ballyhackamore Self Serve	276 Upper Newtownards Road BT4 3EU	A20	(0232) 654149	4USD	GAE
28	375414	BELFAST	Park Lane Self Serve	136 Stockmans Lane BT9 7JE		(0232) 667842	4USD	GAE
29	380070	BELFAST	Knock — Shell	150 Knock Road BT5 6LH	A55	(0232) 797509	4USD	GAE
30	375396	BELLEEK	Shore Road Filling Station	Roscor BT74	A46	(03656) 58262	4USD	GAE
31	375400	BESSBROOK	Carrick Filling Station	109 Camlough Road BT35 7EE	A25	(0693) 830388	4UD	GAE
32	375392	CABRAGH	Cabragh Filling Station	220 Ballygawley Road BT70 1TD	A4	(08687) 61543	4USD	GAE
33	375363	CAMPSIE	Campsie Filling Station	70 Clooney Road BT47 3PA	A2	(0504) 860345	4UD	GAE
34	373131	CARRICKFERGUS	Gallows Green Self Serve	84-88 Belfast Road BT38 8BT	A2	(09603) 51170	4USD	GAE
35	375336	CARRYDUFF	Jamison of Carryduff Ltd	636 Saintfield Road BT8 8BT	A24	(0232) 813348	4USD	GAE
36	375393	COLERAINE	Dunedin Travellers Check	74-76 Lodge Road BT52 1NE	A26	(0265) 44403	4USD	GAE
37	375317	COMBER (CO DOWN)	Crescent Self Serve	Newtownards Road BT23 5AY	A21	(0247) 872512	4USD	GAE
38	375380	COOKSTOWN	Cookstown Filling Station	22 Moneymore Road BT80 8EQ	A29	(06487) 65914	4USD	GAE
39	373169	CRUMLIN	Airport Road Filling Station	11 Tully Road BT42 4RR	A26	(08494) 825706	4USD	GAE
40	373118	DERRY	Lisnagelvin Self Serve	Lisnagelvin Road BT47 1DF	A514	(0504) 49266	4USD	GAE
41	373176	DERRY	Clooney Filling Station	10 Limavady Road BT47 3LS	A2	(0504) 42863	4UD	GAE
42	375358	DERRY	Harkin Brothers	Hollybush, Culmore BT48 8JJ	A2	(0504) 51471	4UD	GAE
43	375384	DOWNPATRICK	College Filling Station	112 Market Street BT30 6LZ	A25	(0396) 615459	4USD	GAE
44	375407	DUNGANNON	Lisnahull Service Station	Ballycowley Road BT70 1TN	A45	(08687) 23829	4UD	GAE
45	384078	DUNGANNON	Oaks Service Station	33 Coalisland Road BT71 6LB	A45	(08687) 24967	4UD	GAE
46	375362	DUNGIVEN	Dungiven Filling Station	Station Road BT47 4LN	B68	(0504) 741245	4USD	GAE
47	299683	ENNISKILLEN	West End Fuel Stop	Sligo Road BT74 7JY	A4	(0365) 324323	4USD	GAE
48	375390	ENNISKILLEN	Dolans Filling Station	Dublin Road BT74 6HH	A4	(0365) 323564	4USD	GAE

Loc. Ref.	Shell Ref.	TOWN	NAME	ADDRESS	Road No.	Tel. No.	Fuel	Cards	24 hour	HGV	Select	Car Wash
49	373193	GARVAGH	Garvagh Self-Serve	Main Street BT51 5AA	A29	(0265) 58300	4USD	GAE				
50	299450	GILFORD	Laurencetown Service Station	208 Banbridge Road BT63 6DW	A50	(08206) 23151	4USD	GAE				
51	540240	GLENAVY	Moira Road Filling Station	71 Main Street BT29 4LP	A26	(08494) 22239	4UD	GAE				
52	375346	GLENGORMELY	Glengormely Self Service	331 Antrim Road BT36 8DY		(0232) 342641	4USD	GAE				
53	375327	HOLYWOOD	Marina – Shell	96-100 Belfast Road BT18 0LR	A2	(0232) 423213	4USD	GAE				
54	375376	KILKEEL	Mourne Garage	Newcastle Street BT34 4AF	A2	(06937) 62240	4UD	GAE				
55	299449	LARNE	Kilwaughter Filling Station	44 Belfast Road BT40 2PH	A8	(0574) 270327	4USD	GAE				
56	299684	LARNE	Kilwaughter Service Station	41 Belfast Road BT40 2PH	A8	(0574) 270544	4UD	GAE				
57	299446	LISBURN	Belsize Service Station	Belsize Road BT27 4DP		(0846) 601455	4USD	GAE				
58	373103	LISBURN	Mayfair – Shell	39 Antrim Road BT28 1AU		(0846) 676935	4USD	GAE				
59	373145	LISBURN	M1 Filling Station	220 Hillsborough Road BT27 5RJ	A1	(0846) 662439	4USD	GAE				
60	373188	LISBURN	Derryvolgie Self Serve	Belfast Road BT27 4AP	A1	(0846) 660459	4USD	GAE				
61	373191	LISBURN	Pond Park Filling Station	95 Pond Park Road BT28 3RF		(08462) 72363	4USD	GAE				
62	375338	LISBURN	McKibbens Service Station	108-112 Queensway, Lambeg BT27 4QP	A1	(0846) 663051	4USD	GAE				
63	375394	LISBURN	Laganvalley – Shell	75-81 Hillsborough Road BT28 1JN	A1	(0846) 603094	4USD	GAE				
64	375365	LISNASKEA	Gannons Filling Station	Main Street BT2 2AA	A34	(03657) 21818	4UD	GAE				
65	373167	LONDONDERRY	Prehen Filling Station	Prehen Road BT47 2NS	A5	(0504) 48831	4USD	GAE				
66	541258	LONDONDERRY	Pennyburn Service Station	27 Culmore Road BT48 7RS	A2	(0504) 269918	4USD	GAE				
67	373167	LURGAN	Silverwood Service Station	Silverwood Industrial Est. BT66 6LN	A27	(0762) 325342	4USD	GAE				
68	299673	LURGEN	Moutrays Filling Station	40 Banbridge Road BT66 7EG	A26	(0762) 323564	4USD	GAE				
69	299447	MOIRA	Broomhedge Service Station	25 Lisburn Road BT67 0JS	A3	(0846) 621305	4USD	GAE				
70	299674	NEWRY	Killens Service Station	Hilltown BT34 2JU	B27	(08206) 38808	4UD	GAE				
71	375387	NEWRY	Glenview Self serve	Dublin Road BT35 8DA	A1	(0693) 66464	4USD	GAE				
72	554190	NEWRY	Greenbank Service Station	Warrenpoint Road BT34 2PS	A2	(0693) 60547	4USD	GAE				
73	299676	NEWTOWNABBEY	Isaac Agnew (Mallusk) Ltd	45 Mallusk Road BT36 8PS		(0232) 342111	4USD	GAE				
74	373114	NEWTOWNABBEY	Abbeycentre Service Station	Longwood Road BT37 9UH		(0232) 860860	4USD	GAE				
75	375322	NEWTOWNARDS	Strangford Filling Station	50 Portaferry Road BT23 3SG	A20	(0247) 810624	4USD	GAE				
76	375404	NEWTOWNBUTLER	J.J. McCaffrey Filling Station	Clonaroo BT74	A34	(036573) 286	4USD	GAE				
77	375403	OMAGH	Penrhyn Self-Serve	Derry Road BT78 5HZ	A5	(0662) 247795	4USD	GAE				
78	375377	PORTADOWN (CO ARMAGH)	Edenderry – Shell	Bridge Street BT63 5AR	A3	(0762) 350940	4USD	GAE				
79	375351	PORTRUSH	Glenvale Garage	Coleraine Road BT51 5HP	A29	(0265) 823702	4UD	GAE				
80	375355	PORTSTEWART	Larkhill Filling Station	Coleraine Road BT55 7HU	A2	(0265) 832722	4USD	GAE				
81	375410	PORTSTEWART	Cahore Service Station	112 Station Road BT55 7PU	B185	(0265) 832221	4USD	GAE				
82	534515	ROSTREVOR	Ghan Filling Station	43 Warrenpoint Road	A2	(06937) 38282	4USD	GAE				
83	375329	SAINTFIELD	Mannis and Morgan	Belfast Road BT24 7JS	A7	(0238) 510229	4UD	GAE				
84	538080	STRABANE	Travellers Rest	Lifford Road BT82 8EP	A38	(0504) 383139	4USD	GAE				
85	375406	TANDRAGEE	Ballymore Service Station	Portadown BT62 2AQ	A27	(0762) 840965	4USD	GAE				

NORTHUMBERLAND

Loc. Ref.	Shell Ref.	TOWN	NAME	ADDRESS	Road No.	Tel. No.	Fuel	Cards	24 hour	HGV	Select	Car Wash
1	357857	ALNWICK	Ords of Alnwick Limited	Willowtree Industrial Estate, South Road NE66 2HA	A1	(0665) 602619	4USD	GAE				
2	363784	ASHINGTON	Ashington – Shell	Newbiggin Road NE63 0TQ	B1334	(0670) 851092	4USD	GAE				
3	366040	BEDLINGTON	Choppington Lane Garage	Choppington Lane NE22 6LA	A1068	(0670) 822318	4UD	GAE				
4	377613	BERWICK-UPON-TWEED	Tweedmouth Self Serve	Main Street, Tweedmouth TD15 2AW	A1167	(0289) 308761	4UD	GAE				
5	380717	BERWICK-UPON-TWEED	Northern Gateway STC	North Road TD15 1QQ	A1167	(0289) 308578	4USD	GAE				
6	366045	BLYTH	Blyth Valley Ford	Cowpen Road NE24 5NF	A193	(0670) 352374	4USD	GAE				
7	366080	CORBRIDGE	Bishops Garages Ltd	Main Street NE45 5LB	B6530	(0434) 632068	4USD	GAE				
8	361943	HALTWHISTLE	Edens Lawn Service Station	Bypass NE49 0HH	A69	(0434) 320476	4USD	GAE				
9	365883	HEXHAM	Dale Garage (Callandale) Ltd	Haugh Lane NE46 3QQ	B6531	(0434) 604527	4UD	GAE				
10	366090	HEXHAM	The Garage	Fourstones NE47 5DQ	B6319	(0434) 674208	4UD	GAE				
11	366330	LYNEMOUTH	Lynemouth Motors	Albion Tae NE61 5SX		(0670) 860249	4UD	GAE				
12	366059	MORPETH	Stannington Filling Station	Great North Road, Stannington NE61 6DW	A1	(0670) 789221	4USD	GAE				
13	366070	MORPETH	Rothbury Motors Ltd	Townfoot, Rothbury NE65 7SL	B6341	(0669) 20516	4UD	GAE				
14	366245	MORPETH	Morpeth – Shell	Grange Road, Stobhill NE61 2UX		(0670) 516203	4USD	GAE				
15	366044	NEWBIGGIN-BY-THE-SEA	C I Young	North Seaton, Newbiggin Road NE64 6XR	B1334	(0670) 812377	4UD	GAE				
16	366095	PRUDHOE	West Wylam Garage Ltd	Front Street NE42 5DH	A695	(0661) 832242	4UD	GAE				
17	357676	WHITLEY BAY	Dale Garage	Astley Road, Seaton Delaval NE25 0DH	A192	091-237 1904	4UD	GAE				

NOTTINGHAMSHIRE

Loc. Ref.	Shell Ref.	TOWN	NAME	ADDRESS	Road No.	Tel. No.	Fuel	Cards	24 hour	HGV	Select	Car Wash
1	355374	BEESTON	Priory – Shell	Derby Road NG9 2TA	A52	(0602) 227923	4USD	GAE				
2	353365	COLWICK	Colwick – Shell	Daleside Road East NG2 4BP	B686	(0602) 612160	4USD	GAE				
3	355372	HUCKNALL	Airways Heating Ltd	Aerodrome Garage, 361-363 Watnall Road NG15 6EQ	B6009	(0602) 633909	4UD	GAE				
4	355431	KEYWORTH	Wolds Service Station	Melton Road, Stanton-on-the-Wolds NG12 5BQ	A606	(0602) 372245	4USD	GAE				
5	433878	KIRKBY-IN-ASHFIELD	Derby Road Garage	Annesley Woodhouse NG15 0AP	A611	(0623) 753257	4USD	GAE				
6	529753	KIRKBY-IN-ASHFIELD	Kingsway Service Station	40 Kingsway NG17 7BP	B6021	(0623) 759514	4UD	GAE				
7	366032	MANSFIELD	Newlands Self Serve	122 Clipstone Road West, Forest Town NG19 0HL	B6030	(0623) 21569	4USD	GAE				
8	366310	NEWARK	North Road Garage	North Road, North Muskham NG23 6HT	A1	(0636) 703232	4USD	GAE				
9	282949	NOTTINGHAM	Plumtree Garage	Station Road, Plumtree NG12 5NA		(0607) 75111	4U	GAE				
10	353045	NOTTINGHAM	Maid Marion Self Serve	Mansfield Road, Redhill NG5 8PG	A60	(0602) 203858	4USD	GAE				
11	353099	NOTTINGHAM	Silverdale Service Station	Clifton Lane, Wilford NG11 7ES	A453	(0602) 813607	4USD	GAE				
12	355361	NOTTINGHAM	Cinderhill – Shell	Nuthall Road, Cinderhill NG8 6AD	A610	(0602) 420077	4USD	GAE				
13	355378	NOTTINGHAM	Wighay Self Serve	Annesley Road, Hucknall NG15 8AY		(0602) 632971	4UD	GAE				
14	355379	NOTTINGHAM	Wilford Hill Self-Serve	Loughborough Road, Ruddington NG11 6LS	A60	(0602) 844904	4USD	GA				

Loc. Ref.	Shell Ref.	TOWN	NAME	ADDRESS	Road No.	Tel. No.	Fuel	Cards	24 hour	HGV	Select
15	355433	NOTTINGHAM	Saxondale – Shell	Saxondale Cross Roads, Bingham NG13 8AY	A46	(0949) 39944	4USD	GAE			
16	355548	NOTTINGHAM	Sherwood Self Serve	383 Mansfield Road, Sherwood NG5 2DG	A60	(0602) 620357	4USD	GAE			
17	355556	NOTTINGHAM	Marmion Filling Station	Carlton Road NG3 2NJ	A612	(0602) 586761	4USD	GAE			
18	355653	NOTTINGHAM	Moorbridge Self Serve	Hucknall Lane, Bulwell NG6 8AJ	A6002	(0602) 278653	4USD	GAE			
19	355781	NOTTINGHAM	Lace Market Self Serve	London Road NG2 3AB	A60	(0602) 501923	4USD	GAE			
20	390755	NOTTINGHAM	Gorse Hill Garage	Mapperley, Mapperley Plains NG3 5RG	B684	(0602) 263341	4USD	GAE			
21	398139	NOTTINGHAM	Woodhouse – Shell	Woodhouse way, Nuthall NG8 6N	A6002	(0602) 750478	4USD	GAE			
22	366034	OLLERTON	Ollerton – Shell	Nottingham Road NG22 9DT	A614	(0623) 823908	4USD	GAE			
23	271443	RETFORD	Hillcrest Service Station	Clarborough DN22 9NJ	A620	(0777) 703415	4UD	GAE			
24	366001	RETFORD	Markham Moor Travellers Check	A1 Northbound Carriageway, Markham Moor DN22 0QU	A1	(0777) 838080	4USD	GAE			
25	550306	RETFORD	Retford – Shell	A1 Southbound, Markham Moor DN22 0PG	A1	(0777) 83304	4USD	GAE			
26	355543	TOTON	Banks Road Service Station	L. Frost & Son Ltd, Banks Road NG9 6HE	B6003	(0602) 734812	4USD	GAE			
27	366005	WORKSOP	Ashlea Service Station Ltd	Doncaster Road, Costhorpe S81 9QY	A60	(0909) 733633	4UD	GAE			

ORKNEY

Loc. Ref.	Shell Ref.	TOWN	NAME	ADDRESS	Road No.	Tel. No.	Fuel	Cards	24 hour	HGV	Select
1	380803	KIRKWALL	Norseman Garage	Rendal KW17 2NZ	A986	(0856) 76208	4UD	GAE			

OXFORDSHIRE

Loc. Ref.	Shell Ref.	TOWN	NAME	ADDRESS	Road No.	Tel. No.	Fuel	Cards	24 hour	HGV	Select
1	353246	ABINGDON	Cornerhouse Garage	Wootton Road, Wootton OX13 6BS	B4017	(0865) 730262	4UD	GAE			
2	353368	ABINGDON	St Helens Self Serve	The Vineyard OX14 3AA	A4183	(0235) 520176	4USD	GAE			
3	538442	ABINGDON	Hartwell (Abingdon) Oxford Ltd	Drayton Road OX14 5JU	B4017	(0235) 522822	4UD	GAE			
4	355357	BANBURY	Cockhorse Self Serve	Warwick Road OX16 7AH	B4100	(0295) 267711	4UD	GAE			
5	355358	BANBURY	Hartwells of Banbury Ltd	Southam Road OX16 7RU	A423	(0295) 251551	4UD	GAE			
6	353244	BICESTER	Layby – Shell	Weston-on-the-Green OX6 8QG	A34	(0869) 51227	4USD	GAE			
7	353371	BICESTER	Chase Filling Stn	London Road OX6 0JL	A41	(0869) 243875	4UD	GAE			
8	308093	CARTERTON	Brize Norton Self Serve	Carterton Road OX8 3PY		(0993) 840022	4USD	GAE			
9	353429	CHIPPING NORTON	Holywell Self Serve	Chapel Cross Roads OX7 5SX	A3400	(0608) 643357	4USD	GAE			
10	347696	DIDCOT	Georgetown Self Serve	Broadway OX11 8SD	B4493	(0235) 812037	4USD	GAE			
11	347726	DIDCOT	Berkshire Downs Filling Stn	A34 Southbound, Chilton OX11 0RW	A34	(0235) 834442	4USD	GAE			
12	353238	OXFORD	Blenheim Service Station	Woodstock Road, Yarnton OX5 1PL	A44	(0867) 52192	4USD	GAE			
13	353239	OXFORD	Headington – Shell	London Road, Headington OX3 7RD	A420	(0865) 62877	4USD	GAE			
14	353372	OXFORD	Humphris (Oxford) Ltd	72 Rose Hill OX4 4HS	A4158	(0865) 748000	4USD	GAE			
15	353374	OXFORD	Oxford Service Area	A34 Peartree Hill Roundabout, Woodstock Rd OX2 8JZ	A34	(0865) 54301	4USD	GAE			
16	353435	OXFORD	Hartwells of Oxford	Watlington Road OX4 5LU	B480	(0865) 777744	4UD	GAE			
17	538440	OXFORD	Faringdon Road	Faringdon Road, Cumnor OX2 9RH	A420	(0865) 862489	4UD	GAE			
18	538441	OXFORD	Seacourt Tower	Westway OX2 03P	A420	(0865) 791798	4USD	GAE			
19	353236	THAME	Thame Service Station	Park Street OX9 3HS	B4445	(0844) 215566	4UD	GAE			
20	347728	WANTAGE	Broadway Motors	Wallingford Street OX12 8BB	A417	(02357) 3632	4USD	GAE			
21	434046	WHEATLEY	Bryants Garages	Station Road OX9 1SR		(0865) 873439	4USD	GAE			
22	353434	WITNEY	Cannon Pool Self Serve	Hailey Road OX8 5HQ	B4022	(0993) 703960	4USD	GAE			
23	353242	WOODSTOCK	Judds Garage	Woodleys OX7 1HT	A44	(0993) 811451	4USD	GAE			

POWYS

Loc. Ref.	Shell Ref.	TOWN	NAME	ADDRESS	Road No.	Tel. No.	Fuel	Cards	24 hour	HGV	Select
1	299862	BRECON	Bishops Meadow Filling Station	Bishops Meadow LD3 95W	B4602	(0874) 2051	4UD	GAE			
2	299861	BUILTH WELLS	North Road Garage	Station Road, Llanelwedd LD2 3SS	A470	(0982) 552600	4UD	GAE			
3	358524	LLANIDLOES	Dolwen Garage	Dolwen SY18 6LQ A470	(05512) 2185		4UD	GAE			
4	358527	LLANIDLOES	Minerva Garages	SY18 6BZ	A470	(05512) 2201	4UD	GAE			
5	299859	LLYSWEN	Wye Garage	CD3 0UR	A4079	(0874) 754217	4UD	GAE			
6	358913	NEWTOWN	W R Davies (Motors) Ltd	Pool Road SY16 3AH	A483	(0686) 625514	4USD	GAE			
7	434496	RHAYADER	Fairfield Filling Station	East Street LD6 5DY	A44	(0597) 810396	4USD	GAE			
8	434498	RHAYADER	Sycamore Garage	East Street LD6 5DY	A44	(0597) 810396	4UD	GAE			
9	308516	SENNYBRIDGE	Riverside Services	LD5 8PS	A40	(0874) 636267	4USD	GAE			
10	299779	WELSHPOOL	Brian Cakebread Car Sales	Border Garage, Newton Road SY21 8RR	A483	(0938) 554444	4UD	GAE			
11	357975	WELSHPOOL	Quarry Service Station	Transport Maintenance, Brook Street SY21 7BL	A590	(0938) 552670	4UD	GAE			
12	358498	WELSHPOOL	W R Davies (Motors) Ltd	Salop Road SY21 7ES	A483	(0938) 552391	4USD	GAE			

	Facilities					

SHETLAND

Loc. Ref.	Shell Ref.	TOWN	NAME	ADDRESS	Road No.	Tel. No.	Fuel	Cards	24 hour	HGV	Select	Car Wash
1	380805	LERWICK	Grantfield Garage	North Road ZE1 0NT	A970	(0595) 2709	4UD	GAE				■
2	330011	SANDWICK	G R Jamieson	Central Stores ZE2 9HH	A970	(09505) 203	4D					

SHROPSHIRE

Loc. Ref.	Shell Ref.	TOWN	NAME	ADDRESS	Road No.	Tel. No.	Fuel	Cards	24 hour	HGV	Select	Car Wash
1	539726	ELLESMERE	Dudleston Heath Garage	Dudleston Heath SY12 9JZ	B5068	(0691) 75655	4UD	GAE				
2	355528	LUDLOW	Ludford Bridge Service Stn Ltd	Ludford Bridge SY8 1PE		(0584) 873909	4USD	GAE				
3	357353	MARKET DRAYTON	Adastra Services	Chester Road, Tern Hill TF9 3QD	A41	(0630) 638729	4UD	GAE		■		
4	398134	MARKET DRAYTON	Williams of Market Drayton	Cheshire Street TF9 3AA	A529	(0630) 652444	4USD	GAE				
5	357351	NESSCLIFFE	The Garage	SY4 1AY	A5	(0743) 81246	4USD	GAE				
6	355493	NEWPORT	Lower Bar Self Serve	Lower Bar TF10 7JA	A519	(0952) 820074	4USD	GAE				
7	357347	OSWESTRY	Cambrian STC	Beatrice Street SY11 1QW	B5069	(0691) 654706	4USD	GAE				
8	357349	OSWESTRY	Oswestry — Shell	Holyhead Road, Weston Rhyn SY11 3EN	A5	(0691) 658615	4USD	GAE		■		
9	355499	SHREWSBURY	Rea Valley Tractors Ltd	Main Road, Pontesbury SY5 0UB	A488	(0743) 790801	4UD	GAE				
10	355485	TELFORD	Sutton Maddock Garage	Sutton Maddock, Shifnal TF11 9ND	A442	(0952) 71251	4USD	GAE				
11	355503	TELFORD	Ketley — Shell	Holyhead Road, Ketley TF1 4DY	A518	(0952) 610433	4USD	GAE		■		
12	355501	TELFORD	Tong Filling Station	Tong, Shifnal TF11 8PS	A41	(0952) 76260	4USD	GAE				
13	357357	WEM	Wem Motor Services Ltd	New Street SY4 5AD	B5476	(0939) 232476	4USD	GAE				
14	357355	WHITCHURCH	Smithfield Garage	Brownlow Street SY13 1QR		(0948) 2826	4USD	GAE				

SOMERSET

Loc. Ref.	Shell Ref.	TOWN	NAME	ADDRESS	Road No.	Tel. No.	Fuel	Cards	24 hour	HGV	Select	Car Wash
1	434562	BATH	Farleigh Service Station	Hinton Charterhouse BA3 6BP	A36E	(0225) 722140	4USD	GAE		■		
2	348347	BRIDGWATER	Bridgwater Self Serve	Bristol Road TA6 4AZ	A38	(0278) 424018	4UD	GAE				
3	348350	BRIDGWATER	Greenway Garage	Quantock Road TA6 7EH	A39	(0278) 423261	4UD	GAE				
4	348330	BRUTON	West End Filling Station	West End BA10 0BQ	A359	(0749) 812753	4USD	GAE				
5	348349	BURNHAM-ON-SEA	Central Garage and Cars	124 Berrow Road TA8 2PG	B3140	(0278) 788186	4UD	GAE				
6	348329	CHEDDAR	Crossroads Filling Station	Upper New Road BS27 3DA	A371	(0934) 742385	4USD	GAE				
7	384299	ILMINSTER	Ilminster — Shell	Horton Cross TA19 9PT	A303	(0460) 53027	4USD	GAE		■		
8	348343	LANGPORT	Taunton Road Garage	Taunton Road, Curry Rivel TA10 0ER	A378	(0458) 251300	4USD	GAE				
9	348495	MINEHEAD	Premier Garage (Alcombe) Ltd	71 Alcombe Road, Alcombe TA24 6AX	A39	(0643) 703459	4UD	GAE				
10	347149	TAUNTON	Taunton Deane MWSA	M5 Southbound, Trull TA3 7PF	M5	(0823) 271111	4USD	GAE				
11	348353	TAUNTON	Taunton — Shell	Priory Bridge Road TA1 1QD	A358	(0823) 336317	4USD	GAE		■		
12	348976	TAUNTON	Williton Filling Station	Fore Street, Williton TA4 4PX	A39	(0984) 33646	4USD	GAE				
13	348994	WELLINGTON	Wellington Motors	Station Road TA21 8NJ	B3187	(0823) 667511	4USD	GAE				
14	347183	WELLS	Easton Service Station	Easton BA5 1DU	A371	(0749) 870343	4UD	GAE				
15	348327	WELLS	Bath Road Garage	Bath Road BA5 3HS	B3139	(0749) 672088	4USD	GAE				
16	353304	WESTON-SUPER-MARE	Sedgemoor MWSA	M5 Motorway North Bound, Edingworth BS24 0LJ	M5	(0934) 750659	4USD	GAE				
17	348379	WINCANTON	Southgate Garage	Southgate Road BA9 9EB	A303	(0963) 33950	4UD	GAE				
18	348489	WIVELISCOMBE	Jones Auto's	West Street TA4 2SK		(0984) 23216	4UD	GAE				
19	348339	YEOVIL	Townsend Garage	Tintinhull BA22 8PF	A303	(0935) 822636	4USD	GAE				
20	348979	YEOVIL	Sparkford — Shell	Camel Hill, Queens Camel BA22 7PH	A303	(0935) 850593	4USD	GAE		■		
21	353319	YEOVIL	Nine Springs S S	Summerhouse Terrace BA20 1NL		(0935) 32167	4USD	GAE				

SOUTH GLAMORGAN

Loc. Ref.	Shell Ref.	TOWN	NAME	ADDRESS	Road No.	Tel. No.	Fuel	Cards	24 hour	HGV	Select	Car Wash
1	348947	BARRY	Redrup Motors (Barry) Ltd	Cardiff Road CF6 6QW	A4055	(0446) 735340	4USD	GAE				
2	347185	CARDIFF	Premier Self Serve	368 Newport Road CF3 7AE	A4161	(0222) 462605	4USD	GAE				■
3	348400	CARDIFF	Westward Ho Self Serve	Llantrisant Road CF5 2PY	A4119	(0222) 843941	4USD	GAE				
4	348429	CARDIFF	Cardinal — Shell	501 Newport Road CF3 7YA	A4161	(0222) 486054	4USD	GAE				■
5	348433	CARDIFF	Windway S/S	637 Cowbridge Road East CF5 1BG	A4161	(0222) 552444	4USD	GAE				
6	348794	CARDIFF	Cardiff — Shell	Caerphilly Road CF4 4QF	A469	(0222) 627314	4USD	GAE				■
7	353275	CARDIFF	Pentwyn S/Stn	Pentwyn Road CF2 7XH	A48	(0222) 733903	4UD	GAE				
8	353281	CARDIFF	Fordthorne Garage	Penarth Road CF1 7TT	A4160	(0222) 223100	4UD	GAE				

SOUTH YORKSHIRE

Loc. Ref.	Shell Ref.	TOWN	NAME	ADDRESS	Road No.	Tel. No.	Fuel	Cards	24 hour	HGV	Select
1	363776	BARNSLEY	Motorway Filling Station	Dodworth Road S70 6PD	A628	(0226) 735368	4USD	GAE			
2	433499	CONISBOROUGH	G.H. Motors Ltd	Doncaster Road, Denaby Main DN12 4ET	A6023	(0709) 868759	4USD	GAE			
3	366233	DONCASTER	Bentley Self Serve	Bentley Road DN5 9AS	A19	(0302) 784125	4USD	GAE			
4	366255	DONCASTER	Sprotborough Road S/Stn	Sprotbrough Road DN5 8AZ		(0302) 784944	4USD	GAE			
5	366270	DONCASTER	Doncaster — Shell	1 Balby Road DN4 0RA	A630	(0302) 340044	4USD	GAE			
6	531742	DONCASTER	Low-Cost	Edlington Lane, New Edlington DN12	B6376	(0709) 862223	4USD	GAE			
7	365976	ROTHERHAM	Mushroom Self Serve	Herringthorpe Valley Road S65 2UG	A6123	(0709) 820070	4USD	GAE			
8	365978	ROTHERHAM	Parkgate Service Station	Broad Street, Parkgate S62 6DP	A633	(0709) 523121	4USD	GAE			
9	365980	ROTHERHAM	Sitwell Self Serve	Whiston S60 4BW	A618	(0709) 365051	4USD	GAE			
10	357755	SHEFFIELD	Sheffield — Shell	Eccleshall Road South S11 8JD	A625	(0742) 731459	4USD	GAE			
11	363385	SHEFFIELD	Woodall Service Area (North)	Motorway Service Area Nth, Harthill S31 8XR	M1	(0742) 486434	4USD	GAE			
12	363387	SHEFFIELD	Woodall Service Area (South)	Motorway Service Area Sth, Harthill S31 8XR	M1	(0742) 486434	4USD	GAE			
13	363841	SHEFFIELD	Norfolk Park Service Station	East Bank Road S2 2AS		(0742) 727411	4USD	GAE			
14	365965	SHEFFIELD	Townend Self Serve	Ridgeway Road S12 2JY	A6102	(0742) 396122	4USD	GAE			
15	365969	SHEFFIELD	The Owl Self Serve	176 Penistone Road North S6 1QA	A61	(0742) 335792	4USD	GAE			
16	365971	SHEFFIELD	Crosshills Self-Serve	The Common, Ecclesfield S30 3WP	A6135	(0742) 468058	4USD	GAE			
17	365982	SHEFFIELD	Crest Self Serve	320 Handsworth Road, Handsworth S13 9BX	A57	(0742) 693054	4USD	GAE			
18	365988	SHEFFIELD	Tinsley Park Self Serve	Greenland Road S9 5HE	A6102	(0742) 446948	4USD	GAE			
19	365999	SHEFFIELD	Wade & Madin	196 Sheffield Road, Killamarsh S31 8ED	B6058	(0742) 486358	4USD	GAE			
20	366003	SHEFFIELD	South Anston — Shell	Worksop Road, South Anston S31 7ES	A57	(0909) 561763	4USD	GAE			
21	366254	SHEFFIELD	St Phillips — Shell	Netherthorpe Road S3 7EZ	A61	(0742) 752103	4USD	GAE			
22	366286	SHEFFIELD	Queens Road Self Serve	500 Queens Road S2 4DT	A61	(0742) 558305	4USD	GAE			

STAFFORDSHIRE

Loc. Ref.	Shell Ref.	TOWN	NAME	ADDRESS	Road No.	Tel. No.	Fuel	Cards	24 hour	HGV	Select
1	380711	BREWOOD	High Green Garage Ltd	High Green ST19 9BD		(0902) 850532	4USD	GAE			
2	355452	BURNTWOOD	Springhill — Shell	150 Cannock Road WS7 0BG	A5190	(05436) 76258	4USD	GAE			
3	353271	BURTON-ON-TRENT	St Peters Self Serve	St Peters Bridge DE15 9AW	A444	(0283) 40024	4USD	GAE			
4	355385	BURTON-ON-TRENT	Belvedere Self Serve	Belvedere Road DE13 0RF	B5017	(0283) 33237	4USD	GAE			
5	360306	BURTON-ON-TRENT	Lesters Garage	Main Street, Yoxall DE13 8NQ	A515	(0543) 472225	4USD	GAE			
6	355454	CANNOCK	Hilltop — Shell	Uxbridge Street, Hednesford WS12 5DE	A460	(0543) 879533	4USD	GAE			
7	355505	CANNOCK	Longford — Shell	Watling Street WS11 1SL		(0543) 572428	4USD	GAE			
8	355444	CHEADLE	Times Service Station	36 Tean Road ST10 1LY	A522	(0538) 753197	4UD	GAE			
9	357943	LEEK	Bridge End Garage	Macclesfield Road ST13 8LD	A523	(0538) 384250	4USD	GAE			
10	355449	LICHFIELD	London Road Self Serve	London Road WS14 9EQ	A5206	(0543) 256517	4USD	GAE			
11	398138	LICHFIELD	Eastern Avenue — Shell	Eastern Avenue WS13 7SA	A5192	(0543) 418299	4USD	GAE			
12	299788	NEWCASTLE-UNDER-LYME	Keele Southbound	Keele Park, Keele ST5 5HG	M6	(0782) 626221	4USD	GAE			
13	357939	NEWCASTLE-UNDER-LYME	Keele Road Garage	Keele Road ST5 5AB	A525	(0782) 610749	4UD	GAE			
14	357941	NEWCASTLE-UNDER-LYME	Higherland Self Serve	Higherland ST5 2TL	A525	(0782) 615780	4USD	GAE			
15	357947	NEWCASTLE-UNDER-LYME	Wolstanton Self Serve	High Street, Wolstanton ST5 0EY	A527	(0782) 613551	4USD	GAE			
16	357962	NEWCASTLE-UNDER-LYME	Keele Northbound	M6 Northbound, Keele ST5 5HG	M6	(0782) 626221	4USD	GAE			
17	358074	NEWCASTLE-UNDER-LYME	Newcastle Discount Giant	Lower Milehouse Lane ST5 9AL		(0782) 623727	4US	GAE			
18	355441	STAFFORD	Great Bridgeford Garage	Great Bridgeford ST18 9SQ	A5013	(0785) 282221	4USD	GAE			
19	355517	STAFFORD	Charles Clark & Son Ltd	Lichfield Road ST19 5DT	A34	(0785) 51366	4U	GAE			
20	355567	STAFFORD	Foregate — Shell	Foregate Street ST16 2PD	A34	(0785) 44883	4USD	GAE			
21	412803	STAFFORD	Bank Top Garage	Stafford Road, Gnosall ST20 0EU	A518	(0785) 82217	4USD	GAE			
22	420518	STAFFORD	R L J Turner & E Turner	Long Street, Wheaton Aston ST19 9NF		(0785) 840286	4USD	GAE			
23	353041	STOKE-ON-TRENT	Normid Burslem	Hamil Road, Burslem ST6 9AL		(0782) 839011	4UD	GAE			
24	353089	STOKE-ON-TRENT	Festival Self Serve	Cobridge Road ST1 5JQ	A53	(0782) 289111	4USD	GAE			
25	357945	STOKE-ON-TRENT	Border Self Serve	Linley Road, Talke ST7 1RZ	A34	(0782) 775192	4USD	GAE			
26	357961	STOKE-ON-TRENT	Mossfield — Shell	Dividy Road, Bucknall ST2 6AJ	B5040	(0782) 212713	4USD	GAE			
27	357985	STOKE-ON-TRENT	Knype Service Station	Tunstall Road, Kynpersley ST8 7AL	A527	(0782) 513551	4USD	GAE			
28	358128	STOKE-ON-TRENT	Normid Talke	Jamage Road, Talke Pits ST7 1QD		(0782) 783541	4UD	GAE			
29	335108	STONE	Aston Garage	Aston-By-Stone ST15 0BH	A34	(0785) 813035	4USD	GAE			
30	355439	STONE	Stone — Shell	Walton ST15 0HH	A34	(0785) 817225	4USD	GAE			
31	355348	TAMWORTH	Wilncote — Shell	Watling Street, Two Gates B77 5AB	A5	(0827) 260809	4USD	GAE			
32	355456	TAMWORTH	Crown Garage	Fazeley Road B78 3HA		(0827) 67371	4UD	GAE			
33	355465	UTTOXETER	Uttoxeter — Shell	New Road ST14 7DA	A50	(0889) 562625	4USD	GAE			
34	355562	UTTOXETER	Blounts Green Filling Station	Stafford Road ST14 8DW	A518	(0889) 562845	4UD	GAE			
35	299835	WOLVERHAMPTON	Hilton Park Southbound	M6 MWSA Southbound, Essington WV11 2RA	M6	(0922) 412237	D	GAE			
36	299836	WOLVERHAMPTON	Hilton Park Northbound	M6 MWSA Northbound, Essington WV11 2AU	M6	(0922) 412237	D	GAE			
37	355479	WOLVERHAMPTON	Oaken Self Serve	Holyhead Road, Codsall WV8 2HX	A41	(0902) 842181	4USD	GAE			

Loc. Ref.	Shell Ref.	TOWN	NAME	ADDRESS	Road No.	Tel. No.	Fuel	Cards	24 hour	HGV	Select	Car Wash

STRATHCLYDE

Loc. Ref.	Shell Ref.	TOWN	NAME	ADDRESS	Road No.	Tel. No.	Fuel	Cards
	468247	APPIN	Duncan Gunn & Sons	Gunns Garage, Tynribbie PA38 4DB	A828	(0631) 73279	4UD	GAE
	380846	ARDRISHAIG	The Lorne Garage	Chalmers Street PA30 8DZ	A83	(0546) 602100	4UD	GAE
	380753	ARDROSSAN	Parkhouse Garage	Parkhouse Road KA22 8AA	A78	(0294) 63654	4USD	GAE
	380735	AYR	Doonfoot Garage	90 Doonfoot Road KA7 4DP	A719	(0292) 442342	4UD	GAE
	380740	AYR	Ingram Motoring Centre (Ayr)	Dalblair Road KA7 1UN	B7024	(0292) 269522	4UD	GAE
	381068	AYR	Woodfield Self Serve	127 Prestwick Road KA8 8ND	A79	(0292) 268071	4USD	GAE
	380466	BELLSHILL	Gopal Motors Ltd	New Edinburgh Road ML4 3HH	A721	(0698) 747995	4UD	GAE
	380483	BELLSHILL	Cross Self Serve	North Road ML4 1QX	B7070	(0698) 748516	4UD	GAE
	380727	BIGGAR	Tinto Garage	Biggar Road, Symington ML12 6LQ	A72	(08993) 200	4UD	GAE
0	380905	BIGGAR	Abington MWSA	M74 Abington ML12 6RG	A74	(08642) 835	4USD	GAE
1	376178	BISHOPTON	Rossland Garage	Greenock Road PA7 5AP	B789	(0505) 862247	4UD	AE
2	433405	BLACKWATERFOOT (ARRAN)	Bannantyne Motors	KA27 8ES	A841	(0770) 86277	4UD	GAE
3	281712	BOWMORE (ISLAY)	Woodrow-Bowmore F/Stn	PA43 7HL	A846	(0496) 81348	4UD	GAE
4	380532	BRIDGEND (ISLAY)	J Campbell	The Stores PA44 7PQ	A846	(0496) 81335	4UD	GAE
5	527262	BRODICK (ARRAN)	Arran Transport	The Pier Buildings KA27 8AX	A841	(0770) 2121	4UD	GAE
6	380952	CAMBUSLANG	J W Gemmell	20/26 Lightburn Road, Halfway G72 8UE	A724	041-641 2212	4UD	GAE
	276922	CAMPBELTOWN	D Oman & Co	The Pier, Carradale PA28 6SQ	B879	(05833) 228	4	GAE
	376158	CARLUKE	Nellfield Garage	Braidwood ML8 4PP	A73	(0555) 772363	4USD	GAE
	381171	CARNWATH	Medwyn Garage	Peebles Road ML11 8NG	A721	(0555) 840249	4UD	GAE
	377623	CARSTAIRS	Rosemount Filling Station	Lanark Road ML11 8QL	A70	(0555) 870320	4USD	GAE
	380506	CLYDEBANK	Clydebank STC	610 Glasgow Road G81 1JA	A814	041-952 7552	4UD	GAE
	377583	COATBRIDGE	Green Park – Shell	331 Bank Street ML5 1EJ	A89	(0236) 432925	4USD	GAE
	381009	COATBRIDGE	Park Lane Self Serve	Whifflet Street ML5 4RX	A725	(0236) 429977	4UD	GAE
	400175	CRAIGHOUSE (JURA)	The Pier Garage	PA60 7XF	A846	(0496) 82222	4	
	276924	CRAIGNURE (MULL)	The Craignure Stores	PA65 6AY	A849	(06802) 301	4UD	GAE
	531931	CRAIGNURE (MULL)	The Bayview Garage	PA65 6AY	A849	(06802) 444	4UD	GAE
	380979	DALMALLY	Cruachan Filling Station	Lochawe PA33 1AW	A85	(08382) 345	4UD	GAE
	380925	DUMBARTON	Cardross Filling Station	Cardross Road, Cardross G82 5PX	A814	(0389) 841377	4UD	GA
	540853	DUNDONALD	Castle Garage Dundonald	3 Drybridge Road KA2 9HA	B730	(0563) 850275	4UD	GAE
	380794	DUNOON	The County Garage	East Bay PA23 8AB	A815	(0369) 3199	4UD	GAE
	381166	DUNOON	Cothouse Filling Station	Kilmun PA23 8SD	A885	(0369) 84333	4UD	GAE
	533073	DUNOON	Baladava Garage	Bullwood PA23 7QN	A815	(0369) 83314	4UD	GAE
	274057	FIONNPHORT (MULL)	McDougall's Garage	PA66 6BW	A849	(06817) 294	4UD	GAE
	380913	GALSTON	Bobbin Garage	Newmills Road KA4 8PA	A71	(0563) 820767	4UD	GAE
	380789	GIRVAN	Scotts Garage	Barrhill KA26 0QT	A714	(0465) 82224	4UD	GAE
	381007	GIRVAN	Glendoune Garage	Glendoune Street KA26 0AA	A77	(0465) 4416	4UD	GAE
B	376138	GLASGOW	Westermains – Shell	31 Glasgow Road, Kirkintilloch G66 1BG	A803	041-777 6631	4USD	GAE
B	377603	GLASGOW	Phoenix Filling Station	Keppochhill Road G21 1SR		041-333 0119	4UD	GAE
B	377628	GLASGOW	White Flag Garage Company Ltd	91 Polmadie Road G5 0BA	B736	041-429 7600	4UD	GAE
B	380465	GLASGOW	Glen – Shell	Rouken Glen Road G46 7HT	B769	041-638 5568	4UD	GAE
B	380469	GLASGOW	Universe T.C. – Shell	2165 Paisley Road West G52 3PF	A737	041-882 1666	4USD	GAE
B	380479	GLASGOW	Old Inns – Shell	A80, Cumbernauld G68 0BJ	A80	(02367) 21864	4UD	GAE
B	380498	GLASGOW	Spring Self Serve	911 Springburn Road G21 1LZ	A803	041-558 5434	4USD	GAE
B	380499	GLASGOW	S M T (Sales & Service) Ltd	177/205 Finnieston Street G3 8HG	A814	041-204 2828	4UD	GAE
B	380502	GLASGOW	St Georges Self Serve	147 St Georges Road G3 6JB	A82	041-332 8773	4UD	GAE
B	380503	GLASGOW	WM Begg & Sons	79 Milngavie Road, Bearsden G61 2DL	A809	041-942 1110	4U	GAE
B	380512	GLASGOW	Clydeview Filling Station	92 Balshagray Avenue G11 7EH	A739	041-339 0647	4UD	GAE
B	380521	GLASGOW	Queen Margaret Drive S/Serve	162 Queen Margaret Drive G20 8NX	A82	041-945 3754	4USD	GAE
B	380529	GLASGOW	Alexandra Parade Self Serve	367 Alexandra Parade G31 3AG	A8	041-554 5171	4USD	GAE
B	380643	GLASGOW	Duncansfield Self Serve	Glasgow Road, Kilsyth G65 9AE	A803	(0236) 823126	4UD	GAE
B	380896	GLASGOW	Fullarton – Shell	2101 London Road G32 8AQ	A74	041-778 9747	4USD	GAE
B	380900	GLASGOW	Whitecraigs Self Serve	80 Ayr Road, Newton Mearns G77 6EP	A77	041-639 3573	4UD	GAE
B	380911	GLASGOW	Anniesland Filling station	Anniesland Road G13 1XD	A82	041-959 2205	4UD	GA
B	380929	GLASGOW	Williamwood Self Serve	690 Clarkston Road G44 3YR	B767	041-637 6578	4USD	GAE
B	380969	GLASGOW	Lowmoss – Shell	Kirkintilloch Road, Bishopbriggs G64 2HS	A803	041-772 3024	4UD	GAE
B	380971	GLASGOW	Douglas Park Self Serve	Main Street, Milngavie G62 6JP	A81	041-956 1126	4USD	GAE
B	380991	GLASGOW	Boundary Self Serve	1628 Cumbernauld Road G33 1AE	A80	041-770 6044	4UD	GAE
B	380993	GLASGOW	McCashins of Cumbernauld	Ring Road, Seafar, Cumbernauld G67 1AP	A8011	(02367) 21686	4UD	GAE
B	381016	GLASGOW	Shaws – Shell	265 Neatherauldhouse Road G43 1LS	B762	041-636 5249	4USD	GAE
B	381033	GLASGOW	Switchback T.C. – Shell	289 Bearsden Road G13 1EQ	A739	041-954 8043	4UD	GAE
B	381048	GLASGOW	Graham Motors (SNM) Ltd	South Carbrain Ring Road, Cumbernauld G67 2UG		(02367) 25574	4UD	GAE
B	381066	GLASGOW	Stonelaw Towers Self Serve	Stonelaw Road, Rutherglen G73 3RL	A749	041-647 1336	4UD	GAE
B	381076	GLASGOW	Garscube Self Serve	2022 Maryhill Road G20 0AB	A81	041-946 6200	4UD	GAE
B	381079	GLASGOW	Mount Ellen Filling Station	Drumcavel Road, Gartcosh G69 8DB	A752	041-779 3412	4UD	GA
	376160	GREENOCK	Victoria Self Serve	Rue End Street PA15 1ET	A8	(0475) 83526	4UD	GAE
	380481	HAMILTON	Portland Self Serve	45-47 Portland Place ML3 7JU	A723	(0698) 286251	4USD	GAE
	380849	INVERARAY	W.D. Semple	Shore Street PA32 8UE	A83	(0499) 2150	4UD	GAE
	380931	IRVINE	Ravenspark Self Serve	Kilwinning Road KA12 8RY	A737	(0294) 78107	4UD	GAE
	377609	KILMARNOCK	Glencairn – Shell	Low Glencairn Street KA1 4DQ	B7038	(0563) 21901	4USD	GAE
	380729	KILMARNOCK	Fenwick Motors	9 Kilmaurs Road, Fenwick by Pass KA3 6AY	A77	(05606) 271	4UD	GAE
	380745	KILMARNOCK	Blair Garage	10-14 Rigg Street, Stewarton KA3 5AG	B769	(0560) 82498	4USD	GAE
	380749	KILWINNING	Howies Garage	4 Stevenston Road KA13 6NJ	A738	(0294) 52687	4UD	GAE
	381085	KIRKMUIRHILL	Fourways Service Station Ltd	Strathaven Road ML11 9RN	M74	(0555) 893498	4UD	GAE
	380721	LANARK	Mansefield Self Serve	West Port ML11 9HE	A73	(0555) 662582	4UD	GAE
	380472	LARKHALL	Ayr Road Garage	Ayr Road, Shawsburn ML9 2TZ	A71	(0698) 883360	4UD	GAE
	380964	LARKHALL	Old Cross Garage	Drygate Street ML9 2AJ	B7019	(0698) 882754	4UD	GAE
	377601	LESMAHAGOW	Lesmahagow Truck Stop	Wellburn Interchange, Milton ML6 9JN	M74	(0555) 894889	4UD	GAE
	434713	LOCHGILPHEAD	Kilmartin Garage	Kilmartin PA31 8RN	A816	(05465) 333	4UD	GAE

Loc. Ref.	Shell Ref.	TOWN	NAME	ADDRESS	Road No.	Tel. No.	Fuel	Cards	24 hour	HGV	Select
79	381003	MAUCHLINE	Tower Filling Station	Kilmarnock Road KA5 5TT	A76	(0290) 50493	4UD	GA			
80	380772	MAYBOLE	John D Cameron	84 High Street KA19 7AH	A77	(0655) 82121	4UD	GAE			
81	380489	MOTHERWELL	Motherwell Self Serve	528-540 Windmillhill Street ML1 2AQ	A721	(0698) 61469	4UD	GAE			
82	380491	MOTHERWELL	Circular Filling Station	Newhouse ML1 5SY	A73	(0698) 860236	4UD	GAE			
83	381063	OBAN	Oban Filling Station	Soraba Road PA34 4HY	A816	(0631) 64050	4UD	GAE			
84	380477	OVERTOWN	Old Toll — Shell	128 Main Street ML2 0QP	A71	(0698) 374094	4UD	GAE			
85	380757	PAISLEY	Tannahill Self Serve	61 Canal Street PA1 2HP	A737	041-887 9888	4UD	GAE			
86	380962	PAISLEY	Archways Self Serve	134 Ferguslie PA1 2TR	A737	041-887 8080	4UD	GAE			
87	330013	PORT ASKAIG (ISLAY)	Port Askaig Stores	PA46 7RB	A846	(0496) 84245	4				
88	281713	PORT CHARLOTTE (ISLAY)	D & N MacKenzie	Main Street PA48 7TL	A847	(0496) 85200	4UD	GAE			
89	279697	PORT ELLEN (ISLAY)	Glenegadale Filling Station	Glenegadale House PA42 7AS	A846	(0496) 2147	4UD	GAE			
90	380732	PRESTWICK	Prestwick — Shell	1 Monkton Road KA9 1AS	A79	(0292) 77415	4USD	GAE			
91	380743	RENFREW	Abbotsinch Self Serve	Inchinnan Road PA4 9AE	A8	041-886 2321	4UD	GAE			
92	380747	RENFREW	Arkleston — Shell	Paisley Road PA4 8XD	A741	041-889 7695	4USD	GAE			
93	380791	ROTHESAY (BUTE)	W & J Duncan	18 Mill Street PA20 0EY	A844	(0700) 503094	4UD	GAE			
94	380796	ROTHESAY (BUTE)	McKirdy & McMillan	East Princes Street PA20 9DN	A844	(0700) 502317	4UD	GAE			
95	380980	SALEN (MULL)	MacDonald's Filling Station	PA62 6JE	A848	(0680) 300326	4UD	GAE			
96	380751	STEVENSTON	Ardeer Self Serve	Glencairn Street KA20 3BE	A78	(0294) 63960	4UD	GAE			
97	380909	STRATHAVEN	Sweetieshop Garage	Glasgow Road ML10 6NL	A726	(0357) 20520	4UD	GAE			
98	381027	TARBERT	Kintyre Filling Station	Barmore Road PA29 6XL	A83	(0880) 820136	4UD	GAE			
99	528174	TARBERT	Clachan Filling Station	Clachan PA29 6XL	A83	(08804) 279	4UD	GAE			
100	299444	TAYINLOAN	D MacDougall	The Stores PA29 6XG	A83	(05834) 226	4U				
101	381176	TAYNUILT	Etive Filling Station	PA35 1JE	A85	(08662) 651	4UD	GAE			
102	380755	WEMYSS BAY	Bay Garage	Greenock Road PA18 6AA	A78	(0475) 520149	4UD	GAE			
103	400182	WHITING BAY (ARRAN)	The Bay Garage	KA27 8TZ	A841	(07707) 345	4U	GAE			
104	380967	WISHAW	Westwood — Shell	Main Street, Newmains ML2 9AT	A73	(0698) 386400	4USD	GAE			

SUFFOLK

Loc. Ref.	Shell Ref.	TOWN	NAME	ADDRESS	Road No.	Tel. No.	Fuel	Cards	24 hour	HGV	Select
1	357011	BECCLES	London Road Garage	London Road, Wrentham NR34 7HJ	A12	(0502) 75391	4USD	GAE			
2	357016	BECCLES	Ingate Garage Ltd	Lowestoft Road NR34 7DE		(0502) 712513	4UD	GAE			
3	357096	BUNGAY	Bungay Filling Station	Beccles Road NR35 1HX	B1062	(0986) 894411	4USD	GAE			
4	356974	BURY ST EDMUNDS	Coronation — Shell	Newmarket Road IP33 3TF	A1302	(0284) 753882	4USD	GAE			
5	357059	BURY ST EDMUNDS	New Lodge Garage	Freckenham IP28 8JY		(0638) 750534	4USD	GAE			
6	357116	BURY ST EDMUNDS	R W M Partridge	Icklingham IP28 6PS	A1101	(0638) 713035	4UD	GAE			
7	384298	BURY ST EDMUNDS	Tim Brinton Cars Ltd	Beddingfield Way IP32 7BT		(0284) 767344	4USD	GAE			
8	355852	FELIXSTOWE	Portside Filling Station	Walton Avenue IP11 8HE		(0394) 675844	4UD	GAE			
9	355693	HAVERHILL	Keith Brown Motors Ltd	Duddery Hill CB9 8DS		(0440) 703606	4UD	GAE			
10	302774	IPSWICH	Ipswich Service Station	162-166 London Road IP2 0DY	A1214	(0473) 287233	4UD	GAE			
11	308239	IPSWICH	Orwell — Shell	Ipswich By Pass, Nacton IP10 0NZ	A45	(0473) 725264	4USD	GAE			
12	356983	IPSWICH	Bourne Bridge Service Station	Wherstead Road IP2 8LR	A137	(0473) 688538	4UD	GAE			
13	356987	IPSWICH	Lady Lane Garage Ltd	Lady Lane, Hadleigh IP7 6AF	B1071	(0473) 822383	4USD	GAE			
14	356990	IPSWICH	Kerridges (Needham Market) Ltd	High Street, Needham Market IP6 8EG	B1113	(0449) 720222	4UD	GAE			
15	356992	IPSWICH	Heath — Shell	23 Woodbridge Road East IP4 5QN	A1214	(0473) 718611	4USD	GAE			
16	356995	IPSWICH	Whitehouse — Shell	665 Norwich Road IP1 6JZ	A1156	(0473) 741500	4UD	GAE			
17	356997	IPSWICH	Ranelagh — Shell	London Road IP2 0DX	A1214	(0473) 257374	4USD	GAE			
18	356998	IPSWICH	Capel St Mary Garage Ltd	London Road, Capel St Mary IP9 2JT	A12	(0473) 310451	4UD	GAE			
19	299995	LOWESTOFT	Kessingland — Shell	High Street, Kessingland NR33 7QF		(0502) 741839	4USD	GAE			
20	299996	LOWESTOFT	Gooch Mtrs — Shell	Mill Road NR33 0PP		(0502) 566562	4UD	GAE			
21	357013	LOWESTOFT	Gunton Garage	Yarmouth Road NR32 4AN	A12	(0502) 730323	4USD	GAE			
22	357019	LOWESTOFT	Oulton Broad STC	Normanston Drive, Oulton Broad NR32 2PT	A117	(0502) 587040	4USD	GAE			
23	356970	SAXMUNDHAM	Stratford — Shell	Main A12, Stratford St Andrew IP17 1LF	A12	(0728) 602322	4USD	GAE			
24	302787	SOUTHWOLD	Reydon Motors	Reydon Corner, Reydon IP18 6NE	A1095	(0502) 723170	4U	AE			
25	356986	STOWMARKET	Stowupland Service Stn	Thorny Green IP14 5AG	A1120	(0449) 612326	4USD	GAE			
26	302821	SUDBURY	Barrett Lee	Northern Road CO10 6XQ	A134	(0787) 370774	4USD	GAE			
27	355791	SUDBURY	Howlett of Lavenham	Sudbury Road, Lavenham CO10 9PJ	B1071	(0787) 247228	4USD	GAE			
28	356964	WOODBRIDGE	Woodbridge — Shell	24 Grove Road IP12 4LH	A12	(0394) 384765	4USD	GAE			
29	356966	WOODBRIDGE	Grove — Shell	Grove Road IP12 4LQ	A12	(0394) 384824	4USD	GAE			
30	357035	WORTHAM	Wortham Garage	Bury Road IP22 1PX	A143	(0379) 898437	4UD	GAE			

SURREY

Loc. Ref.	Shell Ref.	TOWN	NAME	ADDRESS	Road No.	Tel. No.	Fuel	Cards	24 hour	HGV	Select
1	302558	ALDERSHOT	City Ash	Guildford Road, Ash GU12 5HN	A323	(0252) 21976	4USD	GAE			
2	308454	ASHTEAD	Ashtead Park Self Serve	7 The Street KT21 2AD	A24	(03722) 77000	4USD	GAE			
3	302552	BAGSHOT	City Bagshot	14 London Road GU19 5HZ	A30	(0276) 453540	4USD	GAE			
4	302227	BANSTEAD	City Burgh Heath	Brighton Road, Tadworth KT20 6BX	A217	(0737) 363401	4USD	GAE			
5	400027	CATERHAM	Layhams Engineering Ltd	Croydon Road CR3 6XD	B2030	(0883) 349311	4USD	GAE			
6	384082	CATERHAM-ON-HILL	Graystone (Caterham)	49 High Street CR3 5UF	A22	(0883) 344641	4USD	GAE			
7	302481	CHERTSEY	Ottershaw — Shell	Guildford Road, Ottershaw KT16 0PG	A320	(0932) 873298	4USD	GAE			
8	308266	CHERTSEY	Trident Garages Ltd	Guildford Road, Ottershaw KT16 0NZ	A320	(0932) 874411	4USD	GAE			
9	302222	CHESSINGTON	Fleetwood Garage	Leatherhead Road KT9 2HZ	A243	081-397 3636	4USD	GAE			
10	308226	COBHAM	Fairmile S/Stn	270 Portsmouth Road KT11 1HU	A307	(0932) 864455	4USD	GAE			
11	302542	COULSDON	Coulsdon — Shell	93-101 Brighton Road CR5 2BE	A23	081-668 6045	4USD	GAE			
12	302647	COULSDON	Old Coulsdon	215 Coulsdon Road, Old Coulsdon CR3 1EN	B2030	(0737) 551553	4USD	GAE			

Shell Ref.	TOWN	NAME	ADDRESS	Road No.	Tel. No.	Fuel	Cards
308175	DORKING	Carters Garage (Capel) Ltd	Capel Village RH5 4QU		(0306) 711177	4USD	GAE
308192	DORKING	Ockley S/Stn	Stane Street, Ockley RH5 5TP	A29	(0306) 627400	4UD	GAE
302458	EAST MOLESEY	Parkhurst Service Station	195 Hurst Road KT8 9SE	A3050	081-979 2067	4USD	GAE
308136	EGHAM	City Egham (75)	186-187 High Street TW20 9DY	A30	(0784) 437747	4USD	GAE
302225	ESHER	Hinchley Wood – Shell	Kingston by Pass, Hinchley Wood KT10 0PZ	A309	081-339 0141	4USD	GAE
302220	EWELL	Etwelle Service Station	Ewell-by-Pass KT17 2PU	A240	081-393 1421	4USD	GAE
308215	FARNHAM	Henlys Ford (Farnham)	16-20 Firgrove Hill GU9 8LQ	A287	(0252) 733929	4UD	GAE
308220	FARNHAM	Heath End Self Serve	Farnborough Road, Heath End GU9 4AZ	A325	(0252) 22139	4USD	GAE
308464	FRIMLEY	Ivy Cottage Self Serve	13 Chobham Road GU16 5PG	B311	(0276) 691600	4USD	GAE
308213	GODALMING	G. Chandler Ltd	The Green, Elstead GU8 6DA	B3001	(0252) 703135	4UD	GAE
302975	GODSTONE	Godstone STC	Godstone Hill RH9 8BE	B2236	(0883) 742560	4USD	GAE
308228	GODSTONE	Tylers Green Self Serve	Godstone Hill RH9 8BE	B2236	(0883) 742000	4USD	GAE
308270	GUILDFORD	Ladymead – Shell	14 Ladymead GU1 1DL	A25	(0483) 573388	4USD	GAE
308273	GUILDFORD	Woodbridge Hill – Shell	56A Aldershot Road GU2 6AF	A323	(0483) 300062	4USD	GAE
308274	GUILDFORD	Meadows Self Serve	Woodbridge Road GU1 1EF	A322	(0483) 39392	4USD	GAE
308472	GUILDFORD	Chilworth Garage	126 New Road, Chilworth GU4 8LP	A248	(0483) 62221	4USD	GAE
302639	HORLEY	City Horley	Brighton Road RH6 7JU	A23	(0293) 782383	4USD	GAE
308180	HORLEY	Gatwick Self Serve	Reigate Road, Hookwood RH6 0HQ	A217	(0293) 785749	4USD	GAE
302239	KINGSTON UPON THAMES	Home Park Self Serve	34 Portsmouth Road KT1 2NF	A307	081-546 9440	4USD	GAE
302644	LEATHERHEAD	Mole Valley Self Serve	20 Kingston Road KT22 7BL	B2430	(0372) 374404	4UD	GAE
386348	LOWER EASHING	Eashing Service Station	A3 Godalming By Pass GU7 2QG	A3	(0483) 416803	4USD	GAE
308224	REDHILL	Clearview – Shell	19 Horley Road, Earlswood RH1 5AL	A23	(0737) 768846	4USD	GAE
308241	REDHILL	Tollgate Filling Station	Woodhatch Road RH1 5HP	A2044	(0737) 763554	4USD	GAE
302948	REIGATE	Buckland – Shell	Reigate Road, Buckland RH3 7ET	A25	(0737) 844511	4USD	GAE
308232	REIGATE	Reigate Heath Garage	Flanchford Road RH2 8AB		(0737) 244146	4U	GAE
302645	SOUTH CROYDON	Sanderstead – Shell	81 Limpsfield Road, Sanderstead CR2 9LE	B269	081-657 1990	4USD	GAE
302556	STAINES	Staines – Shell	93-101 London Road TW18 4HN	A30	(0784) 456269	4USD	GAE
308261	WEYBRIDGE	St Georges Self Serve	Brooklands Road KT13 0RP	B374	(0932) 353693	4USD	GAE
302983	WOKING	Styles Motor Co	Wych Hill GU22 0EU		(0483) 720322	4UD	GA
308264	WOKING	Send Service Garage	92 Send Road GU23 7EZ	A247	(0483) 222125	4USD	GAE
308276	WOKING	Brookwood Service Station	Connaught Road, Brookwood GU24 0AH	A324	(0483) 797632	4UD	GAE
383385	WOKING	Burnt Common – Shell	Portsmouth Road, Send GU23 7JZ		(0483) 211998	4USD	GAE

TAYSIDE

Shell Ref.	TOWN	NAME	ADDRESS	Road No.	Tel. No.	Fuel	Cards
381209	ARBROATH	Harbour Self Serve	1 Burnside Drive DD11 1NY	A92	(0241) 75086	4UD	GAE
380592	AUCHTERARDER	Loaninghead Filling Station	Loaninghead PH3 1PH	A9	(0764) 682428	4USD	GAE
377633	BALBEGGIE	Lamb & Gardiner Ltd	Main Street PH2 6EZ	A94	(0821) 640662	4UD	GAE
380564	BLAIRGOWRIE	Thomas McNicholl	Perth Road PH10 6EN	A93	(0250) 872598	4UD	GAE
380998	BLAIRGOWRIE	Central Garage	Boat Brae, Rattray PH10 7BJ	A93	(0250) 872485	4UD	GAE
380556	BRECHIN	DF&A Collie	Clerk Street DD9 6AZ	A935	(0356) 622818	4UD	GAE
380561	COUPAR ANGUS	Lamb & Gardiner Ltd	Union Street PH13 9AF	A94	(0828) 27271	4UD	GAE
377630	CRIEFF	Crieff Service Station	East High Street PH7 3JA	A85	(0764) 652273	4UD	GAE
380534	DUNDEE	Caird Park Self Serve	61 Forfar Road DD4 9BS	A929	(0382) 462071	4USD	GAE
380536	DUNDEE	Camperdown Self Serve	Coupar Angus Road, Lochee DD2 3HG	A923	(0382) 611571	4UD	GAE
380538	DUNDEE	Claypots Garage	Arbroath Road, Broughty Ferry DD5 3LB	A92	(0382) 78098	4UD	GAE
380548	DUNDEE	Kingsway East Self Serve	East Kingsway DD4 7PY	A92	(0382) 462089	4USD	GAE
380550	DUNDEE	Tayview Self Serve	394 Perth Road DD2 1JQ		(0382) 662236	4USD	GAE
380977	DUNDEE	Loftus Self Serve	305/309 Queen Street, Broughty Ferry DD5 2HT	A930	(0382) 77709	4USD	GAE
381065	DUNDEE	Coldside Self Serve	166 Strathmartine Road DD3 8DQ		(0382) 89054	4USD	GAE
381204	DUNDEE	Trades Lane Self Serve	Trades Lane DD1 3ER		(0382) 27296	4UD	GAE
380552	DUNKELD	Young's Garage	Perth Road, Birnam PH8 0DN	A9	(0350) 724276	4UD	GAE
380566	EDZELL	H A McKay	18 High Street DD9 7TA	B966	(0356) 648364	4UD	GAE
380583	ERROL	Inchmichael Garage	A.85 Eastbound PH2 7RR	A85	(0821) 670242	4USD	GAE
380574	FORFAR	Fiskens of Forfar Ltd	Queenswell Road DD8 3JA	A926	(0307) 63008	4USD	GAE
381115	FORFAR	Car Services	Dundee Road DD8 1HS	A926	(0307) 63994	4US	GAE
380587	KINLOCH RANNOCH	J & P Brown & Sons	Kinloch Rannoch Garage PH16 5RA	B846	(0882) 632331	4UD	GAE
381082	METHVEN	S Robertson & Son	PH1 3RF	A85	(0764) 683241	4UD	GAE
380568	MONTROSE	North Esk Self Serve	North Esk Road DD10 9AZ	A92	(0674) 73425	4UD	GAE
380943	MONTROSE	South Esk Self Serve	Bridge Street DD10 8AJ	A92	(0674) 73518	4USD	GAE
380579	PERTH	Robert Miller (Car Sales) Ltd	97 Crieff Road PH1 2QB	A85	(0738) 39879	4UD	GAE
380596	PERTH	South Inch Self Serve	4 Edinburgh Road PH2 8AR	A912	(0738) 25712	4UD	GAE
380598	PERTH	Fair City Self Serve	Dunkeld Road PH1 3AB	A912	(0738) 38277	4USD	GAE
380997	PERTH	Goodlyburn Filling Station	Jeanfield Road PH1 1LP		(0738) 25505	4UD	GA

TYNE & WEAR

Shell Ref.	TOWN	NAME	ADDRESS	Road No.	Tel. No.	Fuel	Cards
433255	BLAYDON	Blaydon – Shell	Tyne Street NE21 4JD	A695	091-414 1833	4USD	GAE
366052	CRAMLINGTON	Annitsford – Shell	Annitsford NE23 7BD	A189	091-250 0058	4USD	GAE
357694	GATESHEAD	Priory Vauxhall Lotus	Felling By-Pass (Park Road) NE8 3ER	A184	091-477 8595	4USD	GAE
357750	GATESHEAD	Redheugh Bridge Self Serve	Askew Road West NE8 2JX	A184	091-477 7214	4USD	GAE
366093	GATESHEAD	Windmill Hill Self Serve	96 Bensham Road NE8 1PS	B692	091-477 1921	4UD	GAE
366098	GATESHEAD	Wishaw House Self Serve	Durham Road NE8 4EL	A167	091-478 4295	4USD	GAE
366100	GATESHEAD	Gateshead – Shell	Harlow Green, Low Fell NE9 7TD	A167	091-491 0916	4USD	GAE

Loc. Ref.	Shell Ref.	TOWN	NAME	ADDRESS	Road No.	Tel. No.	Fuel	Cards
8	366342	GATESHEAD	Whitemare Pool — Shell	Whitemare Pool NE10 8YB	A194	091-438 1573	4USD	GAE
9	366075	GOSFORTH	Three Mile Self Serve	Great North Road NE3 2DT	B1318	091-266 4611	4USD	GAE
10	363838	JARROW	Tyne Tunnel Self Serve	Edward Street NE32 3UW	A185	091-489 7663	4USD	GAE
11	357689	NEWCASTLE UPON TYNE	Priory Benton Self Serve	Whitley Road, Long Benton NE12 9SR	A186	091-215 0736	4USD	GAE
12	357757	NEWCASTLE UPON TYNE	Byker Travellers Check — Shell	308 Shields Road NE6 2UU	A187	091-265 0023	4USD	GAE
13	362257	NEWCASTLE UPON TYNE	South Gosforth Self Serve	Benton Park Road NE7 7ED	A191	091-284 6756	4USD	GAE
14	366066	NEWCASTLE UPON TYNE	Clousden Hill Service Station	Great Lime Road NE12 9BE	B5105	091-268 1525	4USD	GAE
15	366069	NEWCASTLE UPON TYNE	Wideopen Service Station	Great North Road, Wideopen NE13 6LW	B1321	091-236 3126	4UD	GAE
16	366073	NEWCASTLE UPON TYNE	Skewbridge Self Serve	Shields Road NE6 4QL	A193	091-262 3301	4UD	
17	366077	NEWCASTLE UPON TYNE	St James Self Serve	Gallowgate NE1 4SQ	A6082	091-232 8199	4USD	GAE
18	366078	NEWCASTLE UPON TYNE	Osborne Garage (Newcastle) Ltd	87 Osborne Road, Jesmond NE2 2AN	B1309	091-281 1677	4UD	GAE
19	366083	NEWCASTLE UPON TYNE	Brambles Self Serve	Westgate Road NE4 9PR	A186	091-273 7478	4USD	GAE
20	366356	NEWCASTLE UPON TYNE	Cochrane Park Self Serve	24 Benton Road NE7 7DT	A188	091-266 0321	4USD	GAE
21	468467	NEWCASTLE UPON TYNE	Metro Filling Station	Derwenthough Road, Swalwell NE16 3BL		091-414 3478	4USD	GAE
22	532850	NEWCASTLE UPON TYNE	Sunniside Garage	Front Street, Sunniside NE16 5SE	A692	091-488 7298	4UD	GAE
23	366284	NORTH SHIELDS	Tynemouth — Shell	Beach Road NE30 2TU	A1058	091-257 4665	4USD	GAE
24	366305	NORTH SHIELDS	3Mile — North Shields	Queen Alexander Road West NE29 9AA	A1108	091-296 0926	4U	
25	366057	SHIREMOOR	Three Mile Garage (Shiremoor)	New York Road, West Allotment NE27 0ER	A191	091-266 4611	4USD	GAE
26	366103	SUNDERLAND	Grindon Broadway Self Serve	The Broadway, Grindon SR4 8LP	A183	091-528 3921	4USD	GAE
27	366109	SUNDERLAND	Alexandra Self Serve	Pallion New Road SR5 2BE	B1405	091-514 4719	4USD	GAE
28	366297	SUNDERLAND	Castle Service Station	Washington Road, Hylton Castle SR5 4RR	B1290	091-549 5130	4UD	GAE
29	366107	WHITBURN	Whitburn Service Station	Coast Road SR6 7NT	A183	091-529 2276	4USD	GAE

WARWICKSHIRE

Loc. Ref.	Shell Ref.	TOWN	NAME	ADDRESS	Road No.	Tel. No.	Fuel	Cards
1	078311	ALCESTER	Barn Service Station	Worcester Road, Cookhill B49 5PP	A422	(0386) 792307	4USD	GAE
2	355571	ALCESTER	Bridge End Service Station	Stratford Road B49 6PQ	A422	(0789) 762191	4USD	GAE
3	398606	ALCESTER	Oversley Mill — Shell	Alcester By-Pass 49 1PB	A46	(0789) 762684	4USD	GAE
4	355245	BIRMINGHAM	Hillcrest Self Serve	Grimstock Hill, Coleshill B46 1LD	A446	(0675) 462456	4USD	GAE
5	355338	BULKINGTON	Arbury Service Station Ltd	366 Nuneaton Road CV12 9RR	B4112	(0203) 313146	4U	GA
6	355838	COVENTRY	Corley Northbound	M6 Northbound, Corley CV7 8NR	M6	(0676) 40111	4USD	GAE
7	355840	COVENTRY	Corley Southbound	M6 Southbound, Corley CV7 8NR	M6	(0676) 40111	4USD	GAE
8	355301	KENILWORTH	Eykins — Shell	Warwick Road CV8 1HY	A452	(0926) 59050	4USD	GAE
9	355297	LEAMINGTON SPA	Comptons Garage	Rugby Road, Cubbington CV32 6DF	B4453	(0926) 423477	4USD	GAE
10	355639	LEAMINGTON SPA	Leamington — Shell	Clarendon Avenue CV32 5PY		(0926) 425355	4USD	GAE
11	353348	NUNEATON	Travellers Check — Shell	Avenue Road CV11 4JF	A4254	(0203) 642422	4USD	GAE
12	355558	NUNEATON	Central Avenue Garage	Central Avenue CV11 5BD	B4114	(0203) 382753	4USD	GAE
13	355319	RUGBY	Rugby — Shell	Leicester Road CV21 1DJ	A426	(0788) 561975	4USD	GAE
14	355269	STRATFORD-UPON-AVON	Stratford upon Avon F/Stn	Evesham Road CV37 9AS	B439	(0789) 204317	4USD	GAE
15	355272	STRATFORD-UPON-AVON	Bridgetown — Shell	Shipston Road CV37 7LP	A3400	(0789) 261313	4USD	GAE
16	389978	STUDLEY	New Park Service Station	109 Alcester Road B80 7NW	A435	(0527) 852297	4UD	GA
17	355354	WARWICK	Oaklands — Shell	Hertford Hill, Hatton CV35 7DZ	A4177	(0926) 491681	4USD	GAE

WEST GLAMORGAN

Loc. Ref.	Shell Ref.	TOWN	NAME	ADDRESS	Road No.	Tel. No.	Fuel	Cards
1	299460	NEATH	Grandison Garage	Pant-yr-Heol SA11 2HD	A474	(0639) 632460	4UD	GAE
2	348725	NEATH	Neath Abbey Self Serve	Neath Abbey Road SA10 7DF	A474	(0639) 643297	4UD	GAE
3	299462	PONTLLIW	Pontlliw Service Station	Swansea Road SA1 1ES	A48	(0792) 892020	4UD	GAE
4	348723	PORT TALBOT	Pinetree Self Serve	Baglan Road SA12 8BH	A48	(0639) 812360	4USD	GAE
5	348735	REYNOLDSTON	Peter Oliver Motors	Knelston SA3 1AR	A4118	(0792) 390903	4UD	GAE
6	348727	SWANSEA	Avenue Garage	Swansea Road, Pontardawe SA8 4AL	A4067	(0792) 775577	4USD	GAE
7	348729	SWANSEA	Halfway — Shell	Mumbles Road, Blackpill SA3 5AU	A4067	(0792) 203451	4USD	GAE
8	348733	SWANSEA	Abertawe Self Serve	1093 Carmarthen Road, Fforestfach SA5 4AL	A483	(0792) 586129	4USD	GAE
9	348737	SWANSEA	Walters Central Garage	Pontardulais SA4 1RH	A48	(0792) 882238	4UD	GAE
10	348739	SWANSEA	Eagle Service Station	Llangyfelach Road, Treboeth SA5 9EW	B4489	(0792) 772571	4USD	GAE
11	348837	SWANSEA	Gellinudd S/Stn	New Road, Portardawe SA8 3DY	A474	(0792) 862312	4UD	GAE
12	348877	SWANSEA	Thames Rico S/Stn Ltd	Fabian Way, Port Tennant SA1 8LD	A483	(0792) 655730	4USD	GAE
13	348988	SWANSEA	Tawe Self Serve	Neath Road, Landore SA1 2JG	A4067	(0792) 792547	4USD	GAE
14	389116	SWANSEA	Llansamlet S/S	Peniel Green Road, Llansamlet SA7 9BA	A48	(0792) 775577	4USD	GAE
15	398336	SWANSEA	Swansea MWSA	M4 MWSA Swansea, Penllergaer SA4 1GT	M4	(0792) 896222	D	GAE

WEST MIDLANDS

Loc. Ref.	Shell Ref.	TOWN	NAME	ADDRESS	Road No.	Tel. No.	Fuel	Cards
1	355303	BALSALL COMMON	Balsall Common — Shell	Kenilworth Road CV7 7DN	A452	(0676) 533149	4USD	GAE
2	353336	BIRMINGHAM	Truckers Rest West Bromwich	Junc 1 M5, Smethwick, Warley B66 1AX	A4252	021-500 5040	4USD	GAE
3	355200	BIRMINGHAM	Valley Self Serve	Highfield Road, Hall Green B28 0BY		021-777 1204	4USD	GAE
4	355208	BIRMINGHAM	Millpool Hill Self Serve	Alcester Road South, Kings Heath B14 5ER	A435	021-430 5133	4USD	GAE

Loc. Ref.	Shell Ref.	TOWN	NAME	ADDRESS	Road No.	Tel. No.	Fuel	Cards
5	355212	BIRMINGHAM	Broad Oaks – Shell	386 Warwick Road, Solihull B91 1BB	A41	021-709 0353	4USD	GAE
6	355226	BIRMINGHAM	Bearwood Self Serve	385-407 Bearwood Road, Warley B66 4DJ	A4030	021-429 6756	4USD	GAE
7	355229	BIRMINGHAM	Rednal Garage	472 Lickey Road, Rednal B45 8UU	A441	021-453 7127	4USD	GAE
8	355235	BIRMINGHAM	Pebble Mill Self Serve	560 Pershore Road, Selly Oak B29 7EN	A441	021-471 4391	4USD	GAE
9	355237	BIRMINGHAM	Abbey Garage	37 Sutton Road, Erdington B23 6QH	A5127	021-382 5000	4UD	GAE
10	355239	BIRMINGHAM	Barr Beacon Self Serve	Beacon Road, Great Barr B43 7BW	B4154	021-360 7725	4USD	GAE
11	355247	BIRMINGHAM	Moorcroft – Shell	Chester Road, Streetly B74 2HN	A452	021-353 7305	4USD	GAE
12	355250	BIRMINGHAM	Gateway Self Serve	Birmingham Road, Great Barr B43 6NT	A34	021-357 1275	4USD	GAE
13	355278	BIRMINGHAM	West Side Self Serve	Bath Row, Edgbaston B15 1LS	B4127	021-643 2931	4USD	GAE
14	355587	BIRMINGHAM	Alcester Road Service Station	78 Alcester Road South, Kings Heath B14 7PT	A435	021-444 2432	4USD	GAE
15	355645	BIRMINGHAM	Linden Road Self Serve	Linden Road, Bournville B30 1PA	A4040	021-458 4242	4USD	GAE
16	355647	BIRMINGHAM	Moseley Road Self Serve	561-569 Moseley Road, Balsall Heath B12 9BS	A435	021-440 3259	4UD	GAE
17	355723	BIRMINGHAM	Acocks Green – Shell	Stockfield Road, Acocks Green B27 6AR	A4040	021-765 4134	4USD	GAE
18	355745	BIRMINGHAM	Mass Garage	1163-1185 Chester Road, Erdington B24 0QY	A452	021-373 1661	4UD	GAE
19	355783	BIRMINGHAM	Druids Heath – Shell	Bells Lane, Druids Heath B14 5QH		021-433 3266	4USD	GAE
20	355785	BIRMINGHAM	Harborne – Shell	Harborne Lane, Harborne B17 0NT	A4040	021-414 1325	4USD	GAE
21	355793	BIRMINGHAM	The Wood Self Serve	Pine Square, Chelmsley Wood B37 5UD		021-770 6385	4USD	GAE
22	355803	BIRMINGHAM	Northfield Self Serve	1020 Bristol Road South, Northfield B31 2QU	A38	021-476 2153	4USD	GAE
23	355837	BIRMINGHAM	Corrida Self Serve	Station Road, Stechford B33 9AX	A4040	021-784 4363	4USD	GAE
24	383658	BIRMINGHAM	Cactus Self Serve	123 Corbett Street, Warley B66 3PU		021-555 5030	4UD	GA
25	390115	BIRMINGHAM	Station Garage	Station Road, Marston Green B37 7AX		021-779 5735	4USD	GAE
26	182405	COVENTRY	Shirleys Garage (Meriden) Ltd	Main Street, Meriden CV7 7HL	B4102	(0676) 22242	4USD	GAE
27	353352	COVENTRY	Binley Woods – Shell	Coventry Eastern By-Pass CV3 2ZZ	A46	(0203) 635929	4UD	GAE
28	355307	COVENTRY	Southbound – Shell	721 London Road CV3 4EX	A45	(0203) 303104	4USD	GAE
29	355309	COVENTRY	Binley Road Self Serve	Binley Road CV3 1HB	A428	(0203) 442046	4USD	GAE
30	355314	COVENTRY	Henley Road Self Serve	Henley Road CV2 1LP	B4109	(0203) 689682	4UD	GAE
31	355345	COVENTRY	Woodway – Shell	124 Hinckley Road CV2 2EU	A4600	(0203) 602928	4USD	GAE
32	355552	COVENTRY	Whitmore Park Service Station	Holbrook Lane CV6 4DG		(0203) 686148	4USD	GAE
33	355819	COVENTRY	Godiva – Shell	Tile Hill Lane CV4 9DS	B4101	(0203) 466458	4USD	GAE
34	355832	COVENTRY	Antelope STC	Allesley Old Road CV5 8BU	A4106	(0203) 691126	4USD	GAE
35	355521	DUDLEY	Woodsetton S/S	Birmingham New Road DY1 4PD	A4123	(0902) 663558	4UD	GAE
36	434016	DUDLEY	Sedgley Service Station	Gospel End Road, Sedgley DY3 3LT	A463	(0902) 663190	4USD	GAE
37	434819	DUDLEY	Merryhill Service Centre	Level Street, Brierley Hill DY5 1UA		(0384) 76312	4USD	GAE
38	355216	HALESOWEN	Manor – Shell	Spies Lane B62 9SR	B4043	021-422 5029	4USD	GAE
39	355223	HALESOWEN	Dudley Road Service Station	Dudley Road B63 3NJ	A459	021-550 1997	4USD	GAE
40	001304	SOLIHULL	Gresswolde Garage	1649 Warwick Road, Knowle B93 0LL	A4141	(0564) 772341	4USD	GAE
41	010409	SOLIHULL	Ring of Bells Garage Ltd	Solihull Road, Hampton-in-Arden B92 0EX	A452	(0675) 53161	4USD	GAE
42	355194	SOLIHULL	Evans Halshaw	639 Stratford Road, Shirley B90 4BA	A34	021-745 5855	4USD	GAE
43	355196	SOLIHULL	Triangle – Shell	Stratford Road, Shirley B90 3LU	A34	021-733 6131	4USD	GAE
44	355206	SOLIHULL	Hockley Heath Service Station	2635 Stratford Road, Hockley Heath B94 6NH	B4439	(0564) 782244	4USD	GAE
45	355519	STOURBRIDGE	Bob Stinton Garages Ltd	220 Stourbridge Road, Lye DY9 7BE	A458	(0384) 892233	4UD	GAE
46	355243	SUTTON COLDFIELD	Central – Shell	Lichfield Road, Four Oaks B74 2XH	A5127	021-308 3737	4USD	GAE
47	355255	SUTTON COLDFIELD	The Green Self Serve	166 Birmingham Road B72 1BX	A5127	021-355 5652	4USD	GAE
48	355224	WALSALL	Wednesbury Motor Services Ltd	Holyhead Road, Wednesbury WS10 7PA	A41	021-556 1315	4UD	GAE
49	355374	WARLEY	Broadway Self Serve	Corner Broadway, Oldbury B68 9HB	A4123	021-422 9719	4USD	GAE
50	355630	WEST BROMWICH	West Brom – Shell	Dudley Street B70 9LS	A4035	021-553 1474	4USD	GAE
51	198703	WOLVERHAMPTON	Wood End Service Station	Wood End Road, Wednesfield WV11 1YD	A4484	(0902) 732702	4USD	GAE
52	353333	WOLVERHAMPTON	Stafford Road – Shell	Stafford Road, Fordhouses WV10 6NR	A449	(0902) 787624	4USD	GAE
53	355487	WOLVERHAMPTON	Triton Self Serve	Tettenhall Road WV3 9NQ	A41	(0902) 771220	4USD	GAE
54	355536	WOLVERHAMPTON	Lichfield Road Service Stn	Lichfield Road, Wendesfield WV11 3HD	A4124	(0922) 409302	4USD	GAE
55	382609	WOLVERHAMPTON	Springfield Garage	201 Penn Road WV4 5TT	A449	(0902) 341421	4USD	GAE

WEST SUSSEX

Loc. Ref.	Shell Ref.	TOWN	NAME	ADDRESS	Road No.	Tel. No.	Fuel	Cards
1	308301	ARUNDEL	City Fontwell – Shell	Arundel Road, Fontwell BN18 0SB	A27	(0243) 544382	4USD	GAE
2	535524	BILLINGSHURST	Roman Way Garage	3 High Street RH14 9RD	A29	(0403) 783728	4USD	GAE
3	308199	BOGNOR REGIS	Bognor Garage	Shripney Road PO22 9NJ	A29	(0243) 821137	4USD	GAE
4	308259	BOLNEY	Bolney Motor Works	London Road RH17 5PZ	A23	(0444) 881273	4USD	GAE
5	308247	BURGESS HILL	Burgess Hill – Shell	173 London Road RH15 8LJ	A273	(0444) 236454	4USD	GAE
6	308086	CHICHESTER	Bartletts of Selsey	High Street, Selsey PO20 0LP	B2145	(0243) 602226	4USD	GAE
7	308123	CHICHESTER	R & G Auto Service Bracklesham	Bracklesham Lane, Bracklesham Bay PO20 8JA	B2198	(0243) 670365	4UD	GAE
8	308210	CHICHESTER	D Rowe & Co Ltd	The Hornet PO19 4JW	A259	(0243) 788100	4USD	GAE
9	308212	CHICHESTER	Stockbridge Stc	Stockbridge Road, Donnington PO19 1SJ	A286	(0243) 531358	4USD	GAE
10	308442	CHICHESTER	Taskergrange Ltd	96 High Street, Selsey PO20 0QG	B2145	(0243) 602737	4UD	GAE
11	308502	CHICHESTER	Bosham Service Station	Bosham Lane, Bosham PO18 8HG		(0243) 572211	4UD	GA
12	999601	CHICHESTER	Chichester Yacht Basin Ltd	Birdham PO20 7EJ		(0243) 512731		
13	539505	COWFOLD	Noah's Ark Garage	Henfield Road RH13 8DT	A281	(0403) 864511	4UD	GAE
14	302875	CRAWLEY	Turners Hill Garage Ltd	Turners Hill Road, Crawley Down RH10 4EY	B2028	(0342) 716322	4U	G
15	308112	CRAWLEY	Pease Pottage MWSA	M23 Motorway Service Area, Pease Pottage RH11 9YA	M23	(0293) 535756	4USD	GAE
16	308451	CRAWLEY	Lex Ford Crawley	Worth Park Avenue RH10 4AB		(0293) 613361	4USD	GAE
17	302841	EAST GRINSTEAD	Sussex Self Serve	147/149 London Road RH19 1ET	A22	(0342) 312650	4USD	GAE
18	308250	HASSOCKS	Hassocks S/Stn	Keymer Road BN6 8AR	B2116	(0273) 843101	4U	GE
19	308150	HAYWARDS HEATH	Birch Service Station	5 Lewes Road RH17 7SE	A272	(0444) 450929	4USD	GAE
20	308167	HAYWARDS HEATH	Caffyns Plc (Haywards Heath)	Market Place RH16 1DB	B219	(0444) 451511	4U	GAE
21	308253	HENFIELD	Henfield Motors	High Street BN5 9DF	A281	(0273) 492108	4UD	GAE
22	302844	HORSHAM	Fishers (Horsham) – Shell	Guildford Road, Broadbridge Heath RH12 3NS	A24	(0403) 256381	4USD	GAE
23	308514	HORSHAM	Hop Oast – Shell	Hop Oast Field, Horsham By-Pass RH13 7AR	A24	(0403) 733532	4USD	GAE
24	308288	LANCING	Ashcraft Service Station	215 Brighton Road BN15 8JP	A259	(0903) 762610	4USD	GAE
25	308291	LANCING	Crabtree Service Station	Crabtree Lane BN15 9NH	A259	(0903) 752390	4UD	GAE
26	308292	LITTLEHAMPTON	Cuff Miller & Co L'Hampton Ltd	Horsham Road BN17 6BX	A259	(0903) 714367	4USD	GAE
27	386819	LITTLEHAMPTON	Eastfield – Shell	Rustington-By-Pass, Rustington BN17 6LE	A259	(0903) 732178	4USD	GAE

Loc. Ref.	Shell Ref.	TOWN	NAME	ADDRESS	Road No.	Tel. No.	Fuel	Cards	24 hour	HGV	Select
28	308280	PULBOROUGH	Ashington Self Serve	London Road, Ashington RH20 3JP	A24	(0903) 892548	4USD	GAE			
29	308299	PULBOROUGH	Turners Garage	London Road, Bury RH20 1NP	A29	(0798) 831417	4UD	GAE			
30	308304	WASHINGTON	Ballamys Garage	London Road RH20 3AJ	A283	(0903) 892431	4USD	GAE			
31	302468	WORTHING	H D Steele & Son (Teville)	Teville Road BN11 1UB	A24	(0903) 237527	4UD	GAE			
32	302514	WORTHING	H D Steele & Son (Goring Way)	104 Goring Way, Goring-by-Sea BN12 4TY	A259	(0903) 243271	4UD	GAE			

WEST YORKSHIRE

Loc. Ref.	Shell Ref.	TOWN	NAME	ADDRESS	Road No.	Tel. No.	Fuel	Cards	24 hour	HGV	Select
1	357506	BRADFORD	Sunwin Self Serve	Thornton Road BD1 2AP	B6145	(0274) 723979	4USD	GAE			
2	362178	BRADFORD	Listers Arms Self Serve	Manchester Road BD5 8DJ	A641	(0274) 722555	4USD	GAE			
3	362197	BRADFORD	Wakefield Road F/Stn	Wakefield Road BD4 7RW	A650	(0274) 721753	4U	GAE			
4	362206	BRADFORD	Apperley Bridge Self Serve	Harrogate Road BD2 3DT	A658	(0532) 508392	4USD	GAE			
5	362208	BRADFORD	Turf Self Serve	Keighley Road BD9 4JR	A650	(0274) 490031	4USD	GAE			
6	365866	BRADFORD	Bowling Bridge Service Stn	Wakefield Road BD4 7PE	A650	(0274) 722886	4UD	GAE			
7	365875	BRADFORD	A Simpson & Co	Highfield Road Garage, Idle BD10 8RD	A657	(0274) 612018	4UD	GAE			
8	365877	BRADFORD	Thornbury Self Serve	935 Leeds Road BD3 8HD	A647	(0274) 663391	4USD	GAE			
9	299712	BRIGHOUSE	Hartshead Moor Westbound	M62 Westbound, Clifton HD6 4JX	M62	(0274) 876584	4USD	GAE			
10	299714	BRIGHOUSE	Hartshead Moor Eastbound	M62 Eastbound, Clifton HD6 4JX	M62	(0274) 876584	4USD	GAE			
11	366333	BRIGHOUSE	Lawson Road F/Stn	Lawson Road HD6 1NY		(0484) 717577	4USD	GAE			
12	394807	BRIGHOUSE	Dews — Shell	Bradford Road HD6 4DH	A641	(0484) 721193	4USD	GAE			
13	357810	CASTLEFORD	Riverside Self Serve	Lock Lane WF10 2JU	A656	(0977) 552277	4USD	GAE			
14	365908	CASTLEFORD	Castleford Self Serve	Park Road, Glasshoughton WF10 4RW	A639	(0977) 511601	4USD	GAE			
15	365909	DEWSBURY	Woodkirk Garage Ltd	Leeds Road, Woodkirk WF12 7JB	A653	(0924) 444655	4UD	GAE			
16	357780	HALIFAX	Almar Self Serve	151 Pellon Lane HX1 5RL		(0422) 353667	4USD	GAE			
17	365893	HALIFAX	Salterhebble — Shell	Salterhebble Hill HX3 0QE	A629	(0422) 381226	4USD	GAE			
18	365895	HALIFAX	Headlands Garage	Denholme Gate Road, Hipperholme HX3 8JX	A640	(0422) 202795	4USD	GAE			
19	277828	HEBDEN BRIDGE	R E Thornton	Burnley Road, Mytholmroyd HX7 5LN	A646	(0422) 883053	4USD	GAE			
20	363835	HEBDEN BRIDGE	Bankfoot Garage	Burnley Road HX7 6BS	A646	(0422) 845103	4USD	GAE			
21	357508	HUDDERSFIELD	Southgate Self Serve	Southgate HD1 6QP	A62	(0484) 515064	4USD	GAE			
22	357797	HUDDERSFIELD	Chapelroyd Garage	58 Church Street, Emley HD8 9RP	(0924) 840126	4UD	GAE			
23	362180	HUDDERSFIELD	Huddersfield — Shell	Westbourne Road HD1 4LE	A640	(0484) 535346	4USD	GAE			
24	365880	KEIGHLEY	Junction Garage	Skipton Road, Cross Hills BD20 7DS	A6068	(0535) 332076	4UD	GAE			
25	365882	KEIGHLEY	Trident Filling Station	Bradford Road BD21 4AH		(0535) 605416	4UD	GAE			
26	535622	KEIGHLEY	Yorkshire Cooperatives Ltd	Hard Ings Road BD21 3NB	A650	(0535) 611766	4USD	GAE			
27	357526	LEEDS	Regent Self Serve	24 Regent Street LS2 7QA	A58	(0532) 468003	4USD	GAE			
28	357776	LEEDS	Pineparks Ltd	Woodlands Motel, Micklefield LS25 4DD	A1	(0532) 864806	4UD	GAE			
29	365831	LEEDS	Alwoodley Self Serve	495 Harrogate Road, Alwoodley LS17 7DA	A61	(0532) 696339	4USD	GAE			
30	365834	LEEDS	Nuthill Self Serve	Great North Road (North), Aberford LS25 3AU	A1	(0532) 813268	4USD	GAE			
31	365843	LEEDS	Bramhope Self Serve	Otley Road LS16 9EB	A660	(0532) 673048	4USD	GAE			
32	365845	LEEDS	Kirkstall Self Serve	217 Kirkstall Road LS4 2AH	A65	(0532) 433667	4USD	GAE			
33	365847	LEEDS	Headingley Lane Self Serve	Headingley Lane LS6 2BW	A660	(0532) 757575	4USD	GAE			
34	365849	LEEDS	Yeadon — Shell	New Road, Yeadon LS19 7HW	A65	(0532) 502778	4USD	GAE			
35	365853	LEEDS	Grandstand Filling Station	Elland Road LS11 8TU	A643	(0532) 710215	4UD	GAE			
36	365897	LEEDS	Victoria Garage	Bruntcliffe Road, Morley LS27 0LF	A650	(0532) 534921	4U	GA			
37	365899	LEEDS	Victoria Filling Station	Bruntcliffe Road, Morley LS27 0LF	A650	(0532) 526777	4USD	GAE			
38	366241	LEEDS	Horsforth — Shell	Broadway Ring Road, Horsforth LS18 4DF	A6120	(0532) 591526	4USD	GAE			
39	366248	LEEDS	Leeds — Shell	303 Dewsbury Road LS11 5LQ	A653	(0532) 760455	4USD	GAE			
40	366278	LEEDS	Roydsbeck — Shell	Ring Road, Lower Wortley LS12 6AN	A6110	(0532) 311978	4USD	GAE			
41	366282	LEEDS	Springfield Self Serve	Victoria Road, Morley LS27 9NU	A643	(0532) 533172	4USD	GAE			
42	366319	LEEDS	Northways STC	Great North Road (North), Aberford LS25 3AU	A1	(0532) 813906	4USD	GAE			
43	365994	MIRFIELD	Three Nuns Self Serve	Leeds Road WF14 0BY	A62	(0924) 495445	4USD	GAE			
44	366235	OSSETT	Ossett — Shell	Wakefield Road WF5 9AD	A638	(0924) 261027	4USD	GAE			
45	365851	OTLEY	Poolbridge — Shell	Pool-in-Wharfdale LS21 1EQ	A658	(0532) 842105	4USD	GAE			
46	362218	PONTEFRACT	Pontefract — Shell	Bondgate WF8 2JP	A645	(0977) 600926	4USD	GAE			
47	365995	PONTEFRACT	Trusthouse Forte N/Areas Ltd	A1 Trunk Road, Wentbridge WF8 3JB	A1	(0977) 620154	4USD	GAE			
48	366383	PONTEFRACT	Trusthouse Forte S/Areas Ltd	A1 Trunk Road, Wentbridge WF8 3JB	A1	(0977) 620154	4USD	GAE			
49	362176	PUDSEY	Thorpe S/Stn	Richardshaw Lane LS28 7NB		(0532) 564646	4USD	GAE			
50	432987	PUDSEY	Prospect Garage	150 Bradford Road, Stanningley LS28 6EP	B6157	(0532) 570417	4UD	GAE			
51	365868	SALTAIRE	Saltaire — Shell	Bingley Road BD18 4DJ	A650	(0274) 530142	4USD	GAE			
52	363787	WAKEFIELD	Grange Self Serve	Denby Dale Road East, Durkar WF4 3BB	A636	(0924) 371209	4USD	GAE			
53	365901	WAKEFIELD	Redbeck — Shell	Doncaster Road, Crofton WF4 1RR	A638	(0924) 862676	4USD	GAE			
54	365905	WAKEFIELD	Sandal Motors Ltd	Barnsley Road WF2 6EH	A61	(0924) 255904	4USD	GAE			

WESTERN ISLES

Loc. Ref.	Shell Ref.	TOWN	NAME	ADDRESS	Road No.	Tel. No.	Fuel	Cards	24 hour	HGV	Select
1	377621	STORNOWAY	Macaskills Filling Station	Laberfeidh Road PA87 2RA	A857	(0851) 702127	4UD	GAE			
2	380861	TARBERT	Ardhasaig Filling Station	Ardhasaig PA85 3AJ	A859	(0859) 2066	4UD	GAE			

WILTSHIRE

Loc. Ref.	Shell Ref.	TOWN	NAME	ADDRESS	Road No.	Tel. No.	Fuel	Cards	24 hour	HGV	Select	Car Wash
1	348526	CHIPPENHAM	Chippenham Motors Ltd	Bristol Road SN14 6NA	A420	(0249) 444000	4UD	GAE				
2	348553	CHIPPENHAM	Devizes Road Garage	Devizes Road, Bromham SN15 2DZ	A342	(0380) 850300	4UD	GAE				
3	348533	CORSHAM	Pickwick Motors	Bath Road SN13 0HS	A4	(0249) 712272	4UD	GAE				
4	348551	DEVIZES	Chirton Garage	Fussell & Wadman Ltd, Chirton SN10 3QL	A342	(0380) 840281	4USD	GAE				
5	353284	MELKSHAM	Herberts Service Station	Sandridge Road SN12 7BQ	A3102	(0225) 702609	4UD	GAE				
6	347862	SALISBURY	Bemerton – Shell	Wilton Road SP2 7JB	A36	(0722) 323916	4USD	GAE			■	
7	347868	SALISBURY	Riverbourne Filling Station	London Road SP1 3HN	A338	(0722) 322897	4USD	GAE			■	
8	347870	SALISBURY	Riverside Garage	Stapleford SP3 4LT	A36	(0722) 790858	4USD	GAE			■	
9	347872	SALISBURY	Amesbury Motor Company	High Street, Amesbury SP4 7ET		(0980) 623377	4UD	GAE				
10	347874	SALISBURY	Salisbury – Shell	Downton Road SP2 8AR	A338	(0722) 337214	4USD	GAE			■	
11	347876	SALISBURY	Parkhouse Garage	Cholderton SP4 0EG	A338	(0980) 64220	4UD	GAE				
12	347920	SALISBURY	Landford Mtr Co (Salisbury)	Landford Road, Landford SP5 2BB	A36	(0794) 23618	4USD	GAE				
13	349089	SALISBURY	Lex Vauxhall of Salisbury	Brunel Road SP2 7PU		(0722) 323522	4U	GAE				
14	384099	SALISBURY	City Amesbury – Shell	Countess Roundabout, Amesbury SP4 7AS	A303	(0980) 623000	4USD	GAE			■	■
15	308056	SWINDON	Marlborough Road Self Serve	Marlborough Road SN3 1NP	B4006	(0793) 615723	4USD	GAE			■	■
16	308094	SWINDON	Oasis – Shell	Great Western Way, Cockleburry/R.About SN2 1BZ		(0793) 619633	4USD	GAE			■	
17	308512	SWINDON	Swindon Automobiles Ltd	Dorcan Way SN3 3RS	B4006	(0793) 612091	4UD	GAE				
18	348531	SWINDON	Headlands Service Station	509 Cricklade Road SN2 1AH	A4311	(0793) 523708	4USD	GAE				
19	348535	SWINDON	Swindon Road Gge	Swindon Road, Highworth SN6 7DE	A361	(0793) 762234	4USD	GAE				
20	348540	SWINDON	Wootton Bassett Self Serve	94 High Street, Wootton Bassett SN4 7HA	A3102	(0793) 852032	4USD	GAE				
21	348875	SWINDON	Fleming Way Services	Fleming Way SN1 2NG	A259	(0793) 521260	4USD	GAE			■	
22	348323	TROWBRIDGE	Reeds of Trowbridge	Bradley Road BA14 0QP	A363	(0225) 752525	4U	GAE				
23	432959	WARMINSTER	Marsh & Chalfont	Boreham Road BA12 9HD	B3414	(0985) 214777	4UD	GAE				

Mileage Chart

The distances between towns on the mileage chart are given to the nearest mile, and are measured along the normal AA recommended routes. It should be noted that AA recommended routes do not necessarily follow the shortest distances between places but are based on the quickest travelling time, making maximum use of motorways or dual-carriageway roads.

Map of the United Kingdom showing the towns listed in the mileage chart: Inverness, Aberdeen, Fort William, Perth, Glasgow, Edinburgh, Stranraer, Newcastle, Carlisle, Middlesbrough, Kendal, York, Hull, Preston, Leeds, Liverpool, Manchester, Sheffield, Holyhead, Stoke-on-Trent, Lincoln, Shrewsbury, Nottingham, Norwich, Aberystwyth, Birmingham, Peterborough, Hereford, Northampton, Cambridge, Carmarthen, Gloucester, Colchester, Oxford, Cardiff, Bristol, LONDON, Guildford, Salisbury, Maidstone, Barnstaple, Taunton, Southampton, Portsmouth, Brighton, Dover, Exeter, Dorchester, Plymouth, Penzance.

The triangular mileage table (each row ends with the named town; read distances against the town labelled in each diagonal column):

Aberdeen	—
Aberystwyth	471
Barnstaple	607 222
Birmingham	434 123 178
Brighton	609 290 205 171
Bristol	517 132 100 88 170
Cambridge	465 231 267 113 121 171
Cardiff	537 118 137 108 205 47 206
Carlisle	234 236 372 198 374 282 258 302
Carmarthen	521 50 199 157 267 110 269 68 285
Colchester	518 289 292 171 112 196 48 231 311 293
Dorchester	599 214 94 170 117 62 181 129 364 191 208
Dover	587 323 275 205 81 209 121 244 397 307 113 204
Edinburgh	126 336 471 298 474 381 336 402 99 385 389 463 458
Exeter	591 206 55 161 172 83 251 121 355 183 275 54 247 455
Fort William	157 446 582 408 585 492 469 512 209 496 522 574 608 133 566
Glasgow	149 336 472 298 474 382 359 402 99 386 412 464 498 46 456 102
Gloucester	483 111 126 54 156 36 123 65 247 127 171 118 195 347 110 458 347
Guildford	566 227 174 128 44 106 91 142 331 204 104 97 100 430 146 542 431 101
Hereford	486 80 143 57 188 54 170 58 250 85 203 135 227 350 128 461 350 31 133
Holyhead	463 105 341 168 344 251 276 205 228 155 334 333 367 327 326 439 328 217 301 157
Hull	361 229 322 141 283 232 140 252 171 301 193 314 262 232 306 382 271 197 241 200 220
Inverness	106 496 632 458 634 542 519 562 259 546 572 624 658 157 616 65 174 507 592 510 487 431
Kendal	286 191 326 153 329 237 253 257 51 241 319 318 352 150 311 262 151 202 287 205 182 165 311
Leeds	328 174 310 120 263 220 148 240 122 224 201 302 269 199 294 333 222 185 220 189 166 60 382 71
Lincoln	390 200 274 88 215 184 94 204 183 253 148 262 216 261 259 394 263 150 173 153 205 48 443 177 73
Liverpool	360 111 274 101 277 184 215 125 168 267 266 300 225 259 336 225 150 234 119 102 127 385 80 72 139
Maidstone	550 286 232 168 49 166 84 202 361 264 76 161 44 421 205 572 461 152 57 184 329 225 621 315 233 179 263
Manchester	355 131 262 88 265 172 161 192 120 181 214 254 288 219 246 331 220 138 222 141 122 99 380 75 44 85 35 251
Middlesbrough	276 245 359 178 321 269 200 289 94 294 253 351 322 147 343 279 194 235 278 238 236 89 306 83 64 125 145 285 115
Newcastle	237 277 391 211 353 302 233 322 59 327 286 383 354 108 376 240 155 267 311 270 268 145 267 101 96 157 177 317 147 40
Northampton	483 173 211 55 133 115 54 162 248 211 119 159 152 347 195 459 348 79 90 110 153 508 203 134 91 150 115 138 190 223
Norwich	490 294 329 176 170 233 63 268 283 331 59 242 170 361 314 494 383 185 161 231 305 152 543 271 173 104 241 134 185 285 257 117
Nottingham	395 161 234 54 196 145 87 165 189 213 140 226 216 266 219 400 289 110 153 113 174 93 449 149 74 36 108 179 70 131 163 66 119
Oxford	506 160 170 68 110 104 100 109 270 171 125 115 149 370 145 481 370 48 67 80 239 191 531 225 171 128 173 106 173 206 217 98 102 103
Penzance	701 317 109 272 284 194 362 232 466 294 386 166 359 566 110 677 566 220 258 238 435 416 726 421 404 369 317 356 453 486 305 423 328 264
Perth	87 384 520 346 522 430 381 450 147 434 434 512 546 42 504 103 62 395 480 398 375 277 114 199 244 306 273 509 268 153 192 396 406 311 419 614
Peterborough	436 206 254 88 159 158 38 195 229 244 51 206 138 371 195 547 436 155 151 206 251 58 486 348 171 58 204 43 77 58 86 348 352 123 171 406 352
Plymouth	632 248 61 203 215 125 293 163 397 225 317 97 290 497 45 608 497 151 189 169 366 347 657 352 335 300 300 248 287 384 354 256 195 77 545 279
Portsmouth	591 245 162 153 50 99 136 160 356 222 148 75 145 455 126 574 456 119 47 151 324 285 616 306 198 85 246 504 161 178
Preston	324 148 283 110 286 193 211 213 89 197 276 275 309 188 268 300 189 159 243 162 139 123 349 44 68 135 36 272 32 107 139 159 235 107 183 377 237 182 308 268
Salisbury	552 186 118 123 87 54 139 101 317 163 166 40 162 416 90 528 417 74 61 106 285 255 577 292 235 192 120 207 292 324 107 201 167 63 202 465 164 133 45 228
Sheffield	369 166 272 92 234 183 223 120 24 206 254 240 257 373 262 148 192 151 67 423 121 36 149 80 148 141 166 162 151 50 79 207 340 134
Shrewsbury	416 74 222 48 224 132 156 110 180 112 214 214 247 280 206 391 280 97 182 52 105 163 440 135 118 125 66 211 70 188 221 98 218 86 121 316 328 130 247 206
Southampton	572 226 141 134 64 78 131 141 336 203 158 54 155 436 114 547 437 100 48 123 305 257 597 291 238 213 239 122 277 294 309 109 193 170 66 225 485 157 157 21 248
Stoke-on-Trent	390 114 222 48 224 132 131 152 155 202 214 254 206 366 255 97 182 100 123 130 415 109 93 92 57 211 45 163 195 98 175 52 177 316 303 102 247 207 66 167 51 38 187
Stranraer	241 344 480 306 482 390 367 410 107 394 420 472 506 132 464 187 85 355 440 358 335 279 266 159 230 291 233 469 228 202 163 366 391 297 379 574 154 338 505 465 197 425 270 288 445 263
Taunton	559 174 50 130 156 51 219 89 323 151 244 45 227 423 35 534 423 77 126 95 292 273 584 278 261 226 184 214 310 343 163 281 186 122 144 472 205 75 114 235 69 224 173 93 173 431
York	322 201 315 134 277 225 157 245 115 251 210 307 278 193 300 326 216 191 234 194 192 38 376 90 24 81 101 241 71 50 90 147 181 87 184 409 238 127 340 279 75 248 60 145 250 179 224 267
LONDON	549 238 216 120 60 120 60 155 313 217 62 129 78 413 200 524 413 103 30 135 282 188 573 268 199 142 216 138 203 256 288 68 115 131 57 310 461 86 241 75 225 88 169 163 80 163 421 167 212